NAMES TO WATCH IN THE '90s

BOYS:	**GIRLS:**

BOYS:

Austin
Bryce, Brice
Caleb
Cameron
Cody, Kody
Colby
Collin
Colton
Connor
Dakota
Donovan
Ethan
Jordan
Kirk
Levi
Logan
Lucas
Mason
Maxwell
Parker
Riley
Skyler
Tanner
Taylor
Trent, Trenton
Zachary, Zachery

GIRLS:

Alexa
Ariel
Ashton
Autumn
Bianca
Briana, Brianna, Breanna
Chelsey, Chelsie
Christa
Ciara
Emma
Hannah, Hanna
Hope
Jordan
Kara, Kiara
Kasey
Katelyn, Kaitlin, Kaitlyn
Kaylee
Kelsey, Kelsie
Kirsten
Madison
Miranda
Sasha
Sierra
Taylor
Tiara
Tonya

BABY NAMES FOR THE '90s

BARBARA KAY TURNER

BERKLEY BOOKS, NEW YORK

BABY NAMES FOR THE '90s

A Berkley Book / published by arrangement with
the author

PRINTING HISTORY
Berkley edition / October 1991

All rights reserved.
Copyright © 1991 by Barbara Kay Turner.
This book may not be reproduced in whole or in part,
by mimeograph or any other means, without permission.
For information address: The Berkley Publishing Group,
200 Madison Avenue, New York, New York 10016.

ISBN 0-425-12938-1

A BERKLEY BOOK ® TM 757,375
Berkley Books are published by The Berkley Publishing Group,
200 Madison Avenue, New York, New York 10016.
The name "Berkley" and the "B" logo
are trademarks belonging to Berkley Publishing Corporation.

PRINTED IN THE UNITED STATES OF AMERICA

20 19 18 17 16 15 14 13 12 11

CONTENTS

INTRODUCTION

All of the ten thousand names listed in this book are in use today in the United States. If you include all the minor spelling variants, misspelled and unique names that can be found in the most recent birth registration records of states across the country, the available name list more than doubles. But consider this:

- Nearly 40 percent of all boys born in 1989 were named from an incredibly short list of just twenty-five names; another twenty-five names sufficed for 30 percent of the girls born the same year.
- Ninety percent of the boys and 75 percent of the girls were given names from a list of only five hundred per gender.
- A large number of names on the five-hundred lists are spelling variants or are related in other ways to the Top 50 names.

Since some four million babies are born in the United States every year, the statistical use of the top names becomes mind boggling. Fortunately this is a big country. There's plenty of room for the thousands and thousands of Christophers and Michaels and Sarahs and Amandas to go to school, play, work and live long lives without developing identity problems because of their names' popularity.

Lists of the top twenty-five, fifty and one hundred names appear from time to time. But if you wanted to find a name

1

less frequently used yet still familiar, wouldn't you like to know that Colin, for example, recently ranked 168th on the Top 500 list, Connor ranked 300th and Marilyn ranked 378th?

Would you like to know what names are moving up the list most rapidly? Or if you were thinking of naming your son Blair, would you like to know that in 1989, 61 percent of the babies named Blair were girls?

Baby Names for the '90s is designed to help you take a much closer look at the Top 500 ranking names for each gender, and a special comparative look at cross-gender names, without neglecting the fascinating potential of nine thousand names in rarer usage. In the research phase of this book, the author has compiled birth registration data from twelve states; lists of first names from Oregon, California, Colorado, Utah, Iowa, Nebraska, Missouri, Wisconsin, Kentucky, South Carolina, Alabama and West Virginia have been carefully analyzed to track frequency of use of names, discover naming trends and provide data for the ranking of the top name lists that are presented in Chapter 2.

But naming a baby is much more than a matter of statistics. The author also conducted a survey of some two hundred men, women and young adults to examine naming preferences and questions of concern to parents and prospective parents today. Respondents' written comments are quoted freely to give a sense of the human feelings involved.

Here's what you'll find in *Baby Names for the '90s*:

Trends: What's happening in the '90s regarding traditional vs. unusual name choices; changes in types of names considered suitable for girls; where name choices are coming from.

Lists: In the second chapter you'll find six lists including

• the Top 100 names for boys and for girls.
• more than sixty names expected to rise in popularity.

- more than sixty cross-gender names in frequent usage today.
- more than fifty names for girls reflecting a major trend.
- special and unique names.

Index: The index of ten thousand names will give you more information than you'll find in any other baby-naming aid today. Names used by both sexes are marked to show the balance of current gender usage. The numerical ranking of each of the Top 500 names for boys and girls is clearly shown. Spelling variants and related names are grouped under the most frequently used version of the main name. Cross-references will lead you to names that are related to the main name but follow different sound patterns or are spelled in distinctive ways.

In addition to notes about origins and meanings, the index also provides a simple pronunciation key for most names, to help parents avoid the formation of unnecessary spelling variants or outright misspellings. Chapter 5 explains how all this information is organized for quick and easy access.

Do enjoy your exploration into the questions of trends and ranking of names. Whether you finally choose a name from the middle of the list of ten thousand names or from the top of the Top 50, you're sure to be much more satisfied that your choice is the right choice for your son or daughter.

1

NAMING TRENDS IN THE '90s

Traditional or Unusual Names—
Which to Choose?

"I like traditional names that are not commonly used," one twenty-something parent responded in the survey. A man in his thirties commented that "classic is a better term than traditional" to describe a name that is familiar but not ordinary. Other comments from the survey:

"I would rather my child have a name that will stand out a little without being too strange."

"I would go somewhere in between—a name that is easy to say and spell, but special."

"Not traditional, but nothing extremely unusual either."

The number one reason for choosing a classic or traditional name is the fact that it will be instantly acceptable by most people in the arenas of school, work and play throughout life. Birth registration lists bear out the continued preference for traditional names, but they also reveal a parental nod to newer names and variants that are now achieving equal ranking with the more traditional names.

Overall, Jessica holds the number one place for girls today, closely followed by Ashley, Amanda, Brittany, Sarah, Jennifer, Stephanie, Samantha, Elizabeth and Megan. In some states, Ashley holds the top place; in South Carolina, West Virginia and Kentucky, Brittany is the top-listed girls' name. For boys, the overall top ten list shows Michael, Christopher, Joshua, Matthew, Daniel, David, Andrew,

Justin, Ryan and Robert. In South Carolina, West Virginia and Kentucky, Joshua takes the lead. Tyler is ranked fourth in Utah, and James is number three in Kentucky and South Carolina. (See Chapter 2 for the complete Top 100 name lists.)

Although rankings vary from state to state and from year to year, the lists are excellent indicators of a name's standing with the majority of parents across the country. Michael, for example, has consistently remained in the Top 50 names for at least five decades and has ranked close to, or in, first place for the past twenty years. Tiffany, considered to be a faddish choice when it came into fashion in the early eighties, is still among the Top 25 choices for girls today, proving that the name itself has enduring appeal. A study of the sound pattern of top names gives clues about their continuing popularity. Girls' names with three syllables, soft endings and the accent on the first syllable follow one favored pattern. If the name rhymes with other liked names, the appeal is increased. Tiffany may owe much of its success to Stephany, Bethany, Brittany and so on.

In the past three years, Kayla has risen from a ranking of 149th to 21st place on the girls' most-popular-name list. Kelsey, Taylor, Jordan, Bianca and Katelyn have all moved well up into the Top 100 names. Two other spellings of Katelyn (Kaitlin and Kaitlyn) have also moved into the Top 100, which could be considered a tripling of the popularity of the basic name. A special liking for names that begin with K seems to be developing as a sub-trend for the nineties. Kayla, Kelsey, Kaitlyn, Kelly, Kristen, Kirsten and Katie are leaders in this category.

Zachary, Jordan and Cody have taken big jumps on the boys' Top 50 list; Austin, Cameron, Corey and Cory, Taylor and Trevor have advanced into the Top 100. Ethan jumped 261 places in three years and is now ranked at 107. Logan, Caleb and Seth are not far behind. Biblical names for boys are well favored today.

Most of these newly arrived top names for boys and girls

have a traditional look and sound; the ones that aren't precisely traditional aren't strikingly unusual either. They fit the pattern of a '90s trend toward a looser definition of "traditional." This is especially apparent with girls' names.

More Tailored Names for Girls

In the survey on name choices for girls in the '90s, 75 percent of the women and 62 percent of the men indicated their belief in a trend toward stronger names for girls. As one respondent commented, "There is a certain strength and tailoredness associated with some of these names." The word *tailored* fits these names very well. They are often borrowed from surname forms and have a crisp, classic look and sound. Names like Whitney, Brook, Paige, Morgan, Kelsey, Madison, Jordan, Taylor and other cross-gender names are good examples. Cross-gender names are usable by both boys and girls; for example, today usage of Jordan is about 78 percent for boys, 22 percent for girls. Usage of Taylor is about 57 percent for boys, 43 percent for girls.

Comments from the survey, particularly from women, were specific about the advantages of cross-gender names for girls:

"Cross-gender names break down barriers of sexual stereotypes."

"In the nineties, when girls are competing for power positions, a cross-gender name could be an asset."

"Our daughter has found it to be an advantage—people remember her name."

"An advantage for girls is that these names often give an impression of adventurousness or strength of character."

Cross-gender Names for Boys

Some 32 percent of the men and women in the survey approved of cross-gender names for boys and girls. An equal percentage disliked them. A majority of the comments expressed the idea that such names were less likely to benefit boys and that care should be taken when choosing the names. Some comments:

"Boys might have problems with being teased. I don't feel a girl would have nearly as many problems."

"Neither a handicap nor an advantage, unless the name leans too much toward one gender or the other."

"I gave my oldest boy a cross-gender name; if I could do it again, he'd be Jack!"

"I've often wished I had one and would probably give one to a daughter, but maybe not for a boy."

"It depends on the name; some are too feminine for boys."

Birth registration lists show that a substantial number of names are consistently being used for both sexes. About 160 are specially noted in the index of this book, marked to show the percentage of use by each gender. These percentages won't necessarily remain the same as time passes, but they do indicate trends for the '90s. Moreover, they give you warning of names that once were cross-gender but are now used almost exclusively by one sex or the other.

What about Junior Names?

The survey showed a definite lessening of interest in giving a child the same name as a parent. Fifty-five percent of the men and fifty-nine percent of the women said they disliked the idea. Twenty-eight percent of the men and twenty-five percent of the women liked the idea, and the rest were indifferent or had no opinion.

New Names on the Block

An exciting trend of the new decade is the influx of very distinctive girls' names to the most popular lists. Savannah, Sierra, Chantel, Madison, Morgan (as a feminine name), Ciara, Dakotah, Destiny, Kiana, Tiara and Keisha are some of the names that are new to baby name listings or have been rarely used in the past.

Again, a major factor of parental acceptance seems to be how well the new names match favored sound and look patterns of other names already on the top lists. For example, Savannah sounds like the immensely popular Samantha. Morgan is just a step away from Megan in sound and effect. Names like Kiana and Brianna take much of their appeal from their similarity to Diana and Deanna. Tierra and Tiara are rhyming variants of Tara, and Sierra and Ciara follow in a natural progession.

Variants of standard names and phonetic spellings like Christa, Brittani, Desirae and Haley confirm parents' liking for the original names at the same time they show the human desire to make them just a little bit different. All these new names and variant forms add considerable interest and variety to the classic and traditional name pool.

Created Names and "La-" Names

Parents have always created new names, either from a desire to give a child a unique name or because the created name has special significance to the family. A favorite kind of name creation is to combine elements of both parents' names. A San Francisco Bay area couple, Larry and Jastelle, relate how Jastelle's name was formed from a combination of Jack and Estelle, the names of her parents. The tradition has been carried on with Larry and Jastelle's own daughter, to whom they've given the name Ellary.

Some classic names, like Vanessa, Jessica, Wendy, Pamela and Lorna, are examples of pure literary invention from past centuries, creations of writers and poets. Obviously the names have intrinsic qualities of lasting appeal, because parents are still happily using them today, while other invented names have been long forgotten.

A third kind of name creation involves giving independent life to name endings and short forms, then adding a variety of new endings, especially diminutives. Nora, for example, once was an ending of names like Eleanora and Leonora; then it came into independent usage. Variants like Noreen and Norissa quickly followed.

Something similar can be seen today in what has become a phenomenon of the eighties and nineties—prefix names. In these names, prefixes like De, Da, Je, Ja, Ki, Le, La, Ma, Na, Ra, Te, Ta and especially She and Sha, are combined with many different name endings such as -kisha, -kita, -lisa, -lana, -neesa, -quisha, -rissa and -naye. These created names sometimes have two syllables, as in names like Janaye, but the preferred pattern for girls follows the form of traditional names like Felicia and Natasha—three syllables with the accent falling on the second syllable. Lakeisha, Latasha, Shalisa and Janaye are examples of very popular prefix names.

Boys' prefix names are created in similar fashion, most often using two syllables, following the pattern of classic names like Jerome and Marcel. In every case, the accent is on the second syllable.

To accommodate the large numbers of contemporary prefix names, they're grouped in the index under the various alphabetical headings as "La-" names, "Sha-" names, and so on. Especially popular names of this type are entered separately. It may be that some of the names listed are actually existing names from other cultures that happen to fit the prefix pattern and thus have been unintentionally included.

Inspiration from the Media

When asked whether names of public figures and real or fictional people in movies and TV shows are likely to influence name choice, 53 percent of the women and 59 percent of the men surveyed answered yes. Birth registrations confirm this response. Comments in the survey made it clear that it is mainly the attention brought to a name by media exposure that causes parents to consider the name for their babies, not a desire to make a child the namesake of a public figure, actor or character.

"They [names in the media] can be a source of ideas, but shouldn't be the sole source."

"I think any place you get ideas for names is helpful."

"Some names are really nice, and I'm sure people wouldn't hear about them if they didn't hear them through the media."

"The names might be traditional names and okay, but if someone named their child Joe Montana Jones, I wouldn't like it."

"I would choose 'normal' names from people that I admire, but not easily recognizable names like Madonna or Sting."

"I think people should choose names because they really like them, not due to media influence."

The survey showed how respondents ranked various sources of name ideas in order of greatest to least important. Men rated suggestions from family and friends first, followed by names in the media, baby name books, personal invention and family traditions (junior and heritage names).

Women rated baby name books as the most important source of ideas, followed by suggestions from family and friends, family tradition, names in the media and personal invention.

2

TOP NAME LISTS

The following pages contain the Top 100 most popular names for boys and girls as well as lists of tailored names for girls, cross-gender names and names expected to rise in popularity during the coming decade. The Names to Watch list is based on increased usage as shown in birth registration records over the past four years.

The listings under the Tailored Names for Girls heading are only samples of the more favored examples of this type; you'll recognize others in the index, as well as more of the cross-gender names. Look also for the lists of special and unique names in this chapter, compiled from birth registration records of some of the more unusual names in use today.

For centuries, a fascinating aspect of naming has been the abiding interest in the use of names of special or unique origin such as nature, geographic locations, aristocratic rank and luxury items. Interest in these special names often comes in waves, based on social developments and current attitudes.

Virtue names like Patience, Hope and Charity came into fashion during the Reformation era of the sixteenth and seventeenth centuries. In the eighteenth century, a trend for the elaboration of simple names brought latinized names into fashion. With the nineteenth century came the Romantic era and many new flower names. Names like Ivy, Olive and Myrtle became as popular as Rose and Violet. Environmental concerns brought more nature names like River and Sunshine into use during the 1970s.

Today, unique names like Destiny, Dakotah, Dallas and Marquis are becoming popular. Shakespeare's Portia has given way to Porsche, and there's little doubt that the reference is to the luxury car, though the sound similarity to Portia gives the name validity. Virtue names have a strong place on current lists, though names that are more difficult to pronounce, such as Chastity, may be replaced by Chasity, a phonetic variant. Aristocratic titles used as names are also popular. Caesar and Cesar are frequently used, and Marquis is fast acquiring its own variants. Of the jewel names, Amber is by far the most popular today.

Top 100 Names for Girls

1. Jessica	35. Maria	68. Nancy
2. Ashley	36. Amy	69. Shannon
3. Amanda	37. Alexandra	70. Kristina
4. Brittany	38. Erica	71. Lindsay
5. Sarah	39. Jasmine	72. Kristin
6. Jennifer	40. Natalie	73. Marissa
7. Stephanie	41. Hannah	74. Patricia
8. Samantha	42. Angela	75. Brooke
9. Elizabeth	43. Kelly	76. Brenda
10. Megan	44. Brittney	77. Angelica
11. Nicole	45. Mary	78. Morgan
12. Lauren	46. Cassandra	79. Adriana
13. Melissa	47. Erin	80. April
14. Emily	48. Victoria	81. Ana
15. Amber	49. Jacqueline	82. Taylor
16. Michelle	50. Jamie	83. Tara
17. Heather	51. Lindsey	84. Jordan
18. Christina	52. Alicia	85. Jenna
19. Rachel	53. Lisa	86. Catherine
20. Tiffany	54. Katie	87. Alexis
21. Kayla	55. Allison	88. Karen
22. Danielle	56. Kristen	89. Melanie
23. Vanessa	57. Cynthia	90. Natasha
24. Rebecca	58. Anna	91. Sandra
25. Laura	59. Caitlin	92. Julie
26. Courtney	60. Monica	93. Bianca
27. Katherine	61. Christine	94. Krystal
28. Chelsea	62. Diana	95. Mayra
29. Kimberly	63. Erika	96. Holly
30. Sara	64. Veronica	97. Alexandria
31. Kelsey	65. Kathryn	98. Monique
32. Andrea	66. Whitney	99. Leslie
33. Alyssa	67. Brianna	100. Katelyn
34. Crystal		

Top 100 Names for Boys

1. Michael	35. Jason	68. Cory
2. Christopher	36. Jeffrey	69. Miguel
3. Joshua	37. Sean	70. Taylor
4. Matthew	38. Jordan	71. Edward
5. Daniel	39. Jeremy	72. Francisco
6. David	40. Travis	73. Trevor
7. Andrew	41. Cody	74. Adrian
8. Justin	42. Nathan	75. Jorge
9. Ryan	43. Mark	76. Ian
10. Robert	44. Jesse	77. Antonio
11. James	45. Charles	78. Shawn
12. Nicholas	46. Juan	79. Ricardo
13. Joseph	47. Samuel	80. Vincent
14. Anthony	48. Patrick	81. Edgar
15. John	49. Dustin	82. Erik
16. Jonathan	50. Scott	83. Peter
17. Kevin	51. Stephen	84. Shane
18. Kyle	52. Paul	85. Evan
19. Brandon	53. Bryan	86. Chad
20. William	54. Luis	87. Alejandro
21. Eric	55. Derek	88. Brett
22. Jose	56. Austin	89. Gabriel
23. Steven	57. Kenneth	90. Eduardo
24. Jacob	58. Carlos	91. Raymond
25. Brian	59. Gregory	92. Phillip
26. Tyler	60. Alex	93. Mario
27. Zachary	61. Cameron	94. Marcus
28. Aaron	62. Jared	95. Manuel
29. Alexander	63. Jesus	96. George
30. Adam	64. Bradley	97. Martin
31. Thomas	65. Christian	98. Spencer
32. Richard	66. Corey	99. Garrett
33. Timothy	67. Victor	100. Casey
34. Benjamin		

Top-listed Tailored Names for Girls

Ashton
Bailey
Blair
Brook, Brooke
Brynn
Cameron
Casey
Cassidy
Chelsey, Chelsie
Christian, Kristian
Dallas
Dana
Darcy
Eden
Hayley, Hailey, Haley
Hollis
Jordan
Kasey, Kacie
Kellen
Kelly, Kelley
Kelsey, Kelsie
Kendall
Kirby
Lee, Leigh
Lindsay, Lindsey, Lyndsey
Loren, Lauren
Mackenzie, McKenzie
Madison
Marlen
McKenna
Meredith
Morgan
Paige
Savannah
Shannon
Shea
Shelby
Skye, Sky
Stacy, Stacey
Sydney
Taylor
Tristan
Whitley
Whitney

Top-listed Cross-gender Names

Alexis
Ali
Angel
Ariel
Ashton
Avery
Blair
Cameron
Carey
Casey
Cassidy
Christian
Codi, Cody
Corey, Cory
Dakota
Dallas
Dana
Daryl

Devon, Devin, Devan	Loren
Dominique	Mackenzie
Dorian	Marlin
Francis	Morgan
Jackie	Noel
Jamie, Jaime	Paris
Jean	Quinn
Jessie	Riley
Jody	Robin
Jordan	Shannon
Kacey, Kasey	Shea
Kelly, Kellen	Shelby
Kendall	Sidney
Kerry	Taylor
Kim	Terry
Kristian	Tory, Torrey
Lee	Tracy
Leslie	Tristan

Names to Watch in the '90s

BOYS:

GIRLS:

Austin	Alexa
Bryce, Brice	Ariel
Caleb	Ashton
Cameron	Autumn
Cody, Kody	Bianca
Colby	Briana, Brianna, Breanna
Collin	Chelsey, Chelsie
Colton	Christa
Connor	Ciara
Dakota	Emma
Donovan	Hannah, Hanna
Ethan	Hope
Jordan	Jordan

BOYS: **GIRLS:**

Kirk   Kara, Kiara
Levi   Kasey
Logan   Katelyn, Kaitlin, Kaitlyn
Lucas   Kaylee
Mason   Kelsey, Kelsie
Maxwell   Kirsten
Parker   Madison
Riley   Miranda
Skyler   Sasha
Tanner   Sierra
Taylor   Taylor
Trent, Trenton   Tiara
Zachary, Zachery   Tonya

Special and Unique Names

VIRTUE NAMES
Amity, Blessing, Charity, Chastity, Constance, Faith, Felicity, Glory, Grace, Harmony, Honor, Hope, Hosanna, Innocencia, Joy, Justice, Loyal, Mercy, Merit, Modesty, Patience, Prudence, Serenity, Solace, True, Verity

FLOWER NAMES
Acacia, Azalea, Camelia, Cherry, Chrysantha, Dahlia, Daisy, Fern, Gardenia, Ginger, Gladiola, Hazel, Heather, Holly, Hyacinth, Iris, Ivy, Jasmine, Jessamine, Laurel, Lily, Linden, Lotus, Magnolia, Marigold, Mimosa, Myrtle, Olive, Peony, Poppy, Rose, Verbena, Viola, Violet, Willow, Zinnia

JEWEL NAMES
Amber, Amethyst, Beryl, Coral, Diamond, Ebony, Emerald, Garnet, Ivory, Jade, Jasper, Jet, Jewel, Onyx, Opal, Pearl, Ruby, Sapphire, Topaz

COLOR NAMES
Amber, Amethyst, Azure, Beige, Burgundy, Carmine, Cerise, Cinnamon, Coral, Ebony, Emerald, Gray, Indigo, Ivory, Lavender, Magenta, Mahogany, Ruby, Saffron, Scarlet, Silver, Viridian

WEATHER NAMES
Breezy, Dusty, Misty, Rainbow, Raine, Sunny, Sunshine, Storm, Stormy, Tempest, Zephyr

CELESTIAL AND EMOTIONAL NAMES
Ambrosia, Angel, Angelica, Antares, Bliss, Blythe, Celeste, Darling, Delight, Desire, Devine, Galaxy, Happy, Heaven, Honey, Jetaime, Jubilee, Lamour, Lovie, Marvel, Miracle, Myrth, Nirvana, Nova, Paradise, Precious, Radiance, Sparkle, Star, Temple, Treasure, Venus

TITLE NAMES
Baron, Caesar, Chancellor, Contessa, Count, Countessa, Czar, Czarina, Duke, Dutchess, Earl, Empress, General, Judge, Khanh, King, Knight, Lady, Laird, Lord, Majesta, Majesty, Major, Marques, Marquesa, Marquis, Marquise, Pharoah, Prince, Princesa, Princess, Queen, Raja, Rani, Regina, Rex, Royal, Sultan, Sultana

LUXURY NAMES
Brandy, Burgundy, Cashmere, Champagne, Chantilly, Chiffon, Lace, Mink, Paisley, Porsche, Sable, Satin, Silver, Velvet

STATES AND CITIES, COUNTRIES AND CONTINENTS
Africa, Albania, America, Arizona, Asia, Atlanta, Australia, Avila, Berkeley, Boston, Britain, Calais, California, Canada, Capri, Cheyenne, China, Colorado, Dakota, Dallas, Denver, Florence, Florida, France, Frisco, India, Indiana, Jericho, Kauai, Laramie, London, Louisiana, Marseille, Martinique, Milan, Montana, Monterey, Montreal, Nevada, Normandy, Odessa, Paris, Persia, Phoenix, Riviera, Sahara, Seville, Venetia, Venice, Verona, Vienna, Virginia

3

DO NAME ORIGINS AND
MEANINGS MATTER?

When survey respondents were asked if they thought name origins and definitions were important, 43 percent of the men and 54 percent of the women said yes. Twenty-one percent of the men and 17 percent of the women said no; the rest said it didn't matter either way or had no opinion. In response to the majority opinion, this chapter briefly outlines some reasons why you might be interested in knowing more about the names you're considering as choices for your child.

Ethnic Origins

Names used in the United States have a particularly wide variety of ethnic origins, due to our history of immigration and assimilation of many different peoples. Today, more and more parents consult name books and name dictionaries to find baby names that match their ethnic heritage. Parents seeking Irish names in this book, for example, will find Sheena, Sinead and Shawn. They'll also learn that those names are Gaelic forms of Jane, Janet and John.

Names like Denise, Ana, Raphael and Martin are so familiar to all of us that their French, Portuguese and Spanish origins may have been forgotten. Scandinavian, Czech, Russian, Slavic, Italian, Arabic and African names have also been assimilated into common usage. The index will

identify many of these and, in some cases, will show even
deeper roots in more ancient languages. The origins of some
names may be unknown, doubtful or so very mixed it's not
possible to state them with any certainty. Still others may
be recent inventions or blends that are simply labeled "contemporary."

Some primary names, like John and Mary, have variants
in dozens of languages. Variants most frequently used in
the United States will be grouped with the main name and
their origins identified where possible; other related names
may be cross-referenced. This provides a valuable bonus:
it's good to know about the common bond we share with
people of many countries through the medium of names.
The Russian Raisa, the Greek Rhoda and the English Rose
are all names chosen by parents with the same beautiful
image in mind—a rose.

The ten thousand names listed in the index also include
a number of names of Polynesian and Asian heritage, with
particular emphasis on Hawaiian and Japanese names that
have some of the sound patterns especially favored in this
country today. Sachiko and Michie aren't that much different from Sasha and Michelle, and names like Nikki and
Kalani are being used by children from various back-
grounds.

Meanings of these names are arrived at differently from
most European and American names, and I am indebted to
Eileen M. Root, author of *Hawaiian Names—English
Names*, for her explanation of meanings for most of the
Hawaiian names included. Meanings of Japanese and other
Asian names are generally derived from the combinations
of pictographic characters used to represent the spoken
names and can vary according to the characters used. Ruby
Yamasaki of San Francisco was most helpful in determining
some of the potential meanings for the Japanese names listed
in the index.

Name Meanings

Name meanings are always fascinating, however fragmentary or obscure or even doubtful they may have become as the original name passed through changes from country to country and century to century. The meanings of some names, especially occupational names like Carter and Taylor, are unmistakable today, many centuries after they came into common usage. Place names, patronymics ("son of" names) and names that describe the color of skin or hair, tallness or shortness, have also retained meanings essentially the same as they were in medieval or earlier times. Teutonic names that involve combinations of name elements, like "ruler," "spear" and "bold," often are given combined meanings today to satisfy the modern taste for a more comprehensive meaning. Thus, a German name might be defined as "bold ruler," rather than "ruler" and "bold." Names that have been compounded might also be shown with a compound meaning, as "beautiful rose" for Rosabella.

Religious and Mythological Origins

In spite of the growing secularization of society, biblical names continue to be very popular. Parents today are not always familiar with the Biblical source of such names as Joshua, David, Elizabeth and Ruth, or of the mythological origins of names like Mark, Diana and Helen. Names like Patrick and Cecilia are rich in historical associations, due not only to their assimilation into Christian usage as saints' names, but also to their more ancient non-Christian origins. Names from Greek, Roman and Scandinavian mythology abound in common usage today.

Is it worthwhile to include in the index listings some reminders of these connections to the past? Definitely!

Whether used by saints or villains, kings or commoners, names that have survived the centuries are an awesome heritage. You'll find it well worth your time to browse through all ten thousand names before you consult the checklist that follows to spot pitfalls you'll want to avoid.

4
CHECKLIST FOR FINAL SELECTION

In the parents' survey, both men and women agreed that five important points should be considered before making final name choices:

- **Psychological impressions** (a name is "weak," "strong," etc.)
- **Ease of spelling and pronunciation**
- **Distinctiveness, originality**
- **Name meaning and origin**
- **Family significance**

Most of these factors are personal to the families involved, but the second point brings up practical aspects that are often overlooked.

The Sound of the Name

Do you like the way the whole name—first, middle and last—sounds when it's put together?

Is it comfortable or awkward to say aloud?

How do just the first and last names sound together?

Are there any rhyming peculiarities using short forms of the first name with the last name (like Dick Pick or Sue Blue)?

The Look of the Name

Write out the full name on paper. Do you like the way it looks?

Was it easy or difficult to spell?

If it's not spelled the usual way, is it a true variant name or would most people think it's just misspelled?

Are you willing to spend extra time teaching your child to spell an unusual name correctly?

Underline the three initials; do the initials alone spell a word you don't care for?

Nicknames

Make a list of the most likely nicknames. Do you think you and your child can live with them?

Do any of the most likely nicknames create problems or make funny or awkward combinations when used with the last name (like Phil Potts for Phillip Potts)? Or do the initials spell an undesirable name (like P.I.G. for Phillip Ivan Gregory)?

Are you willing to spend time and effort to ensure use of the full name rather than nicknames, if that's what you prefer?

A Final Word

While naming a baby is a task to be taken seriously, there's nothing wrong with enjoying the experience. Try out names you like on family and friends. Write possible combinations on bits of paper and stick them on the refrigerator for a few days. Sing lullabies for practice, using different names. In the end, whatever name you choose will be perfect because the time and effort you've spent are proof that you're giving the gift of your love along with the name.

5

HOW TO USE THE INDEX

To find a particular name, look it up alphabetically, of course, but also keep in mind that there may be several different ways to spell it. For example, Cassidy and Cameron will be under "C," but Kassidy and Kameron will be under "K." Use the cross-references to find related names that are spelled or pronounced too differently to be grouped together with the main name.

Depending on the individual name, an index entry may contain up to nine pieces of information: name, ranking in the Top 500, pronunciation key, language origin, meaning of the name, informative comment or historical note, cross-gender usage, cross-references to other names and sub-listings of related names. But don't panic! The average listing contains only three to five elements, and the sample entry shown here proves it's easy to understand.

Basic Entry

HOPE (384): (English) "Expectation, belief." A virtue name.

Notice the number that follows the name; this is the rank number that shows Hope is number 384 on the list of five hundred names most frequently used for girls. (English) shows that the name is of English origin.

Cross-gender Usage

CASEY (100): (Irish) "Alert, vigorous." Usage: boys 66%, girls 34%. See also Kasey.

The usage percentages show the current balance of use between the genders.

Pronunciation and Variant Forms

Where the pronunciation of a name is not obvious, a simplified phonetic key appears close to the name to indicate the pronunciation generally recognized or most widely used in America today. The accent falls on the syllable that is capitalized.

GEOFFREY (246): *(JEF-ree)* (English/French) "Peaceful." See also Jeffrey.

Geoff

The above example also shows a cross-reference to a major variant form that has a different spelling, with the addition of another variant form of the main name.

BOYS' INDEX

A

AARON (28): (Hebrew) "Lofty, inspired." Biblical; Moses' brother Aaron was the first high priest of Israel. The soundalike Scandinavian name Aren means "eagle."
Aron (French, Slavic, Scandinavian), Arron, Aren, Aaren

ABDULLAH: (Arabic) "Servant of God."
Abdul, Abdulla

ABEL (252): (Hebrew) "Exhalation of breath." Biblical; the second named son of Adam. The variant form Able is an English surname.
Able

ABNER: (Hebrew) "Father of light." Biblical; King Saul of Israel's army chief by this name was a valiant warrior and clever strategist.

ABRAHAM (216): (Hebrew) "Father of multitudes." Biblical; Abraham, celebrated for his great faith, was the ancestor-father of Israel and some of the Arabic peoples.
Abe

ABRAM: *(AY-bram)* (Hebrew) "Exalted father." Biblical; the patriarch Abraham's original name was Abram before God changed it.
Abran (Spanish)

ABSALOM: (Hebrew) "Father of peace." Biblical; Absalom was the son of King David renowned for his handsome appearance and ability to win the loyalty and allegiance of others.

27

Absalon

ACE: A nickname given to one who excels. It is also an English surname meaning "noble."

ACHILLES: *(a-KILL-eez)* (Greek/Latin) The mythological hero of the Trojan War famous for his valor and manly beauty.

ADAIR: (Scottish) "From the oak tree ford." In rare use today for both boys and girls.

ADAM (30): (Hebrew) "Earthling man; from the red earth." Biblical; in the Book of Genesis, man was created from the red earth of Eden.
Addam, Adamson

ADAN (387): *(a-DAHN)* (Spanish) Variant form of Adam.

ADDISON: (English) "Son of Adam."

ADIEL: (Hebrew) "God is an ornament." A Biblical name.

ADIN: *(AY-den)* (Hebrew) "Pleasure-given." Biblical; an exile who returned to Israel from Babylon.

ADLAI: *(AD-lay)* (Hebrew) "My ornament." A Biblical name made noteworthy in the 20th century by the presidential candidate Adlai Stevenson.

ADLER: (German) "An eagle."

ADNAN: (Arabic) "Pleasure."

ADOLFO (448): (Teutonic/Latin) "Noble wolf"; (Spanish) Variant form of Adolphus.
Adolph, Adolphus, Adolpho

ADONIS: (Greek) "Handsome; a lord." In Greek mythology, Adonis was a beautiful youth loved by Aphrodite.
Adonai, Adonay

ADRIAN (75): (Latin) From Adria, the Adriatic sea region; also carries the meaning of "dark."
Adrien (French), Adriano (Spanish)

ADRIEL: *(AY-dree-el)* (Hebrew) "Of God's flock." A Biblical name.

ADWIN: (Ghana) "Creative."

AGUSTIN (373): *(a-GUS-tin)* (Latin) "Exalted, sublime"; (Spanish) Variant form of Augustine.
Agustine. See also Agust.

AHMED: *(AH-med)* (Arabic) "Much praised." Two of the many names of the prophet Muhammad.
Ahmad, Amad, Amadi

AIDAN: *(AY-den)* (Latin/English) "Helpful."
Aiden

AKENO: *(ah-KAY-noh)* (Japanese) "In the morning"; "bright shining field."

AL: A short form of names beginning with "Al-."

ALAN (129): (English/Celtic) "Fair, handsome." See also Allen.

ALARIC: *(AL-a-rik)* (German/French) "Rules all." Historically, Alaric was the Gothic king who plundered Rome in A.D. 410.
Alric, Alrick

ALASDAIR: *(AL-as-dare)* A Gaelic form of Alexander.
Alastair, Alistair, Allister, Alister

ALBERT (176): (English/German) "Noble, bright." One of the most famous Alberts was Prince Albert, consort of Queen Victoria, who was noted for his enthusiastic support of the application of science to the modern industrial age. Albert Einstein devised the Theory of Relativity when still a young man.
ALBERTO (151) (Spanish), Adelbert (German)

ALBIN: (Latin/English) "White." Alban and Albin are English surnames probably based on Alba, a Spanish and Italian place name.

ALBION: *(AL-bee-an)* (Latin/Celtic) "White cliffs." Albion is an ancient poetic name for Britain.

ALDEN: (English) "Wise/old, friendly." English surnames occasionally used as given names.
Aldrin, Aldric: "Old/wise ruler."

ALDO (461): (English/Latin) "Old one, elder."

ALEC (323): Scottish short form of Alexander.
Aleck, Alek (Russian), Aleko (Greek)

ALEX (61): English short form of Alexander.

ALEXANDER (29): (Greek) "Defender of mankind." Alexander the Great (356–323 B.C.) conquered and ruled the greater part of the known world before his death at the age of thirty-three. History describes him as a man of physical courage, impulsive energy and fervid imagination.

ALEJANDRO (88), Alexandro (Spanish); Alexandre (French); Alessandro (Italian)

ALEXIS (366): *(a-LEX-is)* (French/Greek) "Helper, defender." Usage: boys 20%, girls 80%.
Alexei (Russian), Alexi, Alexio

ALFONSO (266): *(al-FON-so)* (Spanish/German) "Ready, eager." The name Alfonso has been favored by Spanish royalty.
Alfonse, Alphonse (French); Alphonso (English)

ALFORD: (English) "The old ford."

ALFREDO (171): (Spanish) Variant form of Alfred; (English) "Elf-wise counselor."

ALFRED (346), Alf, Alfie

ALGERNON: *(AL-jer-non)* (French) "Bearded."

ALI (442): (Arabic) "The greatest." Variant form of Allah, title of the Supreme Being in the Muslim faith. The homonym Allie is often a short form of names beginning with "Al-." Usage: boys 80%, girls 20%.
Aly, Allie

ALLARD: (English/French) "Noble, brave."

ALLEN (167): (English/Scottish) Variant form of Alan. The homonym Allon is Hebrew, meaning "great tree."
ALLAN (364) (Scottish); Alain *(al-LAYNE)* (French); Allain, Allyn, Alun (Welsh); Allon, Alon

ALONZO (465): *(a-LON-so)* Spanish/Italian form of Alphonse. See Alfonso.
Alonso

ALTON: (English) "From the old town." Surname.

ALVA: (Arabic/Hebrew) "Sublime." Biblical; Alvah was a place and tribal name.
Alvah, Alvan

ALVARO (333): *(al-VAR-oh)* (German/Spanish) "One who speaks the truth."

Alvar

ALVERN: (Latin) "Spring, greening." See also Elvern.

ALVIN (308): (English) "Wise friend."
Alvyn, Alwin, Alwyn; Alvino (Spanish) "White, fair."

ALVIS: *(AL-viss)* (English) "All-knowing."

AMADEUS: *(ah-ma-DAY-us)* (Latin) "Loves God."
Amadeo (Spanish)

AMBROSE: (Greek) "Immortal."

AMES: (English/French) "Friend." English surname in rare use as a given name.

AMIR: *(a-MEER)* (Arabic) "Prince."

AMON: *(AY-mon)* (Hebrew) "Trustworthy, faithful." Biblical. Also the name of one of the gods of Thebes in Egypt.

AMORY: *(AM-er-ee)* (English/German) "Brave, powerful."
Amery

AMOS: *(AY-muss)* (Hebrew) "Bearer of burdens." Biblical; the prophet who wrote the Book of Amos.

ANDERS: Scandinavian form of Andrew.
Anderson

ANDREW (7): (Greek) "Manly, brave." Biblical; the first chosen of the twelve apostles; Andrew is called the patron saint of Scotland and Russia.
ANDRE (179) (French/Portuguese); Aundre (Contemporary); ANDRES (152) (Spanish); Andreus, Andreas (Greek); Andrei (Italian); Andreo (Spanish); Andric, Andrian, Andru, Andriel (Contemporary)

ANDY (222): Short form of Andrew.
Andino

ANGEL (114): *(AHN-hail* or *AIN-jel)* (Latin/Greek) "Messenger." Biblical; name for the spirit creatures sent by God to men as His messengers. Usage: boys 82%, girls 18%.
ANGELO (340) (Italian/Portuguese/Spanish), Angelino

ANGUS: (Gaelic/Scottish) "Singular, choice."

ANSELL: (German/English) "God's protection."

Ansel, Anselmo

ANSON: (English) "Anne's son." An English surname.

ANTARES: *(an-TARE-ees* or *an-TAHR-ees)* (Greek) The name of a giant red star, the brightest in the constellation Scorpio.

ANTHONY (14): (English) Variant form of Antony, (Latin) "Highly praiseworthy." Mark Antony (82–30 B.C.), Roman triumvir and general, shared a throne and a tempestuous political career with Queen Cleopatra of Egypt. St. Anthony founded the first Christian monastic order and is traditionally renowned for his resistance to temptation by the Devil.

ANTONIO (78) (Spanish/Italian); Antonino, Antony (Italian); ANTOINE (453) (French) *(AN-twan)*, Anton (Russian/German/Czech); Antone (American)

APOLLO: (Greek) "Destroyer." The Greek and Roman god of light, music and poetry. Apolonio is a Greek name meaning "belongs to Apollo." Biblical; one of the early Christian disciples.

Apolonio, Apollos

ARAM: *(AIR-am)* (Assyrian) "High, exalted."

ARAMIS: *(AIR-a-miss)* (French) In fiction, the famous swordsman from Alexander Dumas's *Three Musketeers*, notable for his ambition and religious aspirations.

ARCHER: (English/French) "A bowman." An English surname.

ARCHIBALD: (English) "Valuable, bold."

Archie

ARDELL: *(ar-DELL)* (Latin) "Eager, industrious." In rare use for boys and girls.

ARDEN: (Celtic) "Lofty, eager." In rare use for boys and girls.

Ardon (Hebrew) "Bronze." A Biblical name.

ARI: (Hebrew) "Lion." Also can be a short form of names beginning with "Ari-."

ARIC: (English/Norse) "Rule with mercy." See also the soundalike name Eric.

Arick, Aaric

ARIEL (479): (Hebrew) "Lion of God." Biblical; a name for Jerusalem. Shakespeare gave this name to a prankish spirit in *The Tempest*. Usage: boys 29%, girls 71%.

ARION: The name of a Greek poet and musician. Also the name of the mythological magic horse born to Poseidon and Demeter.

ARLANDO: Variant form of Orlando.

ARLEN: (Hebrew) "Pledge."
Arlin, Arlan, Arland

ARLEY: Variant form of Harley.
Arlie, Arleigh

ARLO: (Latin) "Strong, manly;" (Italian) Variant form of Charles.

ARMANDO (153): (Spanish) "Army man." Variant form of Herman.
Armand (French); Arman (Russian), Armond; Armondo (Italian)

ARMON: (Hebrew) "High place."
Armen, Armin

ARNAN: (Hebrew) "Quick, joyful." A Biblical name.
Arnon "torrent valley."

ARNOLD (497): (English/German) "The eagle rules."
Arnoldo (Spanish); Arno (Italian); Arnie, Arnel, Arnell, Arnett, Arne, Arni

ARSENIO: *(ar-SEE-nee-oh)* (Spanish) Variant form of Arsenius; (Greek) "Virile, masculine." St. Arsenius the Great tutored the sons of the Roman emperor Theodosius. The actor/television personality Arsenio Hall has brought the name into prominence.
Arcenio

ARTHUR (191): (Celtic) "Noble, courageous." King Arthur of Britain (sixth century) and his Round Table of knights have become legendary figures.
ARTURO (179) (Spanish), Artur (Portuguese), Artie, Art

ARVIN: (English) "The people's friend."
Arwyn, Arwin

ASA: *(AY-sah)* (Hebrew) "Healer, physician." Biblical; name of the third king of Judah.
Ase

ASH: (English) "Ash tree." Typically an English surname used as a given name. Ash and its variants are English surnames used as given names. Ashley is used now almost entirely as a name for girls. See also Ashton.
Ashford, Ashley

ASHER: (Hebrew) "Happy, happiness." Biblical; Asher, the eighth son of Jacob, was promised a life blessed with abundance.

◄ ASHTON (431): (English) Place name and surname. Usage: boys 54%, girls 46%.
Ashtin

AUBREY: *(AW-bree)* (English/French) "Rules with elf-wisdom." Usage: boys 13%, girls 87%.
Aubry

AUDEN: (English) "Old friend."
Audie, Audel, Audley

AUDRIC: (English) "Old/wise ruler."

AUGUST: (Latin) "Majestic dignity; grandeur." St. Augustine was the first archbishop of Canterbury.
Augustine, Augustus (German)

AURELIO: *(aw-REE-lee-oh)* (Spanish) Variant form of Aurelius; (Latin) "Golden."
Aurelius, Aureliano (Spanish)

AUSTIN (57): (French/English) Variant form of Augustine. Usage of Austen: boys 83%, girls 17%.
Austen, Austyn

AVERY: *(AY-vree)* (English/French) "Rules with elf-wisdom."

AXEL: (Scandinavian) "Sacrifice to God."

AXTON: (English) "From the peaceful town."

AYERS: (English) "Heir to a fortune."

B

BAILEY: (English/French) Comes from the word meaning steward or public official; man in charge. Usage of Bailey: boys 8%, girls 92%.
Bayley

BANNER: (English/Scottish) "Flag; ensign bearer."

BARAK: *(BARE-ek)* (Hebrew) "Flash of lightning." Biblical; a valiant army leader who cooperated with the prophetess Deborah to win victory in a battle against overwhelming odds. See also Barric.
Barrak, Baruch

BARAN: (Russian) "The ram; forceful, virile." See also Baron.

BARCLAY: (English/Scottish) "The birch-tree meadow." Place name.
Bartley

BARD: (Celtic) "Minstrel; a singer-poet."
Baird, Barden, Bardon

BARNABAS: (Hebrew) "Son of comfort." Biblical; a first-century missionary companion of Paul.
Barnaby (English), Bernabe, Barney

BARNETT: (English) "Of honorable birth."
Barnet, Barney

BARON: (English/French) A title of nobility used as a given name. The Hebrew phrase Bar Aaron, "son of Aaron."
Barron, Barr

BARRETT: Variant form of Barnett.
Barret

BARRIC: (English) "Grain farm." A place name. See also the soundalike name Barak.
Barrick, Beric

BARRY (431): (Celtic) "Spearman, marksman."
Barrie, Barrington

BART: A short form of names beginning with "Bart-."

BARTHOLOMEW: (Hebrew) "The son of Tolmai (the

farmer).'' Biblical; one of the twelve apostles, known as the patron saint of tanners and vintners. Variant forms listed here are related English surnames.

Barton, Bates, Bardo, Bartel, Barth

BARTRAM: (English) ''Glorious raven.'' The raven was sacred to Odin, the Norse god of war; the raven is also the emblem of the Danish royal standard. See also Bertram.

BARUCH: (Hebrew) ''Blessed.''

BASIL: *(BAZ-el)* (Greek) ''Royal, kingly.''

BAXTER: (English) ''Baker.'' An occupational name.

BAYARD: *(BAY-erd)* (English/French) ''Auburn-haired.'' The name of a sixteenth-century French knight and national hero renowned for his valor and purity of heart.

Bay, Baylen

BEALE: (English/French) ''Handsome.''

Beal, Beall

BEAU (317): (French) ''Handsome, beautiful.''

Beauregard ''well thought of''; Beaumont ''beautiful mountain.''

BEN (469): Short form of names like Benjamin and Benedict.

Benny, Bennie, Benito (Spanish/Italian), Benji, Benjy, Benn (English)

BENEDICT: (Latin) ''Blessed.'' A name used by fifteen popes and a monastic order, the Benedictines. Shakespeare's Benedick in *Much Ado About Nothing* is a self-assured, witty bachelor.

Benedick, Benedetto (Italian)

BENJAMIN (34): (Hebrew) ''Son of the right hand.'' Biblical; the twelfth and most beloved son of the patriarch Jacob.

BENJIRO: *(ben-jee-ROH)* (Japanese) ''Enjoy peace; be in peace.''

BENNETT: Variant form of Benedict.

Bennet, Benson

BENTLEY: (English) ''Grassy meadow.''

BENTON: (English) "Settlement in a grassy place." Place name.

BERKLEY: (Irish) "The birch-tree meadow." See also Burke.
Berke, Berkeley, Berk

BERLYN: (German) "Son of Berl." See also Burl.
Berl, Berle, Burlin

BERNARD (457): (Teutonic) "Strong as a bear."
Bernardo (Spanish/Portuguese), Bernie, Bern (Scandinavian) Berne, Bernelle, Burnard, Barnard

BERT: (English) "Illustrious."
Bertie, Berton, Bertin

BERTRAM: (Teutonic/English) "Glorious raven." See also Bartram.
Bertrand (French)

BEVAN: (Welsh) "Son of Evan."
Bevis

BILLY (213): Nickname for William, now often used as an independent name. Usage of Billie: boys 38%, girls 62%.
Bill, Billie

BIRCH: (English) "Bright, shining; the birch tree." A nature name and surname.
Birce

BJORN: *(bee-YORN)* (Scandinavian) "Bear." Famous name bearer: the Swedish tennis champion Bjorn Borg.

BLADE: (English) "Knife, sword." This surname has been in use since medieval times.

BLAINE (387): (Scottish/English) "Thin, lean." Blaine is very rarely used for girls. Variant forms listed here are related English surnames.
Blayne, Blane, Blaney

BLAIR: (Scottish/Gaelic) "Field of battle." Usage: boys 39%, girls 61%.

BLAISE: (Teutonic/English) "Torch; burning fire." Blaise Pascal was a brilliant seventeenth-century child prodigy, mathematician, scientist and philosopher; he invented the

calculating machine and hydraulic press before he died
at age thirty-nine.

Blaize, Blayze, Blaze, Blase, Blais, Blaisdell

BLAKE (111): (English/Scottish) "Dark, dark-haired." Can
also mean the reverse: "fair, pale." Very rarely used for
girls.

Blakeman, Blakely

BO: A nickname and short form occasionally used as an
independent name for boys and, due to actress Bo Derek,
for girls. Usage: boys 85%, girls 15%. See also Beau.

BOBBY (216): Short form of Robert. Usage of Bobbie: boys
27%, girls 73%.

Bob, Bobbie

BODEN: (Scandinavian) "A shelter."

Bodin, Bodie, Bodine

BOONE: (English/French) "Good, a blessing." Daniel
Boone, the modest American frontier hero, has influenced the use of the surname as a given name.

BORAK: (Arabic) "The lightning." According to legend,
Al Borak was the name of the magical horse that bore
Muhammad from earth to the seventh heaven.

BORG: (Scandinavian) "Castle."

BORIS: (Russian) "Fighter." St. Boris is known as the patron saint of Moscow.

BOSTON: (English) Place name and surname rarely used
as a given name.

BOWEN: (Welsh) "Son of Owen."

Bohannon (Irish)

BOYCE: (English/French) "Lives near the wood."

BOYD: (Celtic/Scottish) "Blond, fair-haired."

BRAD (371): (English) "Broad, wide."

Bradd, Braddock "Broad-spreading oak."

BRADEN: (English/Irish) "Broad hillside."

Bradon, Braddon, Braeden, Braedon, Brayden, Braydon

BRADLEY (65): (English/Scottish) "Broad clearing in the
wood." Also related English surnames.

Bradlee, Bradford, Bradshaw

BRADY (270): (Irish/English) "Broad."

BRAM: (English/Scottish) "Bramble; a thicket of wild gorse." Short form of Abraham, Abram. A noted name bearer was Bram Stoker, author of *Dracula*.

BRAND: (English/German) "Fiery torch; beacon."
Brandt (German), Brando (Italian), Brandell

BRANDON (19): (English) "Beacon on the hill."
BRANDEN (265), Brandin, Brandan, Brandyn

BRANNON: (Irish) Variant form of Brandon.
Brannan, Brannen, Branson

BRANT: (English) Variant form of Brand. Joseph Brant was a Mohawk Indian, a renowned strategist who fought on the British side during the American Revolution. He was also a devout scholar who translated Christian religious works into his native Indian tongue.
Brantley, Branton

BRAXTON: (English) Place name and surname sometimes used as a given name.

BRECK: (Irish/Gaelic) "Freckled."
Brexton

BRENDAN (207): (Irish) Variant form of Brandon. Brendan Behan was a noted Irish playwright and wit.
BRENDON (457), Brenden

BRENNAN (404): (Irish/Gaelic) "A sip of water."
Brennen, Brennon, Brannon, Brenn, Brenan, Brenen

BRENT (139): (English) "From the burnt field."
BRENTON (461), Brenten, Brendt, Brentley, Brently

BRETT (89): (English/French) "Brit." A native of Brittany (France) or Britain (England). Rare usage of Britt is about equal for boys and girls.
BRET (373), Britton, Brittan, Brittain (English); Bretton (Scottish); Britt (Dutch)

BREWSTER: (English) "One who brews ale." See also Webster.

BRIAN (25): (Celtic) "He ascends." Brian Boru (tenth century) was king of Ireland and one of its greatest national heroes. See also Bryan.

Brien, Brion, Briant, Bryant (French)

BRICE (495): (English/French) A given name of medieval origin. See also Bryce.

Briceson

BRICK: (English) "Bridge."

Brickman, Brigham

BROCK (317): (English/German) Variant form of Brook. The related surnames are English and German/Jewish variant forms of names like Baruch.

Brockman, Brockton, Broxton

BRODERICK: (Scandinavian/Scottish) "Brother."

Broderic, Brodrick, Brodric

BRODIE: (Scottish) Place name. There is a Castle Brodie in Scotland.

Brody

BRONSON: (English/German) "Brown's son."

Bron

BROOKS: (English) "Water, stream." Usage of Brook: boys 37%, girls 63%.

Brook

BRUCE (279): (English/Scottish) Surname used since medieval times, now a common given name, especially in Scotland. The tale of "the Bruce" (Robert, king of Scotland in the fourteenth century), who watched and learned the value of perseverance from a spider spinning a web, has become a part of the world's folklore.

BRUNO: (Italian/Portuguese) "Brown."

Braun (German)

BRYAN (54): (English) Very popular variant form of Brian. BRYANT (194), Bryon

BRYCE (158): (Scottish) Surname form of Brice.

BRYSON (479), Brycen, Bryston

BUCHANAN: (bew-KAN-an) (Scottish/Gaelic) "House of the clergy."

BUCK: (English) The word for a male goat or deer, used as a given name or nickname. Buck is also an English slang word used to describe a sportsman or a dandy.

Buckley

BUD: A familiar form of "brother." Nickname used since medieval times.

Buddy

BUELL: *(BEW-el)* (German) "Hill dweller." Use of surnames like Buell, Buford and Beauregard as given names stems from the custom of naming sons after commanding officers during and after the Civil War. In the North, names like Grant and Scott became popular choices.

Buford

BURDETT: *(ber-DETT)* (English/French) Surname used as a given name.

Burdette

BURKE: (English) "Fortified hill."

Bourke

BURL: (English) "Fortified." See also Berlyn.

Burle, Burleigh

BURNE: (English/Irish) "Bear, brown." See also Byrne.

Burnell, Burnette, Burney

BURT: (English) "Fortified."

Burton

BYRNE: *(Burn)* (Celtic/Scottish) "Field in the heights."

BYRON (254): *(BYE-ron)* (English/French) Surname often used as a given name. The English variant form Biron was the name of a character in Shakespeare's *Love's Labours Lost*.

Biron

C

CABLE: (English) "Ropemaker." A common English surname.

Cabe

CADELL: *(kay-DELL)* (Celtic) "Spirit of battle." See also Kade.

Cade, Caden, Cayden

CAELAN: *(KAY-lan)* (Gaelic/Irish) "Powerful in battle."
See also Cale.
Calan, Calin

CAESAR: *(SEE-zar)* (Latin) Caesar was the title of the Roman emperors after Augustus Caesar. Czar (Russian) and
Kaiser (German) are variant forms. See also Cesar.

CAIN: (Hebrew) "Something produced." Biblical; Cain,
the firstborn son of Adam, killed his brother in jealous
anger and spent the rest of his life as a wanderer in exile.

CAINE: (English/French) Place name and surname. No
connection to the biblical Cain. See also Kane.

CAL: Short form of names beginning with "Cal-."

CALDER: (English/Scottish) "Rough waters."

CALE: (English) Surname derived from Charles. See also
Caelan.
Calen, Calin (Spanish), Caley

CALEB (120): *(KAY-leb)* (Hebrew) "Dog; tenacious and
aggressive." Biblical; Caleb, a companion of Moses and
Joshua, was noted for his astute powers of observation
and fearlessness in the face of overwhelming odds.

CALHOUN: (Gaelic) Place name and surname.

CALLUM: (Gaelic) "Mild, gentle."
Caelum

CALVERT: (English) "Cowherd, cowboy."
Calbert

CALVIN (211): (Latin) "Bald." A Roman family clan
name. See also Kalvin.

CAM: Short form of names beginning with "Cam-."

CAMDEN: (Gaelic/Scottish) "Winding valley."

CAMERON (62): (Gaelic) Nickname meaning "bent
nose." This nickname of a specially valorous ancestor,
became the surname of one of the oldest clans in Scotland. Usage: boys 97%, girls 3%.
Camron

CAMILO: *(ka-MEE-lo)* (Latin) "Freeborn child; noble."
Masculine form of Camille.
Camillo

CANTRELL: (Latin) "Singer."

CARDELL: (English/French) Surname.

CAREY: (Welsh/Celtic) "Friendly, loving." Usage: boys 63%, girls 37%. See also Cary.

CARL (198): (German/Scandinavian) Variant form of Charles. See also Karl.

CARLOS (59): (Latin) "A man." Variant form of Charles. Carlo

CARLTON: (English) "Charles's town." Surname and place name. Carlin is a German diminutive form, "little Charles."
Carleton, Carlson, Carlisle, Carlin, Carlen, Charlton

CARMELO: (Hebrew) "Fruitful orchard." Also refers to Mount Carmel in Palestine.

CARNE: *(karn)* (Gaelic/Welsh) Variant of English surname Cairn, meaning a landmark or memorial made of piled-up stones.
Carney

CARNELL: (English) "Defender of the castle."

CARRICK: (Scottish) "From the rugged hills."

CARRINGTON: (English/Celtic) Place name and surname.

CARSON (469): (English/Scottish) "Son of Charles."

CARTER: (English) "One who transports goods."

CARY: (Welsh, English) "Loving." See also Carey.

CASEY (100): (Irish) "Alert, vigorous." Usage: boys 66%, girls 34%. See also Kasey.
Case, Cace

CASHMAN: (English) Surname in rare use as a given name.
Cash

CASIMIR: *(KAH-zee-meer)* (Slavic) "Enforces peace." See also Kasimir.
Casimiro

CASPAR: (Persian) "Keeper of the treasure." In medieval tradition, Caspar was one of the Three Magi who traveled from afar to find the baby Jesus.
Casper

CASSIDY: (Irish/Welsh) "Curly headed." Usage: boys 22%, girls 78%.
Cass, Cassian

CASSIUS: *(KASH-us)* (Latin) Roman clan name. Shakespeare's *Julius Caesar* depicts Caius Cassius as politically ambitious. In modern times, Cassius Clay was the birth name of the heavyweight boxing champion Muhammad Ali.

CECIL: *(SESS-ul)* (Latin) "Unseeing." Masculine form of Cecilia.

CEDRIC: (Welsh) "Gift of splendor." Cedro and Cidro are Spanish short forms of Isadoro.
Cedrick, Cedro, Cidro *(SEE-dro)*

CESAR (132): (Spanish/Portuguese/Italian) Variant form of Caesar.
Cezar, Cesario (Spanish/Italian), Cesare *(CHEZ-a-ray)* (Italian)

CHACE: (English) "Huntsman." See also Chase.
Chayce

CHAD (87): A name dating from medieval England. Also a short form of various surnames.
Chadd, Chadwick, Chadwell, Chadrick

CHAN: (Spanish) Nickname for John. Also used as a short form of various English surnames. Chano and Chayo are similar Spanish short forms for names ending in "-ano" and "-rio." Chan is also a Chinese family name.
Chano, Chayo

CHANCE (340): (English/French) Variant form of Chauncey, often used in the sense of "fortune; a gamble."
Chauncey, Chauncy, Chaunce

CHANCELLOR: *(CHANCE-ler)* (Latin) "Secretary; keeper of the keys." English surname. Also a title used for high-ranking government officials or educators.

CHANDLER: (English/French) "Candlemaker." Usage: boys 79%, girls 21%.

CHANNING: (English/Irish) "Young wolf."
Chann, Channe, Channon

CHARLES (46): (German/French) "A man." French variant form of Carl, adopted by the English especially since the seventeenth century, when Kings Charles I and II ruled. Charles and its variant forms have been favored by the royalty of several countries, including the present Prince of Wales. See also Carlos and Karl.

CHARLIE (414): Short form. Variant forms are related English surnames. Usage of Charley: boys 71%, girls 29%. Charly: boys 64%, girls 36%.
Charley, Charly, Charlton, Charleston, Charleson

CHARRO: (Spanish) Nickname for a cowboy, especially in Argentina.

CHASE (127): (English) "Huntsman." See also Chace.
Chasen

CHAZ (404): Nickname for Charles, used as independent name.
Chas, Chuck, Chick

CHE: *(chay)* (Spanish) Short form of Jose, made familiar as a given name by the South American revolutionary Che Guevara.

CHEROKEE: (American Indian) "People of a different speech." The name of one of the largest tribes, used as a given name.

CHESTER: (English) Place name and surname used as a given name.
Chet, Chess, Cheston

CHEVY: (French) "Horseman, knight." A short form of Chevalier. Chevy Chase, the actor-comedian, has brought the name into modern notice.
Chevell *(sha-VELL)*, Cheval *(she-VALL)*, Chevalier

CHEYENNE: *(shy-ENN)* (French/American Indian) An Algonkin tribe of the Great Plains. Also the name of the capital city of Wyoming. Usage: boys 14%, girls 86%.

CHEYNE: (Scottish) "Oak-hearted."
Chayne, Chane, Chaney, Cheney

CHICO: (Spanish) "Boy, lad." Also a Spanish short form of Ezekiel.

Chiko *(CHEE-koh)* (Japanese) "Arrow; arrow shaft; promise, pledge."

CHRIS (414): Short form of names beginning with "Chris-" also used as an independent name.
Cris (Spanish)

CHRISTIAN (66): "Follower of Christ, the Anointed." The "Cr-" spellings are Spanish forms. Usage of Christian: boys 91%, girls 9%.
CRISTIAN (270), Cristos, Criston, Christan, Christos

CHRISTOPHER (2): (Latin) "With Christ inside."
Christofer, Christoffer (German); Christophe, Christofor (French); Cristofer, Cristofor, Cristoval (Spanish)

CISCO: *(SISS-co)* Spanish diminutive of Francisco.

CLANCY: (Irish) "Redheaded."

CLARENCE (421): (Latin) "Bright, shining, gentle."

CLARK (491): (English) "Cleric, secretary."
Clarke

CLAUDE: (English/Latin) "Lame."
Claudio, Claud, Claudius

CLAYTON (181): (English) "Earth." Place name and surname derived from Clay.
Clay, Clayborne, Clayburn, Claiborne

CLEAVON: *(KLEE-von)* (English) "Cliff."

CLEMENT: (Latin) "Clemency, mercy." A name borne by fourteen popes.
Clemente, Clemens (Danish), Clem

CLEON: "Renowned father." Based on Cleopas.

CLETUS: *(KLEE-tus* or *KLAY-tus)* (Greek) "Illustrious."
Cleytus, Cleo, Cleon

CLEVELAND: (English) "Land of cliffs."
Cleve

CLIFFORD (356): "Cliff-side ford." English place name and surname.
Clifton (English) "Town by the cliff." Cliff

CLINTON (233): (English) "Hillside town."
Clint, Clintwood

CLIVE: *(Kleeve* or *Klyve)* (English) "Cliff."

CLOVIS: (Latin/German) "Renowned fighter." Variant form of Louis.

CLYDE: (Scottish/Irish) Given name from the Clyde River in Scotland.

COBURN: (Scottish/English) Surname and place name.
Coby

COCHISE: *(ko-CHEECE)* (American Indian) The name of a renowned warrior, chief of the Chiricahua Apache, in rare use today as a given name.

CODY (41): (Irish/Gaelic) "Helpful." Very rarely used for girls.
Codie, Codey

COLBY (272): (English) "Dark, dark-haired."
Colbey, Colbert (French)

COLE (269): (English) "Conqueror." Short form of Nicholas.
Coleman, Colman, Colson

COLIN (168): (English/French) Short form of Nicholas.
COLLIN (256), Collins, Colan, Colino (Italian), Colyn

COLLIER: (English) "Coal-miner."

COLT: (English) "Young horse; frisky." Variant forms are English surnames used as given names.
Colter, Coulter, Coltrane

COLTON (161): "Coal-town."
Colten, Coltin

CONAN: *(KOH-nan)* (Celtic/Irish) "Mighty; high one."

CONNAL: (Celtic/Irish) "Mighty; valorous."
Connell, Conal

CONNOR (300): (Irish) "Desiring."
Conor, Conner

CONRAD (469): (Teutonic) "Brave, wise."

CONROY: (Irish/Gaelic) "Wise advisor."

CONSTANTINE: (Latin) "Constant, steadfast." Most famous name bearer was Constantine the Great, the fourth-century emperor who made Christianity the official state religion of the Roman Empire.

CONWAY: (Welsh) Place name and surname.

COOPER: (English) "Barrelmaker." May also be the English form of a German surname meaning "copper-smith."

CORBETT: (Latin/French) "Raven."

CORBIN (435): (Latin/French) "Raven-haired." Variant forms are English surnames used as given names.
Corben, Corbyn, Corvin, Corby

CORDELL: "Cordmaker." English surname.
Cordale, Cord

COREY (67): (English/Irish) "Hill hollow." See also Cory.
Correy, Corrick, Corley, Corky

CORMAC: *(KOR-mak)* (Irish) "Raven's son." Cormac was the name of the third-century Irish king who founded schools of military science, law and literature at Tara.
Cormack, Cormick

CORNELIUS: *(kor-NEEL-yus)* (Latin) "Horn, horn-blower." Biblical; Cornelius was a Roman centurion who was baptized by Peter.
Cornell, Cornel

CORRIGAN: (Irish) "Spearman."

CORRIN: (Irish) "Spear-bearer."
Corin, Corran, Corren, Corlan

CORT: (English/French) "Courtier; court attendant." Today Courtney is primarily used for girls. See also Curt and Kurt.
Court, Cortland, Courtland, Courtney, Courtenay

CORTEZ: *(kor-TEZ)* (Spanish) "Courteous." Variant form of Curtis. Surname of the Spanish explorer and adventurer who with a small expeditionary force conquered the Aztec civilization of Mexico.

CORWIN: (Gaelic) "From beyond the hill."
Corwyn

CORY (69): (English/Irish) Surname. Very rarely used for girls. See also Corey.
Correy, Corry

COYAN: *(KOY-an)* (French) "Modest."
Coyne

COYLE: (Irish) "Leader in battle."

CRAIG (164): (Scottish/Welsh) "Rock, rocky."

CREED: (Latin/English) "Belief; guiding principle."
Creedon is an Irish surname.
Creedon

CREIGHTON: (Gaelic/Scottish) "Border dweller."
Crayton

CRISPIN: (Latin/English) "Curly haired." St. Crispin was
a third-century martyr now known as the patron saint of
shoemakers.
Crespin

CROYDON: (English) Surname and place name.
Croy

CRUZ: *(krooz)* (Spanish/Portuguese) "Cross."

CULLEN: (Irish/Gaelic) "Good-looking lad."
Cullin, Cullan

CURRAN: (Gaelic) "Dagger."
Curry, Currie

CURT: (English) "Courtier." See also Cort and Kurt.

CURTIS (125): (English/French) "Courteous."
Curtiss

CYD: Variant short form of Sydney.
Cydney

CYRANO: *(SEER-ah-no)* (French) Cyrano de Bergerac was
a seventeenth-century soldier/science-fiction writer. His
talents and his extraordinary nose provided the inspiration for Rostand's *Cyrano de Bergerac.*

CYRIL: *(SEER-el)* (Greek) "Master, ruler."
Cyrill, Cy, Ciro (Spanish)

CYRUS: (Persian/Greek) "Enthroned." Historical; Cyrus
the Great conquered Babylon at the height of its powers
and founded the Persian Empire.

CZAR: *(ZAR)* (Russian) "Caesar, emperor."

D

"DA-" and "D'-" names: (Contemporary) Blends of "Da-" plus various endings, with pronunciation on the second syllable. Names beginning with "D'-" (meaning "of") follow an Italian style of surnames. See also Damario and "De-" names.

DaJon, DaJohn, DaJuan, D'Angelo, DaMar, Damarco, Damarko, D'Amico, D'Amante, Damont, DaMonte, DaSean, DaShae, DaShaun, DaShawn, DaVar, DaVon, DaWayne

DACE: *(dayce)* (English/French) "Of the nobility." Dacio is a Spanish name meaning "from Dacia."
Dacey, Dacio

DAEGAN: *(DAY-gan)* (Gaelic/Irish) "Black-haired." Variant form of Deegan.
Dag *(dahg)* (Scandinavian) "day," Dagen, Daeg, Deegan

DAI: *(dah-EE)* (Japanese) "Large," "generation." Surname.
Daini *(dah-ee-nee)* "big ear," "second greatest."

DAKOTA (295): *(da-KOH-tah)* (American Indian) "Friend, ally." Tribal name. Usage: boys 86%, girls 14%.
Dakotah

DALE (317): (English) "Valley." Very rare usage for girls.
Dael

DALLAS (323): (Scottish) "From the dales, the valley meadows." Name of the Texas city and surname used as a given name. Usage: boys 87%, girls 13%.

DALLIN: (Contemporary) Blended name; Dallin and its variants are rhyming variants based on the name Alan. See also Daylon
Dallon, Dallen, Dallan, Dalan, Dalon, D'Alan

DALTON (469): *(DOLL-ton)* (English) "From the valley town."

DAMARIO: *(da-MAH-ree-oh)* (Spanish) Masculine form of Damaris (Greek) "gentle."

Demario

DAMIAN (296): *(DAY-mee-en)* (Latin) Variant form of Damon. The Belgian priest, Father Damien, is honored as
the man who gave his life helping the lepers of Molokai
in Hawaii. St. Damian (third century) is known as the
patron saint of physicians.

DAMIEN (350) (French); Damion, Damiano (Spanish)

DAMON (373): *(DAY-mon)* (Greek) "One who tames,
subdues."

Damone *(da-MONE)*, Daymon

DAN: (Hebrew) "Judge." Biblical; Dan was the fifth son
of Jacob and founder of one of the twelve tribes of Israel.
While Dan is an independent name, it can also be used
as a short form of Daniel.

Dann

DANA: *(DAY-na)* Variant form of Daniel or Dane. Usage:
boys 15%, girls 85%.

DANE (297): (Scandinavian) "From Denmark." Variant
forms Daine and Dayne are English/French surnames
occasionally used as given names. Danford means
"Dane's Ford."

Dayne, Dain, Daine, Dayner, Danon *(DAY-non)*, Danford

DANIEL (5): (Hebrew) "God is my judge." Biblical; Daniel the prophet and writer of the Book of Daniel was a
teenager when he was taken to Babylon after the destruction of Jerusalem in 607 B.C. He survived two death sen-
tences, first in a lions' den, then in a fiery furnace. Many
prominent men have had the name since, among them
Daniel Webster the statesman and Daniel Boone the frontiersman.

DANNY (129); Dannie, Danilo (Spanish), Danell

DANNO: *(DAH-noh)* (Japanese) "Field gathering." Surname.

DANTE (448): *(DAHN-tay)* (Italian/Spanish) "Enduring."
Historical; Dante Alighieri, considered one of the greatest poets of all time, wrote *The Divine Comedy*, notable

for the graphic description of the medieval version of Hell
known as Dante's Inferno. See also Donte.
Daunte, Dantel

DANTON: *(dan-TONE* or *dan-TAHN)* (French) Variant
form of Anthony.
D'Anton

DARBY: (English) Place name and surname. In usage for
both boys and girls.

DARCEL: *(dar-SELL)* "Dark." Variant form of the French/
Irish surnames Darcy or D'Arcy. Very rarely used for
boys.
Darcell, Darcy, D'Arcy, Dorcey

DARENCE: (Contemporary) "Shining, gentle, open."
Blend of Darell and Clarence.
Darrence, Darrance, Derrance

DARIN: (Greek) "Gift." See also Darren.
Daron, Daren, Daran, Daryn (Welsh), Darrin, Darron,
Darryn, Derrin, Derren, Derrian

DARIO: *(DAR-ee-oh)* (Spanish) Short form of Darius and
Darian.
Dayo

DARION: "Gift." Variant form of Darin. Of unknown origin, the soundalike name Darien has poetic significance;
John Keats described the moment of discovery when ex-
plorers stood "silent, upon a peak in Darien."
Darien, Darian, Darrien, Darrian, Darrion

DARIUS (436): *(da-RYE-us* or *DARE-ee-us)* (Medo-
Persian) Possibly a royal title, like Caesar. Historical;
Darius the Mede assumed the kingship of Babylon after
its conquest by Cyrus.
Darrius, Dario

DARNELL (421): (English) "Hidden." Place name and
surname. Very rarely used for girls.
Darnel

DAROLD: (Contemporary) Blend of Daryl and Harold or
Gerald.
Darrold, Derrold, Derald

DARRELL: (English/French) "Open." Surname that dates from at least the 11th century. See also Darryl.

Darel, Dareau *(da ROW)* (French), Dariel, Dariell, Darroll, Derrall, Derrell, Derrill, Derell

DARREN (203): "Gift." Variant form of Darin. See also Darin.

DARRICK: (Gaelic/Scottish) "Strong, oak-hearted." Contemporary form of Darroch or a variant of Derrick. See also Derek.

Darick, Daric, Darroch, Darrek

DARRYL (286): Daryl is occasionally used for girls (12%), boys (88%). See also Darrell.

DARYL (418), Daryll, Daryle, Darryll, Darrel, Derryl

DARTAGNAN: *(dar-TAN-yan)* (French) Literary; Dumas's swashbuckling tale *The Three Musketeers* was based on the real d'Artagnan's memoirs.

DARVELL: (English/French) "Town of eagles."

DARVIN: (Contemporary) Blend of Daryl and Marvin.

Dervin

DARWIN: (English) "Dear friend." Historical; Charles Darwin, nineteenth-century naturalist, was the first major exponent of human evolution.

Darwyn

DASHIELL: *(DASH-ell)* A name of uncertain origin made famous by mystery writer Dashiell Hammett, author of *The Maltese Falcon*. The short form Dash is also an English surname that refers to the ash tree.

DAVID (6): (Hebrew) "Beloved." Biblical; one of the most remarkable personalities in the Scriptures. David was a shepherd, musician, poet, soldier, statesman, prophet and king. He wrote about half of the Psalms and very likely composed music for them as well. He is the only David mentioned in the Bible; his name occurs there more than a thousand times. Today there are variants of the name in almost every language group.

Dave; Davin (French); Davyn (Welsh); Davey, Davie (Irish); Davy, Davion, Davian, Daveon, Daviel, Daviot

DAVIS: (English) Surname. Variant form of David.

Davies (Welsh), Davison, Davidson, Dawson, Dayson, Dayton

DAX: (French) Place name; a town in southwestern France that dates from before the days of Roman occupation.

Daxton, Dack (English)

DAYAN: (Hebrew) "Judge." Moshe Dayan was a renowned twentieth-century Israeli military leader and statesman.

DAYLAN: (Contemporary) Daylan and its variants probably are rhyming variants of the name Waylon.

Daylen, Daylin, Daylon, Deylin, Dalen

"DE-" names: (Contemporary) Blend, of "De-" plus various endings, with pronunciation emphasis on the second syllable. These given names follow the French aristocratic style of surnames using the prefix "de." Capitalizing the second syllable is optional and often appears both ways in contemporary usage. See also DeAndre, DeShawn and "Da-" names.

DeAnthony, Deonte, Deante, DeAngelo, DeJohn, DeJon, DeJuan, DeLeon, Delon, Deloran, Delorean, DeMar, DeMario, DeMauri, DeMarco, DeMarcus, Demarcos, DeMarr, Demond, Demonte, Deondre, Deontae, Derelle, DeRoyce, DeShay, DeVal, DeVell, DeVane, DeVaughn, DeVaun, DeVonn, Devonte, DeWayne

DEACON: *(DEE-ken)* (Greek/English) "Dusty one; servant."

Deakin, Deke, Dekle, Dekel

DEAN (299): *(deen)* (English) "From the valley." Dean is a surname and a "title" name, signifying a church official or the head of a school.

Deane, Dene

DEANDRE (314): *(dee-AHN-dray* or *dee-ahn-DRAY)* An especially popular "De-" name.

DeAndre, Deandrae, D'Andre

DECLAN: *(DECK-lan)* The name of an Irish saint. Decker

and Dekker are homonym Dutch and German surnames in rare use as given names.

Decker, Dekker

DEDRICK: *(DEE-drick)* (English) Variant form of the Dutch name Diederick meaning "gifted ruler." See also Dirk.

Dedric, Diedrick; Dietrich, Dieter (German)

DEL: (French) Surname prefix meaning "of the." Used today as an independent name and as a short form of names beginning with "Del-."

DELANEY: *(de-LANE-ee)* (French/Irish) "From the elder tree grove." Very rarely used for boys.

Delane, Delaine, Delancy, Delano *(DELL-a-no)*

DELBERT: (English) "Noble, bright."

Dalbert

DELFINO: *(del-FEE-noh)* (Latin) "Dolphin." Also "from the oracle of Delphi."

DELMAR: (French) "Of the sea."

Delmer, Delmore

DELMON: (English/French) "Of the mountain." The English surname Delman means "man from the valley."

Delman, Delmont

DELROY: (French) "Of the King."

Delron

DELTON: (English) "From the town in the valley." Surname.

DELVIN: (English) "Godly friend."

Delvon; Delwin, Delwyn (Welsh)

DEMETRIUS (395): (Greek) "Of Demeter." Greek mythology; Demeter is the goddess of corn and harvest; her withdrawal for the part of the year that her daughter Persephone must spend with the god of the underworld is the reason for winter. See also Dimitri.

Demitrius; Demetrio (Spanish); Demetri, Demitri

DENNIS (149): (English) Variant form of the Greek Dionysius. Greek mythology; Dionysius is the Greek god of wine, responsible for the growth of the vines in spring and the originator of winemaking; he is equivalent to the Roman god Bacchus.

Denny, Dennie, Denney, Dennison, Denis, Denys (French)

DENTON: (English) "Valley town."

DENVER: (English/French) Possibly a variant form of the English surname Danvers, meaning "from Anvers." Contemporary use is most likely in reference to the name of the capital city of Colorado.

DENZEL: (English) A place name in Cornwall.
Denzell, Denzil

DENZO: *(den-zoh)* (Japanese) "Report with discretion; discreet."

DEREK (56): (German/English) "Gifted ruler." From Theodoric. See also Darrick and Dirk.
DERRICK (143) (Dutch), DERICK (384), Dereck, Derrek, Derrik, Derik, Deryk, Darek, Deryck

DERRY: A short form for names beginning with "Der-." Also an Irish surname. Very rarely used for girls. Derris may be a contemporary variant blend based on Derry plus Ferris.
Derris

DERWIN: (Contemporary) This blend of Derek and Irwin could be given the combined meaning "gifted friend." Derwent is a similar sounding English surname referring to the Derwent River in England.
Derwyn, Durwin, Derwent, Dervin, Dervon

DES: *(Dez)* Short form of names beginning with "Des-," occasionally used as an independent name.

DESHAWN: See also "De-" names. DeShawn is an especially popular form of this contemporary name style.
DeSean, Deshaun, Deshon, Deshane

DESI: *(DEZ-ee)* (Latin) "Yearning, sorrow"; (Spanish) Short form of Desiderus.
Dezi

DESMOND: (Gaelic) "From South Munster." An Irish

surname referring to Munster, one of the five regions of ancient Ireland.

Desmund, Dezmond

➤ DESTIN: *(DESS-tin* or *dess-TEEN)* (French) "Destiny." The soundalike French surname Destan means "by the still waters."

Deston, Destan

DESTRY: *(DESS-tree)* (English) Variant form of a French surname. Destry has the flavor of the American West, due to the classic western film *Destry Rides Again*.

Destrey

DEV: Short form of names beginning with "Dev-."

DEVEREL: *(DEV-er-al)* (English/French) Place name and surname.

Deverell, Deveral, Devereau, Devereaux; Devery, Deverick (contemporary variants)

DEVIN (112): (Latin/French) "Divine, perfect." Usage: boys 85%, girls 15%. See also Devon.

DEVLIN: (Irish) "Misfortune."

Devlyn, Devlon, Devland

DEVON (221): (English) Name of the county in England, noted for its beautiful farmland. Usage: (Devon) boys 72%, girls 28%; (Devan) boys 68%, girls 32%. See also Devin.

DEVAN (438); Deven, Devyn, Devion, Deveon, Devron, Deavon

DEWEY: *(DOO-ee)* (English) Place name and surname.

DEXTER (491): (Latin) "Right-handed."

Dex

DIAMOND: (Greek/English) "Unyielding, brilliant." The gemstone used as a given name. Usage: boys 25%, girls 75%.

Dimond, Dymond, Daymond

DICK: One of the rhyming nicknames from medieval times. Richard was shortened to Rick, then rhymed to Dick, and variants like Dickson and Dix (which is also the French word meaning "ten") followed. Today Dick is rarely used as an independent name.

Dickson, Dixon, Dix

DIEGO (189): *(dee-AY-go)* (Spanish) Variant form of James.

DIJON: *(di-JAHN)* (French) The name of a town in eastern France. In contemporary usage as a given name, Dijon is a homonym of the "De-" name DeJon.

DILLON (240): (Irish/French) "Like a lion." The popularity of this name may be affected by its sounding like Dylan.

Dillen, Dilan

DIMITRI: *(de-MEE-tri)* (Slavic) Variant form of Demetrius. In Catholic tradition, Dimas was the name of the compassionate thief who died with Jesus at Calvary.

Dimetrius, Dimitrios, Dimas *(DEE-mas)*

DINO: *(DEE-no)* (Italian/Spanish) Short form ending of names like Bernardino, used as an independent name.

DION: *(DYE-on)* Short form of Dionysius. See also Dennis. Diandre and Diondre are blends of Dion and Andre.

Deon, Dionte, Diondre, Diandre, Dondre

DIRK: (German) "Wealthy"; (Dutch) Variant form of Derek and Dietrich. See also Dedrick.

DOLAN: (Irish) "Dark, bold."

DOLPHUS: "Noble wolf." Short form of Adolphus.

DOMINGO: *(doh-MEEN-goh)* (Spanish) Variant form of Dominic. Domingo is also the Spanish name for Sunday, the "Lord's day."

DOMINIC (195): (Latin) "Of the Lord." The French spelling of Dominique is used for boys as well as for girls; boys 29%, girls 71%.

DOMINIQUE (286), DOMINICK (445), Dominik, Domenico (Spanish), Dominico

DON (438): Short form of names beginning with "Don-." Don is also a Spanish/Italian courtesy title (see Donna in girls' index). The use of the Welsh-Gaelic surname Donne as a given name may be in honor of John Donne, the seventeenth-century poet.

Donn, Donne, Donnie, Donny

DONAHUE: (Gaelic) "Brown-haired fighter."

DONALD (106): (Gaelic) "Great chief." Donald is one of the clan names of Scotland. See also Donnell.

DONATO: *(doh-NAH-toh)* (Spanish/Italian) "Gift from God." Historical; Donatello (Italian) is the name of a Florentine sculptor (fourteenth to fifteenth century) who created bronze statues of power and dramatic action. Today Donatello is familiar to young people as the name of one of four cartoon fantasy creatures, the Ninja turtles. See also Raphael, Leonardo and Michelangelo.

Donatello, Donzel

DONNELL: *(DON-el or don-NEL)* (Scottish/Irish) Variant form of Donald. Donal is also an Irish form of Daniel.

Donal, Donell, Donnel

DONOVAN (304): (Gaelic) "Brown-haired chieftain."

Donavon, Donavan

DONTE: *(don-TEE, don-TAY or DON-tee)* (Contemporary) Donte and its variants are spelling variants of Dante. See also Dante.

Dontae, Dontay, Dontaye, Dontell

DORIAN: (Greek) "Gift." Literary; in Oscar Wilde's novel *The Picture of Dorian Gray*, Dorian was granted the wish that a portrait of himself would change to show the ravages of time while he himself would retain perpetual youth and beauty. Usage: boys 81%, girls 19%.

Dorion, Dorien, Dorean

DORRAN: (Irish/English) "Stands firm." Surname. Contemporary usage of Dorran and other related surnames listed here as variants is probably influenced by the similarity of sound to favored names such as Darren, Torrance and Darryl.

Dorren, Doran, Doron, Dorrin, Dorrance, Dorrell, Dorrel

DOUGLAS (122): (Scottish) "From the dark river." Historical; there were two branches of this powerful Scottish clan and family, the Black Douglases and the Red Douglases. The lords of these clans are key figures in Sir Walter Scott's novels.

Douglass, Doug

DOV: (Hebrew) "Bear."

DOVER: (Welsh) "Water." Name of the British seaport on the English Channel, in rare use today as a given name.

DOYLE: (Gaelic) "Dark stranger."

DRAKE: (English) Variant form of Drakon. (Greek) "Dragon". Historical; Sir Francis Drake was an adventurous privateer who was also the first Englishman to sail around the world.

Drago *(DRAY-go)* (Italian/French), Draco (Latin), Draken, Drakon, Dracon *(DRAY-ken)*; Drayce (Contemporary)

DREW (184): "Manly, brave." Short form of Andrew. Rarely used for girls (8%).

Dru (French), Drue

DRURY: (English/French) "Beloved friend, sweetheart."

DUANE: *(d'wain)* (Irish) "Dark." See also Dwayne. (Historical note: many Irish and Scottish names have the meaning "dark" or "black." Most Gaels had brown hair and darker skin coloring that contrasted with the fair hair and pale skins of Scandinavian invaders.)

Duayne, Duwayne; Duante *(d'wan-TAY)* (Contemporary)

DUARTE: *(d'-WAR-tay)* (Spanish) "Prosperous guardian." Variant form of Edward.

Duardo

DUGAN: *(DOO-gen)* (Gaelic) "Dark."

DUKE: (English) Title used as a nickname or given name. Duke is also a short form of Marmaduke.

DUMONT: (French) "Of the mountain."

DUNCAN: (Irish/Scottish) "Brown-haired."

DUNSTAN: (English) "Hill stone."

DURAND: (Latin/English) "Firm, enduring."

Duran, Durant (French), Durante

DURBIN: (Latin/German) "City-dweller."

DUREAU: *(dur-ROW)* (French) "Strong."

Durrell, Durell (English), Duron, Durango

DUSTIN (50): (English) "A fighter." The exposure given to this name by actor Dustin Hoffman has been a major influence on its popularity with parents over the past twenty years. Popularity is also influenced by the rhyming similarity to another favored name, Justin.
Dustan, Dustyn, Duston, Dusty

DUVAL: (French) "Of the valley."

DWADE: (Contemporary) This blend of Dwayne and Wade could be given the combined meaning "dark traveler."

DWAYNE (399): (Irish) "Dark." See also Duane.
Dwain, Dwaine, Dwane, Dewayne, DeWayne

DWIGHT (479): (Scottish/Scandinavian) "Valiant."

DYLAN (124): (Welsh) "From the sea." See also Dillon.
Dyllon, Dyllan

E

EAGAN: (Irish) "Fiery, forceful."
Egan, Egon

EAMON: *(EE-mon* or *AY-mon)* "Prosperous protector." Irish form of Edmund.
Eames

EARL (453): (English) "Nobleman." Name based on the English title.
Earle, Erle

EASTON: (English) "From East town."
Eston

EBEN: *(EBB-an* or *EE-ben)* (Hebrew) "Stone." Biblical; a memorial stone erected by the prophet Samuel to mark a critical defeat and a victory in Jewish history.

EDDIE (212): Short form of names beginning with "Ed-." Edlin is a German diminutive of Ed.
Eddy, Ed, Edlin

EDER: *(EE-der)* (Hebrew) "Flock." Biblical; the tower of Eder near Hebron was built as a watchtower from which shepherds could watch their flocks. The name became a symbol of God's watchfulness over his people.

EDGAR (82): (English) "Fortunate and powerful."
Edgardo (Spanish), Edgard (French)

EDISON: (English) "Son of the fortunate warrior."
Edson

EDMUND: (English/French) "Prosperous protector."
Edmond, Edmundo, Edmon

EDRIC: (English) "Power and good fortune."
Edrick, Edrik

EDSEL: (German) "Noble, bright."

EDWARD (72): (English) "Prosperous guardian." A favorite name of British royalty.
EDUARDO (91) Edwardo (Spanish/Portuguese); Eduard (German); Edouard (French)

EDWIN (154): "Rich in friendship."
Edwyn

EFRAIN (352): *(eff-rah-EEN)* Spanish form of Ephraim; (Hebrew) "doubly fruitful." See also Ephraim.
Efren, Efrem (Spanish), Efran,

EFRON (Hebrew) "Young stag."

EGON: *(EE-gan)* (English) "Strong, active."
Egan

EINAR: *(EYE-ner)* (Scandinavian) "Warrior chief."

EKON: (Nigerian) "Strong."

ELAM: *(EE-lam)* (Hebrew) Biblical; one of the five sons of Noah's son Shem.

ELBERT: (German) "Bright, famous."

ELDRED: (English) "Old/wise ruler."
Eldrick, Eldridge, Elder

ELEAZAR: *(el-ee-AY-zor)* (Hebrew) "God has helped." Biblical; the son of Aaron and later his successor as high priest of Israel.
Eliezer, Eliazar (Spanish)

ELFORD: (English) "The alder tree ford."

ELGAR: (German) "Sword."

ELGIN: (Celtic/English) "Noble, white."

Elgine (*el-GEEN*), Eljin

ELI (352): (*EE-lye*) (Hebrew) "Ascended" or "my God."
Biblical; Eli was a high priest who judged Israel for forty
years and instructed the boy Samuel.
Ely.

ELIAS (294): (*eh-LEE-as* or *ee-LYE-as*) (Greek/Spanish)
Variant form of Elijah.
Elia

ELIHU: (*ee-LYE-hoo* or *ee-LYE-hew*) "My God is He."
Biblical; a young man whose fiery defense of God's righ-
teousness is recounted in the Book of Job.

ELIJAH (279): (*ee-LYE-jah*) (Hebrew) "My God is Jehovah." Biblical; Elijah was one of the foremost prophets
of Israel. The Book of Kings recounts many miracles per-
formed for and by him.
Elija

ELISHA: (*ee-LYE-sha*) (Hebrew) "God is salvation."
Biblical; faithful attendant and successor to the prophet
Elijah. See also Elisha in the girls' index.

ELLERY: (English/Greek) "Joyful, happy."

ELLIOT (311): (English) Variant form of Elijah.
ELLIOTT (350), Eliot, Eliott

ELLIS: (English) Variant form of Elias, from Elijah.
Ellison, Elliston, Elson, Elston

ELMER: (English) "Famed, noble." Elmo is a short form
of Erasmus, the name of a noted Dutch scholar.
Elmo, Elmore

ELOY: (Latin) "Chosen one." Short form of Eligius. A
French saint's name.

ELROY: (Latin) "The king." Elrick and Elrod are contemporary blends in the same pattern as Elroy and with the
same essential meaning.
Elrick, Elrod

ELSWORTH: (English) Place name and surname used as a
given name.

ELTON: (English) "From the old town."
Elston, Elson, Eldon, Elden, Elder

ELVERN: "Spring, greening." Variant form of Alvern.

ELVIN: "Elf-wise friend." Variant form of Alvin.
Elwin, Elwyn, Elvyn

ELVIS: Variant form of Elvin. Brought into popularity by singer/actor Elvis Presley, the name continues to be quietly but steadily used for boys today.

ELWOOD: (English) "Forest dweller."

ELY: See Eli.

EMERSON: (English/German) "Brave, powerful."

EMILIO (321): (*eh-MEEL-ee-o*) (Latin) Spanish form of Emil, from a Roman clan name with the possible meaning "industrious." The German/English form Emil is in rare use today.
Emiliano (Italian); Emil *(AY-mul)*, Emile (ay-MEEL) (French); Emlyn (Welsh), Emlen *(EMM-lin)*

EMMANUEL (220): (*ee-MAN-yoo-ul*) (Latin) Variant form of Immanuel; (Hebrew) "With us is God." Biblical; a name-title applied to the Messiah. See also Manuel.
EMANUEL (397) (Spanish), Emanuele

EMMETT: Male variant form of Emma, a girl's given name from pre-medieval times.
Emmet

EMORY: (English/German) "Brave, powerful." A variant form of Amory.
Emery

ENOCH: (*EE-nok*) (Hebrew) "One trained and dedicated." Biblical; Enoch was the father of Methuselah, the oldest living man named in the Bible.

ENRIQUE (190): (*en-REE-kay*) (Spanish) "Rules his household." Variant form of Henry.
Enrico (Italian), Enzo

EPHRAIM: *(EFF-ram)* (Hebrew) "Doubly fruitful." Biblical; one of Joseph's two sons by his Egyptian wife Asenath. See also Efrain.
Ephrem, Efraim

ERIC (21): (Scandinavian) "Ever kingly." Scandinavian legend relates that the Viking sea-rover Ericson (son of

Eric the Red) landed on the shores of America five hundred years before Christopher Columbus. Today actor Eriq La Salle has generated interest in the French spelling, Eriq. See also Aric.

ERIK (83), ERICK (199), Erich (German), Eriq (French), Erickson, Ericksen, Ericson, Erikson (Scandinavian), Eryk, Erix

ERIN: Gaelic poetic name for Ireland. Today usage as a boy's name is very rare. Eron is a Spanish variant form of Aaron.

Eran (Hebrew) "Roused, awakened," Eron, Eri

ERNEST (263): (English/German) "Serious, determined."
ERNESTO (195) (Spanish); Ernie, Earnest

ERROL: (German) "Earl, nobleman."
Erroll

ERSKINE: (*ERS-kin*) (Scottish) "Ascending."

ERVIN: "Friend." Variant form of Irving. See also Irving.
Erwin, Erving, Ervine

ESAU: (*EE-sah*) (Hebrew) "Hairy." Biblical; Esau, the older twin brother of Jacob, was a skilled and adventurous hunter.

ESMOND: (English) "Protector from the east."
Esmund

ESSEX: (English) "From the east."

ESTEBAN (275): (*ess-TAY-ban*) (Spanish) Variant form of Stephen; (Greek) "Crown, wreath."
Estevan, Estevon

ETHAN (107): (*EE-than*) (Hebrew) "Enduring, overflowing." Biblical; a man of Israel noted for his wisdom.

ETIENNE: (*eh-T'YIN*) (French) Variant form of Stephen; (Greek) "Crown, wreath."

EUGENE (300): (Greek) "Well born."
Eugenio (Spanish)

EUSTACE: (*YOOS-tiss*) (Greek) "Productive."
Eustis, Estes

EVAN (86): (Welsh) "Jehovah has shown favor." Variant form of John.

Evann, Evin, Evyn

EVERARD: (English/German) "Hardy, brave."
Everardo, Evarado (Spanish); Ewart (German)

EVEREST: (English) Place name and surname. The similar sounding Evaristo is the Spanish form of a Greek name meaning "well, good"; it was the name of four saints and one of the early popes of Rome.
Evaristo

EVERETT: (English) Variant form of Everard.
Evert (German); Everet, Everton

EVIAN: (*EV-ee-an*) Contemporary usage may be as a variant of Evan, influenced by the town in France famous for Evian spring water. If considered a blended name (Evan and Ian), Evian could take on the meaning "John-John."

EWAN: (Celtic) "Well-born."
Ewen, Euan

EZEKIEL: (*ee-ZEE-k'yul*) (Hebrew) "God strengthens." Biblical; Ezekiel was a prophet who was among the captives taken to Babylon at the first fall of Jerusalem; he wrote the Book of Ezekiel while in captivity. See also Zeke.
Ezequiel, Esequiel (Spanish)

EZRA: (Hebrew) "Help." Biblical; fifth-century B.C. Jewish priest, scholar, copyist and historian who wrote the two Chronicles and the Book of Ezra and began the compiling and cataloging of the other books that formed the Hebrew Scriptures, the Old Testament.
Esra, Ezrah

F

FABIAN (262): (Latin) From Fabius. Roman clan name, also the name of several Roman emperors and sixteen saints. English pronunciation is *FAY-bee-en*; Spanish is *fah-bee-AHN*.
Fabien, Favian, Fabion, Fabiano, Fabio, Favio, Faber

FAINE: (English) "Good-natured." Fane is an ancient given name, now a Welsh surname.
Fane

FALCO: (Latin) Surname having to do with falconry. See also Hawk.
Falcon (English), Falken, Falk (Scandinavian), Falke (German)

FARAJI: (*FAHR-a-jee* or *fah-RAH-jee*) (Swahili) "Consolation."

FARGO: (English) Surname used as a given name.

FARID: (*fah-REED*) (Arabic) "Exceptional, unequaled."

FARLEY: (English) "Fair meadow." Surname.
Farleigh, Farlow

FARON: (*fare-ow*) Spanish form of Pharaoh, the title of ancient Egyptian rulers. Faro is a Spanish short form, which also may be used in reference to the card game.
Farren: (English) "adventurous." Variants Farren and Farrin are in rare use for boys and girls. See also Ferron.

FARRELL: (*FARE-el*) (Irish) "Brave."
Farrel, Ferrell

FARRIS: (English) "Iron-strong."
Faris, Ferris

FELIPE (289): (*feh-LEE-pay*) (Spanish) "Fond of horses." Variant form of Philip.
Felippe

FELIX (348): (Latin) "Happy." Biblical; Roman procurator of Judea during Paul's time; a wily politician.
Feliciano

FERGUS: (Scottish) "A man of strength."
Ferguson

FERNANDO (115): (Spanish) "Adventurer."
Ferdinand (German/Spanish), Fernand (French)

FERRON: (English/French) "Ironworker." See also Faron.
Ferrin

FIDEL: (*fee-DELL*) (Latin) "Faithful."
Fidal, Fidello

FINLEY: (Gaelic) "Fair champion."
Finlay

FINN: (Gaelic/Irish) "Fair." Historical; Finn Mac Cumhail was a legendary third-century Irish hero somewhat like the English Robin Hood. His warrior-followers were called Finians.
Finnegan, Finian

FITZ: (French/English) Surname prefix meaning "son of."
Fitzgerald, Fitzhugh, Fitzpatrick, etc.

FLETCHER: (English/French) "Arrow-maker."

FLINT: (English) Place name and surname. Also a name from nature, referring to the hard quartz that produces a spark of fire when struck by steel.

FLORIAN: (Latin) "Flower." Italian masculine form of Flora. Florian is also a Czech and Hungarian name.

FLOYD: (English) Variant form of Lloyd; (Welsh) "Grey."

FLYNN: (Irish) "Son of a red-haired man."
Flinn, Flyn

FONSO: Short form of Alfonso.
Fonzo, Fonzie

FONTAINE: (*fon-TANE*) (French) "Fountain; water source."
Fontayne, Fonteyne, Fontane, Fontana (Italian)

FORD: (English) "A shallow place used to cross a river or stream." Surname.
Forde

FORREST (479): (English) "Woodland."
Forest; Forrester; Forester, Foster "forest-ranger"

FORTINO: (*for-TEEN-o*) (Latin) "Strong, fortunate."
Fortunato

FRANCIS (399): (Latin) "From France." The feminine spelling is Frances.

FRANCISCO (73): (*frahn-CEES-ko*) (Spanish) Variant form of Francis.
Francesco (Italian), Frisco

FRANK (121): (English/French) "Free; a free man."

FRANKIE (414); Franky; Franco (Spanish); Franz (German); Francois (French)

FRANKLIN (304): (English) "Free landholder; farm owner."
Franklyn

FRASER: (*FRAY-zer*) (Celtic/Scottish) "Of the forest men." One of the major clans of Scotland.
Frazer, Frazier, Frasier

FREDERICK (302): (German) "Peaceful ruler."
Fredrick, Fredric, Frederic, Frederico, Frederik, Fredrik, Federico (Spanish), Friedrick, Fritz (nickname), FREDDY (335); FREDDIE (457); FRED (438)

FREEMAN: (English) Surname used as a given name. Literally, a free man, one freed from bound servitude to an overlord.
Freman; Fremont (French)

G

GABRIEL (90): (Hebrew) "God's able-bodied one." Biblical; the Archangel Gabriel is the only angel besides Michael named in the canonical Scriptures.
Gabe, Gabian (Spanish), Gavriel (Jewish)

GAGE: (French) "Pledge."

GALEN: (*GAY-lan*) (Greek) "Tranquil." The name of a second-century physician whose research provided a basis for accepted medical practices for fifteen hundred years.
Gaelan, Galyn; Galeno (Spanish)

GAMALIEL: (*ga-MAY-lee-el*) (Hebrew) "God gives due reward." Biblical; a respected teacher of Jewish law.

GANNON: (Gaelic/Irish) "Fair-haired."

GARDNER: (English/French) "Keeper of the garden."
Gard, Gardiner

GARETH: (Welsh) "Gentle." Sir Gareth, noted for his modesty and bravery, was a knight of King Arthur's Round Table.

Garreth

GARLAND: (French) "Wreath, prize."

Garlen

GARNET: (*GAR-net* or *gar-NET*) (English/French) "Keeper of grain." Surname. In rare use for boys and girls.

Garnett, Garner

GARRAD: (*GARE-ad* or *JARE-ad*) (English) Variant form of Garret. See also Jarrod.

Garred, Gared, Gerred

GARRETT (100): "Spear-strong." English variant form of Gerald.

GARRET (486); Garett; Gerrit, Gerritt (Dutch)

GARRICK: (English/German) "Rules by the spear."

GARRISON: (English/German) "Spear-fortified town."

Garson

GARRON: (German/French) "Guards, guardian."

Garan, Garin, Garon, Geron, Garen, Garion, Garrion

GARRY: (English/German) "Spear." Also a short form of names beginning with "Gar-."

GARTH: (German) "Garden."

GARVYN: (English/German) "Spear-friend, ally."

GARY (128): (English/German) "Spear."

GATES: (English) "Gatekeeper; lives near the gates."

GAVIN (364): (Welsh/Scottish) "White hawk." A form of the medieval name Gawain.

Gavino (Italian), Gavan, Gavyn

GAYLORD: (English/French) "Cheerful, jolly."

GENARO: (*HAY-nah-roh*) (Spanish) Variant form of Januarius. (Latin) "Consecrated to God". The name of many saints; also refers to Janus, the Roman two-headed god for whom the first month of the year is named.

GENE: Short form of Eugene.

GENTRY: (English/French) "Well-born."

GEOFFREY (246): (*JEF-ree*) (English/French) "Peaceful." See also Jeffrey.

Geoff (*jef*)

GEOMAR: (*joe-MAR*) (Teutonic) "Famous in battle."
Giomar

GEORDAN: (*JOR-dan*) (Contemporary) Variant spelling of
Jordan.

GEORGE (97): (Greek) "Farmer." St. George, a knight
and the patron saint of England, achieved legendary status
through the medieval depiction of his struggle with a fire-
breathing dragon, symbolic of the Devil.
Georgio (Italian)

GEOVANNI: (*joe-VAHN-ee*) (Italian) Variant form of John.
See also Giovanni.
Geovanny, Geovani, Geovany

GERALD (242): (German/English) "Rules by the spear."
See also Jerald.
Geraldo (Spanish), Gerrell (German), Gerrald, Gerold

GERARDO (174): (German/French) "Spear-strong";
(Spanish) Variant form of Gerard. See also Jerard.
Gerard (*je-RARD*), Gerrard; Gerhard (*GARE-hard*) (Ger-
man); Gerad, Gerrod

GERMAN (390): (German) "People of the spear." Spanish pronunciation is *hare-MAHN*. See also Jermaine.
Germain, Garman

GERONIMO: (*hare-ON-ee-mo* or *jer-ON-ee-mo*) (Greek/
Spanish) "Sacred name." Variant form of Jerome, a
saint's name. The American Indian Geronimo (nine-
teenth century) was one of the last of the renowned
Apache warrior chiefs.
Gerome

GERRY: Short form of names beginning with "Ger-." See
also Jerry.

GERSON: (Hebrew) "Alien resident." Variant form of
Gershom.

GERVAISE: (*zher-VASE*) (French) Variant form of Jarvis;
(Teutonic) "Spearman."

GIACOMO: (*JOCK-a-mo*) (Italian) Variant form of James
and Jacob.

GIAN: (Italian) Short form of John, often used in combination with other names. Gianni is equivalent to Johnny. Gianni, Giancarlo, Gianfranco, etc.

GIDEON: (*GIH-dee-on*) (Hebrew) "One who cuts down." Biblical; a judge of Israel who won battles through skillful planning and faith rather than strength of arms alone.

GIL: Short form of names beginning with "Gil-." Gil is also an Israeli name meaning "joy."

GILBERT (239): (Celtic/German) "Bright lad."
GILBERTO (290) (Spanish)

GILES: (jiles) (Greek) "Young shield."

GILMORE: (Gaelic/Scottish) "Sword bearer."
Gilmer, Gilmar

GILROY: (Gaelic/Scottish) "Serves the king."

GINO: (*GEE-no*) (Italian) Short form of names like Gian and Giovanni.
Geno (Spanish)

GIOVANNI (274): (*joe-VAHN-ee*) (Italian) Variant form of John. See also Geovanni and Jovan.
Giovani, Giovanny, Giovany, Giovonni

GITANO: (*hee-TAHN-oh* or *qui-TAHN-oh*) (Spanish) "Gypsy."

GIULIANO: (*joo-lee-AHN-o*) (Italian) Variant form of Julian, Julio.
Giulio (*JOO-lee-o*)

GIUSEPPE: (*jeh-SEP-ee*) (Italian) Variant form of Joseph.

GLENN (314): (Gaelic) "Valley."
GLEN (402), Glendon, Glendyn

GODFREY: (English/German) "God's peace."

GONZALO: (Spanish) "Safe through the battle."

GORDON (477): (English/Scottish) "From the marshes." Name of one of the great Scottish clans.

GOWAN: (Scottish) Variant form of Owen.

GRADY: (Irish) "Man of rank."
Graden

GRAHAM (445): (*GRAY-em*) (English/Scottish) "Farm home."
Graeme

GRANT (188): (French/English) "Bestow" or "great, tall."
Grantland

GRAYSON: (English) "Gray-haired; son of the Gray family; son of Gregory."
Greyson, Gray, Grey, Graysen

GREG: Short form of Gregory. The double consonant ending on a short form usually indicates an English surname, as in Gregg.
Gregg

GREGORY (60): (Greek) "On the watch." Historical; the first of the sixteen popes to bear the name was called Gregory the Great. He founded monasteries, reorganized papal administration and fostered the development of the Gregorian chants.
Gregorio (Italian/Spanish/Portuguese); Grigor (Russian); Gregor (German); Gregori (French); Grischa (Slavic)

GRIFFIN: (Welsh) "Fighting chief; fierce." Greek mythology and medieval legend; the gryphon was a fierce creature with the foreparts of an eagle and the hindquarters of a lion.
Griffen, Griffith, Griff

GROVER: (English) "Grove dweller."

GUADALUPE (495): (*gwah-da-LOO-pay*) (Spanish/Arabic) "Wolf Valley." Well-used in Spanish-speaking families; refers to Mary as Mexico's "Our Lady of Guadalupe." Usage: boys 15%, girls 85%.

GUILLERMO (256): (*gui-YARE-mo*) (Spanish) Variant form of William.
Guillaume (*gui-AHM*) (French), Gillermo

GUNTHER: (German) "Battler, warrior."
Gunnar (Swedish)

GUSTAVO (195): (Spanish) Variant form of Gustav; (German) "Royal staff."
Gus, Gustav, Gustave, Gustaf

GUY: (Latin) "Lively."
Guido

GWAYNE: (Welsh) "White hawk." Variant of the medieval name Gawain.

H

HADRIEN: (*HAY-dree-an*) "Dark." Variant form of Adrian. The Roman Emperor Hadrian (second century A.D.) was a gifted writer and architect; he caused the Hadrian Wall to be built in Britain.
Hadrian

HAKIM: (*hah-KEEM*) (Arabic) "Wise."
Hakeem

HAL: Short form of names beginning with "Hal-." Also a nickname for Henry.

HALDEN: (English) "From Denmark."
Haldane

HALEN: (*HAY-len*) (Swedish) "Hall."
Hale

HALIM: (*ha-LEEM*) (Arabic) "Gentle."

HAMID: (Arabic) "Thankful to God." A variant form of Muhammad.

HAMILTON: (Scottish) Place name and surname of one of the great noble families of Scotland.

HAMPTON: English place name and surname.

HANK: Nickname for Henry.

HANS: (Scandinavian/German/Dutch) Variant form of John.
Hanson, Hansen (Dutch/Scandinavian); Han (Czech)

HARI: (*HAH-ree*) (Hindi) "Princely."

HARLEY: (English) "Meadow of the hares." Variants listed are related surnames.
Harlan, Harland, Harlen, Harlow

HARMAN: (French) Variant form of Herman. Harmon (Hebrew) "palace" is a biblical place name.
Harmon

HAROLD (383): (English/Teutonic) "Army commander."
Herald is also literally "one who proclaims."
Herald; Harald (Scandinavian); Harrell

HARPER: (English) "Harpist, minstrel."

HARRISON (344): (English) "Harry's son." Harry is an
English version of the French pronunciation of Henri; It's
used as a nickname of Henry as well as of variant forms
like Harrison and Harris.
HARRY (390), Harris, Harriman

HART: (English) "Stag; male deer."
Hartman, Harte

HARVEY: (Celtic/Scottish) "Eager for battle."

HASSAN: (*hah-SAHN*) (Arabic) "Good-looking."

HAVEN: (*HAY-ven*) (English) "A place of safety; shelter."

HAWK: (English) "A hawk, falcon." Surname and a name
from nature. The name is used in American Indian tribal
names as well. See also Falco.
Hawke; Hakon, Haakon (Scandinavian)

HAYDEN: (English) "The hill meadow."
Hayden, Haydon

HEATH: (*heeth*) (English) Surname and place name. Heath
is a word for untended land where certain flowering
shrubs grow. Heather is the equivalent name for girls.

HEBER: (*HEE-ber*) (Hebrew) "Partner." An ancestor of
Abraham.

HECTOR (116): (Greek) "Steadfast." In Homer's *Iliad*,
Hector was a prince of Troy.

HENRY (157): (English/German) "Rules his household."
A favored royal name of England and France. The second
son of the current Prince of Wales is named Henry.
Henri (French), Heinrich (German), Henrick, Hendrick
(Scandinavian)

HERBERT: (German/French) "Illustrious warrior."

HERCULES: (*HER-k'yu-lees*) (Greek) "In Hera's service." In Greek mythology, Hercules was a son of Zeus
who possessed extraordinary strength.

HERMAN: (German) "Soldier."

HERMES: (*HER-mees*) (Greek) "Messenger." Mythology; Hermes was messenger for the gods on Olympus and was himself the god of eloquence. He was called Mercury by the Romans.

HERNANDO: (*her-NAHN-do*) (Spanish) "Adventurous." Variant form of Ferdinand.
Hernan (*her-NAHN*)

HERSCHEL: (Yiddish) "Deer."
Hershel, Hirsch

HILARIO: (*hih-LAH-ree-oh*) (Spanish) Variant form of Hilary; (Greek) "joyful, glad." The name of more than thirty saints.

HIRAM: (*HIGH-ram*) (Hebrew) "My brother is exalted." Biblical; the King of Tyre, friendly to King David and King Solomon.

HOLDEN: (English) "Sheltered valley."
Holman "man from the valley"

HOLLIS: (English) "The holly tree." Very rare usage for boys and girls.

HOLMES: (English/Scandinavian) "Home by the river."

HOLT: (English) "By the forest."

HOMER: (Greek) "Given as hostage; promised." Two of the greatest works of Greek epic poetry, the *Iliad* and the *Odyssey*, are attributed to Homer.
Homar

HORACE: (Latin) From Horatius, a Roman family clan name.
Horacio, Horatio

HOSEA: (*ho-SEE-ah*) (Hebrew) "Saved by Jah." Biblical; a prophet and writer of the Book of Hosea.

HOUSTON: (*HEW-ston*) (Scottish) Place name and surname. The name's association with the American West is due to the Texan general Sam Houston and the city in Texas given his name.

HOWARD (413): (English/Scandinavian) "Noble watch-

man.'' Surname of one of the great houses of English
nobility.
Howie
HUBERT: (German) ''Bright, intelligent.''
HUGO (227): (Latin) Variant form of Hugh; (German) ''a
thinker.''
Hugh, Huey, Huw (Welsh)
HUMBERTO (385): (*oom-BARE-toh*) (Spanish) Variant
form of Humbert; (German) ''big, bright.''
HUME: (H'yoom) (English) ''Home.'' Surname taken from
the name of an ancient fortified town in Saxon England.
A rare given name made familiar today by actor Hume
Cronyn.
HUMPHREY: (German) ''Peace, strength.''
HUNTER (307): (English) ''Pursuer.''
Hunt, Huntington, Huntley
HUSSAIN: (*hoo-SAIN*) (Arabic) ''Good.'' Hussein was the
name of the founder of Shiite Islam.
Hussein
HYATT: (English) Surname used as a given name.

I

IAN (77): (*EE-an*) (Scottish) Variant form of John.
Iain, Iban (*ee-BAHN*) (Spanish)
IBRAHIM: Arabic form of Abraham.
IGNACIO (373): (*eeg-NAH-see-oh*) (Latin) ''Fiery.'' St.
Ignacius of Loyola was the founder of the Catholic Jesuit
order.
Inigo, Ignacius
IGOR: (*EE-gor* or *EYE-gor*) (Russian/Scandinavian) ''War-
rior of peace.''
ILYA: (*ILL-yah*) (Russian) Short form of Elijah.
IMMANUEL: Variant form of Emanuel.
INGRAM: (Scandinavian) ''Raven of peace.''
IRA: (*EYE-rah*) (Hebrew) ''Full-grown.'' Biblical; name of
a priest or chief minister to King David.

IRVING (414): (English) "Friend." See also Ervin.
IRVIN (442), Irwin, Irvine, Irvyn, Irven

ISAAC (135): (Hebrew) "Laughter." Biblical; the only son
of Abraham by his wife Sarah. Today Itzhak Perlman is
one of the world's greatest violinists.
Issac, Izaac (Dutch), Izaak, Itzhak (Israeli)

ISADORE: (Greek) "Gift of Isis." One of the many pagan
names made acceptable to the Christian world through
use by early Christians who became saints.
Isidro (Spanish/Portuguese), Isadoro, Isidore

ISAIAH (251): (eye-ZAY-ah) (Hebrew) "Salvation of Jehovah." Biblical; one of the major prophets and writer
of the Book of Isaiah.
Isaias (Spanish), Isiah

ISMAEL (286): (EES-mah-el) (Spanish) Variant form of
Ishmael; (Hebrew) "God listens." Biblical; the son of
Abraham by Sarah's Egyptian slave woman Hagar.
Ishmael

ISRAEL (242): (EES-rah-el) (Hebrew) "God perseveres,
contends." Biblical; when Jacob was in his nineties, God
changed his name to Israel as a token of blessing.

IVAN (138): (ee-VAHN or EYE-van) Slavic, Russian form
of John. Ivanhoe is a medieval variant form Sir Walter
Scott used for the Saxon hero of Ivanhoe.
Ivanhoe

IVES: (English) Variant form of Yves, from Ivar; (Teutonic) "archer's bow."
Ivar, Ivor, Ivo

J

"JA-" names: (Contemporary) Blends of "Ja-" plus various
endings, with pronunciation emphasis on the second syllable. See also "Je-" names.
Jamar, Jamarr, Jamari, Jamelle, Jamaine, Jamon, Ja-
mond, Jaray, JaRonn, JaVaughn, Javon, Javell, Jayvon

JABARI: (Swahili) "Valiant."

JABIN: (*JAY-bin*) (Hebrew) "God has built." A Biblical name.

JACAN: (*JAY-kin*) (Hebrew) "Trouble." A Biblical name. Jachin

JACINTO: (*ha-CEEN-to*) (Greek) "Alas"; (Spanish) Masculine form of Hyacinth.
Jax

JACK (193): (English) Name based on John or Jacques, the French form of Jacob. Usage of Jackie: boys 25%, girls 75%.
JACKSON (399), Jackie, Jacky, Jacques (*zhahk*), Jock (Scottish); Jaxon, Jax (Contemporary)

JACOB (24): (Hebrew) "Supplanter." Biblical; the son of Isaac and Rebekah and twin brother of Esau. Jacob fathered twelve sons and a daughter, who became the ancestors of the nation of Israel. See also Jake.
Jakob (Scandinavian/German), Jacobo (Spanish), Jacques, Jacobus (Latin)

JADON: (*JAY-don*) (Hebrew) "Jehovah has heard." Biblical.
Jaydon, Jaedon, Jaden

JADRIEN: (*JAY-dree-en*) (Contemporary) Blend of Jay and Adrien.

JAEGAR: (*JAY-ger*) (German) "Hunter." The soundalike Jagur, a biblical place name, is an Aramaic name meaning "heap of stones; marker."

JAGO: (*JAY-go*) (English) Variant form of James.

JAHAN: (French) An early medieval variant form of John.
Jehan

JAIME (141): (*HYE-may*) (Spanish) and (*JAY-mee*) (Scottish) Variant form of James, used frequently for both boys and girls. Usage: (Jaime) boys 82%, girls 18%; (Jamie) boys 12%, girls 88%.
JAMIE (258) (Scottish)

JAIRO (474): (*HYE-roh*) (Spanish) Variant form of Jairus. (Hebrew) "Jehovah enlightens".
Jairus (*JARE-us*)

JAKE (160): Short form of Jacob used as an independent name.

JAKEEM: (*ya-keem*) (Hebrew/Arabic) "Raised up."

JAMAL (411): (*ja-MAL*) (Arabic) "Handsome."
Jamaal, Jamahl, Jamall, Jahmal, Jamael, Jamel, Jamil, Jameel, Jamile, Jamiel

JAMES (11): (English) Variant form of Jacob. Biblical; one of the twelve apostles, who possibly was also a cousin of Jesus. See also Jaime and Jimmy.
Jamieson (Scottish), Jameson, Jamison, Jaymes, Jayme

JAMIN: (*JAY-min*) (Hebrew) "Right hand of favor." Biblical.
Jaymin

JAN: (Dutch/Slavic) Variant form of John. Usage: boys 71%, girls 29%.
Janek, Jansen

JAPHETH: (*JAY-feth*) (Hebrew) "May He grant ample room." Biblical; the oldest of Noah's three sons.

JARAH: (*JAY-rah*) (Hebrew) "He gives sweetness; honey." Biblical; a descendant of Jonathan. Jarrah is an Arabic name meaning "vessel." See also Jerah.
Jarrah

JARED (63): (*JARE-ed*) (Hebrew) "Descending." A pre-flood biblical name. The current popularity of Jared may have started due to the character Jared on the late sixties TV western "The Big Valley." Many variants with the same sound have come into use. See also Jarrod and Jerrod.
Jerad (Hebrew), Jarod, Jarad, Jaryd

JAREK: (Polish) "January child." See also Jerrick.

JARELL: (*JARE-el* or *ja-RELL*) (Contemporary) Blend of Jar- and Darell. See also Jerrell.
Jarrell, Jarrel, Jarel, Jaryl

JARETH: (*JARE-eth*) (Contemporary) Blend of Jar- or Jer- and Gareth.
Jarreth, Jereth

JARL: (Scandinavian) Variant form of Earl.

JARON (453): (*JARE-on*) (Israeli) "Cry of rejoicing." Some of the many contemporary names similar to Jaron may be based on a blend of the sounds of Jared or Jerry and Darren.
Jarron, Jaren, Jaran, Jarin, Jarren, Jarran, Jerron, Jerren, Jerrin, Jeran, Jeren

JARRETT (465): (English) Surname, variant form of Garrett. "Spear-strong."
Jarett, Jarret, Jerrett, Jerett

JARROD (326): (English) Variant and surname form of Garrett, from Gerald. See also Garrad, Jared and Jerrod.
JARRED (404), Jarrad, Jarryd

JARVIS: (English) Variant form of the French name Gervaise, meaning "spearman."
Jervis

JASON (35): (Greek) "A healing." Biblical; an early Christian contemporary of Paul. Greek mythology; Jason was leader of a group of warrior heroes called the Argonauts.
JAYSON (469), Jasen, Jase, Jaison, Jaysen, Jaycen, Jace, Jayce

JASPER: (Arabic) Variant form of Caspar or Gaspar. Jasper is also a semi-precious gemstone, red or reddish brown.
Jaspar

JAVIER (117): (*HA-vee-air*) (Spanish/Portuguese) "Bright." Variant form of Xavier.

JAY (226): (Latin) The name of the bird used as a nickname or independent name.
Jaye, Jae, Jai (Hindi)

JAYCEE: (Contemporary) Phonetic name based on initials.
Jayar, Jayvee, Jaydee

"JE-" names: (Contemporary) With pronunciation emphasis on the second syllable. See also "Ja-" names.
JeMar, JeMario, Jerae, Jeron, Jerone, Jevan, Jevon, Jerell, Jerelle

JEAN: (*Jeen* or *zhahn*) (French) Variant form of John. Usage: boys 43%, girls 57%. Jean is sometimes hyphenated

with a second name, and the French pronunciation (*zhahn*) may be used. See also Jon.
Jeanpierre, Jean-Luc, Jean-Paul, Jean-Carlo

JED: Short form of names beginning with "Jed-"
Jedd

JEDIAH: (*je-DYE-ah*) (Hebrew) "Jehovah knows." Biblical.
Jedaiah

JEDIDIAH: (Hebrew) "Beloved of Jehovah." Biblical; a "blessing" name given in infancy to King Solomon, David's second son by Bathsheba.
Jedediah, Jedadiah

JEDREK: (*JEDD-rick*) (Polish) "A strong man."
Jedrick

JEFFORD: (English) Surname and place name.

JEFFREY (36): (English) "Peaceful." Variant form of Geoffrey. The three-syllable spelling alternate Jeffery has been used since medieval times.
JEFFERY (155), Jeff, Jefferson, Jeffry

JEHU: (*JAY-hew*) (Hebrew) "Jehovah is He." Biblical; Jehu was a military commander of Israel, later king, who was noted for his pell-mell style of chariot driving.

JEMAL: Variant form of Jamal.

JERAH: (Hebrew) Given name as well as the name of a Hebrew lunar month. See also Jarah.
Jerrah

JERALD: (English) Variant and surname form of Gerald.
Jerold, Jerrold, Jerrald, Jeraldo (Spanish)

JERARD: (*je-RARD*) (French) "Spear-strong." Variant form of Gerard. Jerrard is also an English surname.
Jerrard, Jerardo (Spanish)

JEREMIAH (156): (*jare-ah-MYE-ah*) (Hebrew) "Jehovah exalts." Biblical; one of the major prophets, a scholar. Besides writing the Book of Jeremiah and Lamentations, Jeremiah compiled and wrote the histories of first and second Kings.
Jeremias (Spanish)

JEREMY (39): (*JARE-a-mee*) (English) Variant form of Jeremiah. In use since the Middle Ages.
Jeramy, Jeremie, Jeramie

JERIAH: (*jer-RYE-ah*) (Hebrew) "Jehovah has seen." Biblical.

JERICHO: (*JARE-a-ko*) (Arabic) "City of the moon." Biblical; a city in Canaan destroyed when its walls fell down.
Jerico (Spanish)

JERMAINE: (*jer-MAIN*) "People of the spear." Variant form of Germaine.
Jermain, Jermane, Jermayne, Jamaine

JEROME (345): (*jer-ROME*) (Greek) "Sacred name." See also Geronimo.
Jeronimo (Spanish)

JERRELL: "Strong, open-minded." Contemporary blend of Jerold and Darell. See also Jarell.
Jerel, Jerrel, Jerrall, Jerryl, Jeryl, Jeriel, Jerriel

JERRICK: (Contemporary) "Strong, gifted ruler." Variant form based on a blend of Jer- and Derrick. See also Jarek.
Jerick, Jerric

JERROD: (Contemporary) Variant form of Garrett. See also Jared and Jarrod.
Jered, Jerad, Jerod, Jerrad, Jerred, Jerryd

JERRY (172): Used as an independent name, Jerry is also a short form of names beginning with "Jer-." See also Gerry.

JESSE (45): (Hebrew) "Jehovah exists." Biblical; the father of King David. Usage of Jessie: boys 61%, girls 29%. Jesiah is a variant form of Joshua.
JESSIE (228), Jessy, Jess, Jessey, Jesiah

JESTIN: (*JESS-tin*) (Welsh) Variant form of Justin.
Jesstin, Jeston

JESUS (64): (Latin/Greek/Hebrew) Short form of Joshua, from Jehoshua. "Jehovah is salvation." The name of the biblical Christ is very frequently used as a given name in

Spanish-speaking families. Spanish/Portuguese pronunciation is *hay-SOOS*.

JETHRO: (*JETH-ro*) (Hebrew) "Overflowing, abundance." Biblical; Moses' father-in-law, a priest of Midian.

Jett

JIMMY (166): Short form of James frequently used as an independent name.

Jim, Jimmie, Jem

JIRO: (*jee-roh*) (Japanese) "Second son"; "next son."

JOAQUIN (404): (*wah-KEEN*) Spanish short form of the Hebrew name Jehoichin, meaning "Jehovah has established." Joaquin Miller was a noted and colorful nineteen-century poet-adventurer of the American West.

JOB: (*jobe*) (Hebrew) "Persecuted." Biblical; a man called by God "blameless and upright." Job is proverbial as an example of patience under trial.

Jobe, Joby

JOBEN: (*JOE-ben*) (Japanese) "Enjoy cleanness."

JODY: (*JO-dee*) Nickname for Joseph and Jude. Usage: boys 37%, girls 63%.

JOE (185): Short form of Joseph.

JOEY (331)

JOED: (*JO-ed*) (Hebrew) "Jehovah is witness." Biblical.

JOEL (104): (*JO-el*) (Hebrew) "Jehovah is God." Biblical; a prophet and writer of the Book of Joel.

JOHN (15): (Hebrew) "Jehovah has been gracious; has shown favor." Biblical; the name of the longest-lived of the twelve apostles, who was especially loved by Christ. Also the name of John the Baptist, who baptized Christ in the Jordan River. Dozens of variant forms, given names and surnames, male and female, have been created in almost every language. See also Jon, Jean, Juan, Jonathan, Ivan, Evan, Giovanni, Sean and Shane.

JOHNNY (134), Johnnie, Johnson, John-Paul, Johnn, Jan (Czech/Dutch); Janos (Czech); Jansen (German/Dutch); Johan, Johann, Johannes, (German); Jantzen (Danish);

Jensen, Jenson (Scandinavian); Jhon (Contemporary);
Joao (Portuguese)

JOHNATHAN: See Jonathan.

JOMEI: (*joe-MAY*) (Japanese) "Spread light."

JON (230): Variant form of John or short form of Jonathan.
Jon is sometimes used in the French fashion, hyphenated
with a second name. See also Jean.
Jon-Paul, Jon-Carlo, Jonny, Jonn, Jonnie

JONAH: (*JOE-nah*) (Hebrew) "Dove." Biblical; because
Jonah was on board a ship when God caused it to sink,
sailors have traditionally used the name to personify
someone who brings bad luck.
Jonas (Spanish)

JONATHAN (16): (Hebrew) "Jehovah has given." Biblical; the son of King Saul, Jonathan was noted for his
manliness, generosity and unselfishness. He saved David's life when Saul would have killed him.
JOHNATHAN (136); JONATHON (146); JOHNATHON
(255)

JONTE: (*jahn-TAY*) (Contemporary) Variant form of Jonathan, combining Jon with the favored end-sound of Dante.
Johnte, Jontae, Johntay

JORAH: (*JOR-ah*) (Hebrew) "He has reproached." Biblical.

JORAM: (*JOR-am*) (Hebrew) "Jehovah is exalted." Jorim
was an ancestor of Mary.
Jorim

JORDAN (38): (*JOR-dan*) (Hebrew) "Downflowing."
Name of the major river in Palestine, used as a given
name since the Crusades. Usage: boys 78%, girls 22%.
JORDON (421), Jorden, Jordin, Jourdan (*jor-DAN*)
(French), Jourdon, Jordain, Jourdaine, Jordy, Jordi

JORELL: (*jor-ELL*) Contemporary usage possibly inspired
by the fictional character Jor-el, father of Superman.
Jorel, Jorrel, Jorrell, Jurell

JOREN: (*JOR-en*) (French) Variant form of George.
Joron, Jorn, Jory, Jorry, Jorey

JORGE (76): (*HOR-hay*) (Spanish/Portuguese) Variant form of George.
Jorje, Jorgen

JOSEPH (13): (Hebrew) "May Jah give increase." Biblical; the son of Jacob who, sold into slavery, rose to become a supreme power in Egypt. Also, Jesus' legal father, a carpenter.
JOSE (22) (Spanish/Portuguese), Joselito (Spanish), Josef (German/Czech), Jozef, Josephus (Latin), Jomar (combination of Joseph and Mary)

JOSHUA (3): (Hebrew) "Jehovah is salvation." From Jehoshua. Biblical; Joshua was an attendant and helper to Moses during the Israelites' forty-year trek through the Sinai wilderness. He was appointed by God to lead the Israelites after the death of Moses.
JOSUE (235) (Spanish), Josh

JOSIAH (356): (*jo-SYE-ah*) (Hebrew) "Jehovah has healed." Biblical; king of Judah at age eight, after his father was assassinated, Josiah ruled ably and well for thirty-one years.
Josias

JOTHAM: (*JO-tham*) (Hebrew) "May Jehovah complete." Biblical; a king of Judah during a time of military strife.

JOVAN: (*jo-VAHN*) (Latin) "Father of the sky"; (French) Variant form of Jupiter (Jove). Mythology; Jupiter was the supreme deity of Roman mythology, corresponding to the Greek Zeus. Some twenty saints have used the Latin form of the name, Jovanus. The Jovani variants may also be phonetic forms of Giovanni.
Jovin, Jovon, Jovi, Jovito, Jovani, Jovany, Jovanni, Jovanny, Jeovany, Jeovani, Jeovanni

JUAN (47): (*wahn*) (Spanish) Variant form of John, often used in combination with other names.
Juancarlos, Juanito "little John," Juanluis, Juanpablo

JUBAL: (*JOO-bal*) (Hebrew) "The ram." Biblical; Jubal was the inventor of the harp and the pipes, and the founder of music-making.

JUDAH: (*JOO-dah*) (Hebrew) "The praised one." Biblical; Judah was the fourth of Jacob's twelve sons. Judas, the Greek form of Judah, is very rarely used, due to the infamy of Judas Iscariot.
Jude, Judd, Judson

JULIAN (131): (*JOO-lee-en*) (Latin) "Jove's child"; (English) Variant form of Julius, the family clan name of several of the most powerful Roman emperors. Biblical; Julius, a Roman centurion, saved Paul's life during a hazardous voyage.
JULIO (169) (*HOO-lee-oh*) (Spanish), Julius; Juliano; Julien, Jules (French)

JURO: (*joo-ROH*) (Japanese) "Tenth son"; "best wishes"; "longevity."

JUSTIN (8): (Latin) "Just, upright, righteous"; (French/English) Variant form of Justus. Justus is a New Testament biblical name, and the soundalike Justice is a virtue name.
Justyn; Justino (Spanish/Portuguese); Justus, Justis, Justice

K

KACEY: (*KAY-see*) (Contemporary) Based on the initials "K.C." In rare use for boys and girls. See also Kasey.
Kacy, K.C., Casey

KADE: (Scottish/Gaelic) "From the wetlands." Kado is a Japanese surname meaning "additional door"; "gateway." See also Cadell.
Kaden, Kado

KADIR: (*kah-DEER*) (Arabic) "Spring greening."

KAELAN: (*KAY-lan*) (Gaelic) "Powerful in battle." Variant form of Caelan. See also Kellen.
Kalen, Kalin, Kalan

KAEMON: (*kah-AY-mon*) (Japanese) "Joyful; right-handed." Old samurai name.

KAHLIL: (*ka-LEEL*) (Arabic) "Friend."

Kalil

KAI: (*kye*) (Welsh) "Keeper of the keys." Variant form of Kay. Usage: boys 82%, girls 18%. Kai is also Hawaiian, meaning "the sea." Kaimi (*kye-EE-mee*) is a Hawaiian name meaning "the seeker."

Kaimi

KALANI: (*kah-LAH-nee*) (Hawaiian) "The sky; chieftain."

KALEB (402): See Caleb.

KALLUM: "Mild, gentle." See also Callum.

Kailum

KALVIN: See also Calvin.

Kalvyn

KAMDEN: "Winding valley." See also Camden.

KAMERON (395): See also Cameron. Usage: boys 85%, girls 15%.

Kamron

KANA: (*KAH-nah*) (Hawaiian) A Maui demigod who could take the form of a rope and stretch from Molokai to Hawaii. Kano is Japanese: "one's masculine power, capability."

Kano (*kah-noh*)

KANE: (Irish/Gaelic) "Fighter." Kane (*kah-NAY*) is also a Japanese surname meaning "putting together"; "money." See also Caine.

Kaine, Kain, Kayne

KANNON: (Japanese) Variant form of Kuan-yin, the Chinese Buddhist deity of mercy.

Kannen

KANOA: (*ka-NO-ah*) (Hawaiian) "The free one."

KAORI: (*kah-oh-ree*) (Japanese) "Add a man's strength."

KARIM: (*ka-REEM*) (Arabic) "Generous; a friend." The Koran lists generosity as one of the ninty-nine qualities of God.

Kareem

KARL (314): (German) "Man, manly." See also Carl.

Karle, Karlo, Karlos, Karson, Karlin, Karlton, Karel

KASEY (479): (Irish) "Alert, vigorous." Variant form of Casey. Usage: boys 22%, girls 78%. See also Kacey.

KASIMIR: (*KAZ-e-meer*) (Slavic) "Enforces peace." The name of the patron saint of Poland; also a favored name of Polish royalty. See also Casimir.
Kazimir

KASPAR: (Polish) "Keeper of the treasure." Variant form of Caspar.

KASSIDY: "Curly-headed." See also Cassidy. Usage: boys 20%, girls 80%.

KASSIM: (*kah-seem*) (Arabic) "Divided."
Kasim

KEANE: (English/Irish) "Quick, brave." Keandre (*kee-AHN-dray*) is a contemporary blend of "Ke-" and Andre, meaning "manly, brave."
Keene, Keandre

KEARN: (Irish/Gaelic) "Dark."
Kearne

KEATON: (*KEE-ton*) (English) "Place of the hawks."

KEDRICK: "Gift of splendor." Variant form of Cedric.
Kedric

KEEFE: (Irish/Gaelic) "Kindly, good." See also Kiefer.
Keefer

KEEGAN (438): (Irish) "A thinker; fiery." Variant form of Hugh.
Kegan, Keagan, Kagan, Kagen

KEENAN (481): (Irish) Surname.
Kenan, Keenon

KEIJI: (*KAY-jee*) (Japanese) "Director"; "govern with discretion."

KEIR: (Irish/Gaelic) "Dusky; dark-haired." A name made familiar by the actor Keir Dullea.
Keiron, Kieran, Kieron, Kerr

KEITARO: (*kay-tah-ROH*) (Japanese) "Blessed"; "person big in providence."

KEITH (108): (Scottish) "Woodland." Surname and place name.

KELBY: (Scandinavian/Gaelic) "Place by the fountain; spring." Very rarely used for girls.

KELLEN (499): (Gaelic) "Powerful in battle." Usage: boys 86%, girls 14%. See also Kaelan.
Kellan, Keelan, Keillan, Kelle, Kelden

KELLY (293): (Gaelic/Irish) "Lively, aggressive." Usage: boys 8%, girls 92%.

KELVIN (411): (Celtic) "River man."
Kelven

KEN: (English) Short form of names beginning with "Ken-." Ken is also a Japanese name meaning "strong, physically healthy"; "law, regulation." Kenn is an English surname.
Kenn

KENDALL (421): (English) "Royal valley." Surname referring to Kent, England. Usage: boys 27%, girls 73%.
Kendell, Kendal, Kendel, Kendale

KENDREW: (Scottish) "Manly, brave." Variant form of Andrew.

KENDRICK: (Gaelic/Welsh) "Royal chieftain." Surname.
Kendrik, Kendric, Kendrix

KENJI: (*KEN-jee*) (Japanese) "Intelligent second son, strong and vigorous."
Kenjiro (*ken-jee-ROH*) "Second son who sees with insight; longsighted."

KENNARD: (Gaelic) "Brave chieftain."
Kenner, Kendon

KENNETH (58): (Gaelic/Scottish) "Good-looking, fair."

KENNY (368): (Scottish) Surname; also a short form of names beginning with "Ken-."
Kenney, Kennan, Kinney, Kennon

KENT (436): (Celtic) "Royal chieftain." Kent and the other English surname variants listed here all share the basic meaning of "royal" or "royal power."
Kenton, Kentrell, Kenrick

KENTARO: (*ken-tah-ROH*) (Japanese) "Sharp, big boy."

KEOKI: (*kee-OH-kee*) (Hawaiian) Variant form of George.

KEON: (*KEE-on*) (Irish) Variant form of Ewan, from John.
Kian

KEONI: (*kee-OH-nee*) (Hawaiian) Variant form of John.

KERRICK: (English) "King's rule." English surname.

KERRY: (Irish/Gaelic) "Dusky, dark." Surname and name of the county in Ireland. Usage: boys 36%, girls 64%. Kerrigan is an Irish surname with the same meaning.
Kerrigan

KERWIN: (Irish/Gaelic) "Friend from the wetlands."

KEVIN (17): (Irish/Gaelic) "Handsome child." Name of a famous Irish hermit-saint. There are many spelling variants, but Kevin is by far the most popular.
Keven, Kevan, Kevyn, Kevon, Kevinn, Keveon, Kevion, Kevis

KHANH: (*kahn*) (Turkish/Arabic) "Prince." Title used by central Asian tribal chieftains or ruling princes.

KIEFER: (*KEE-fer*) (German) "Barrelmaker." Variant form of Cooper. See also Keefe.
Keifer, Kee

KIEL: (*KYE-el*) (Irish/Gaelic) "Good-looking." See also Kyle.

KILIAN: (*KIL-ee-an*) (Irish/Gaelic) "Trouble."
Killian

KIM: (English) Short form of Kimball or Kimberly. Usage: boys 18%, girls 82%. Kim is also a Vietnamese name meaning "precious metal; gold," used for both boys and girls.

KIMBALL: (Celtic/English) "Bold kin." The related name Kimberly is almost entirely used for girls today.

KIMO: (*KEE-moh*) (Hawaiian) Variant form of James and Jim.

KINGSLEY: (English) "King's field." King is one of several titles occasionally used as given names. Other male title-names are Prince, Duke, Earl, Count, Marquis, Caesar, Czar and Khanh.
King, Kingston, Kinsley

KIRBY: (English) "Church farm." Usage: boys 32%, girls 68%.

KIRK (261): (Scandinavian/English) "Church." In Scotland kirk is still used as a word meaning "church."
Kirkland, Kirklin, Kirklyn, Kerk, Kyrk, Kyrksen

KIT: Nickname for Christopher rarely used today. Notable name bearer, frontiersman Kit Carson.

KLINTON: "Hillside town." See also Clinton.

KNUTE: (*k'NOOT*) (Scandinavian) "Knot." Variant form of Canute, the name of an eleventh-century king of Denmark and England.

KODY (325): "Helpful." See also Cody.
Kodey, Kodie

KOI: (*KO-ee*) (Hawaiian) "Urge, implore." Also the Hawaiian equivalent form of Troy.

KOLBY: "Dark, dark-haired." Koby is a German/Polish short form of Jacob. See also Colby.
Kelby, Koby

KOLTON: "Coal-town." See also Colton.
Koltin, Kolten

KONNOR: "Desiring." See also Connor.

KONRAD: (Polish/German) "Bold advisor." See also Conrad.

KORBIN: "Raven-haired." See also Corbin.

KORDELL: "Cordmaker." See also Cordell.
Kord

KORRIGAN: "Spearman." See also Corrigan.

KORT: (German/Dutch) "Courtier." Variant form of Cort.

KORY (335): See also Cory.
KOREY (429), Korry, Korrey

KRAIG: "Rock; rocky." See also Craig.

KRIS: Short form of names beginning with "Kris-."

KRISTIAN: (Scandinavian) Variant form of Christian.

KRISTOPHER (177): (Scandinavian) Variant form of Christopher.
Kristofer, Kristoffer, Krystopher, Khristopher, Kristoff (Czech), Kristof

KRUZ: "Cross." See also Cruz.

KURT (303): (German) "Brave, wise."

KURTIS (321): "Courtier." See also Curtis.
Kurtiss

KYLE (18): (Gaelic) "Chief." See also Kiel.
Kyler, Kylan, Kylar, Kylen, Kye, Kyrell

L

"LA-"names: (Contemporary) Blends of "la" plus various endings, with pronunciation emphasis on the second syllable. Second syllable might or might not begin with a capital. See also Lamar, Lamont and "Le-" names.
Ladale, Lajon, Lamarcus, Larell, Laronn, Ladell, LaRay, Larenzo, LaRico, Laron, LaRon, Laroy, LaSean, LaShawn, Laval, Lavante, Lavaughn, Lavell, Lavelle, Lavon, Lavonte

LACHLAN: (*LOCK-lin*) (Gaelic/Scottish) "From the land of lakes."

LAFAYETTE: (*lah-fay-ett*) Historical; the Marquis de Lafayette, a French nobleman, was only twenty when he came to serve four years in the American Revolutionary cause.

LAIRD: "Lord." Scottish landholder's title.

LAMAR (485): (French) "Of the sea." Surname.
LaMarr, Lamarr

LAMONT: (Scandinavian/Gaelic) "Man of law." Lamond is a Scottish clan name.
Lamonte, Lamond

LANCE (186): (French) "Lance, lancer." Mythology; in the tales of King Arthur, Sir Lancelot (or Launcelot) was the most renowned Knight of the Round Table. Lantz is a Yiddish name meaning "lancet."
Lancelot, Lantz

LANDON (290): (English) "Landowner."

LANE: (English) "Path, roadway."
Layne

LANGDON: (English) "From the long hill slope." Related
English surnames: Langley "long meadow"; Langston
"long stone."
Langley, Langston

LANNY: Short form of names beginning with "Lan-."
Lannie

LANZO: (*LAHN-zo*) (Italian) Variant form of Lance. See
also Lonzo.
Lanza

LARAMIE: (*LARE-a-mee*) (French) Surname with Western
associations because of Laramie, Wyoming, a town on
the Overland Trail, route of the Pony Express.

LARNELL: (*lar-NELL*) (Contemporary) Blend of Larry and
Darnell.

LARRY (175): Short form of Lawrence and Laurence, often
used as an independent name.

LARS: (Scandinavian) Variant form of Lawrence.
Larson

LASALLE: (*la-SAL*) (French) "The hall."

LATHAN: (Contemporary) Rhyming variant of Nathan.

LAUREAN: (Latin) Masculine form of Laurel.

LAWRENCE (204): (Latin/English) "From the place of the
laurel trees." Lawrence, a later English form of Laurence, currently is preferred by American parents by about
ten to one over Laurence. See also Loren and Lorenzo.
Laurence, Lauro (Italian), Laureano, Laurent (French),
Laurian, Laurenz (German), Lawson, Lawton

LAZARO: (*LAH-za-ro*) (Spanish) Variant form of Lazarus.
(Hebrew/Greek) "God has helped." Biblical; Lazarus,
brother of Mary and Martha, was a close friend of Jesus.
Lazarus's resurrection by Jesus was one of the miracles
recorded in the New Testament.
Lazarus, Lazar (Slavic), Lasar (German)

"LE-" names: (Contemporary) With pronunciation empha-
sis on the second syllable. See also "La-" names.
Ledell, Lemar, Leondre, LeRon, Lerone, LeSean, Le-
Shawn, LeTroy, Levell, Levelle, Levon, LeWayne

LEANDRO: (Spanish) "Lionlike man." Variant form of Leander.
Leandre (French); Leander (English); Leandrew (Contemporary)

LEE (230): (English) Surname frequently used in the American South as a given name in honor of the Confederate general Robert E. Lee. Usage: boys 87%, girls 13%.

LEIF: (*life*) (Scandinavian) According to Norse legend, the Viking Leif Ericson landed his longboat on American shores some five hundred years before Columbus arrived.

LEIGHTON: (*LAY-ton*) (English) "Meadow town."
Layton

LELAND: (English) "Pasture ground."
Leeland

LEMUEL: (Hebrew) "Belonging to God." Biblical; a king mentioned in Proverbs 31 who was given a detailed description of the value and capabilities of a good wife.

LENNOX: (Scottish) Surname and clan name. Lennox, a Scottish nobleman, appears in Shakespeare's *Macbeth*.

LENNY: Short form of names beginning with "Len-" and Leonard.
Len, Lenn, Lennie, Lennell

LEO (409): (Latin) "Lion."

LEON: (Latin/Greek) "Lion." The lion is a central figure in the art and religious symbolism of many different cultures, usually meaning kingliness, grandeur and courage. See also Lionel.
Lion

LEONARD (304): (*LEN-ard*) (German) "Lion-bold." Notable name bearer of Leonardo is Leonardo da Vinci, considered to be one of the most brilliant and creative men who ever lived.
LEONARDO (333) (*lay-o-NAR-do*) (Italian/Spanish/Portuguese), Lenard, Lennard (English), Leonidas, Leonides (Greek)

LEOPOLDO: (Spanish) Variant form of Leopold; (German) "A bold man."

Leopold

LERON: (*le-RON*) (French) "The circle"; (Israeli) "my song."

LEROUX: (*la-ROO*) (French) "The red-haired one."
Larue

LEROY: (French) "The king."
LeeRoy, Leroi, LeRoy

LESLIE: (*LEZ-lee*) (Scottish) Surname of royalty. Once considered a male name, Leslie now is used almost entirely for girls (96%).
Les

LESTER: (English) "Fortified place."

LEVI (183): (*LEE-vye*) (Hebrew) "Joined." Biblical; Levi, third of Jacob's twelve sons, became father of the tribe that was later assigned priestly duties.

LEWIS (418): (Teutonic) "Renowned fighter." See also Louis and Luis.
Lew

LEX: (Latin) "Law." Also a short form of Alexander.

LIAM: (*LYE-am*) (Irish) Variant form of William.
Lyam

LIN: (Chinese) Family name; (English) Short form for names beginning with "Lin." In rare use for boys and girls.

LINCOLN: (*LINK-an*) (Latin/Welsh) "Lakeside colony." The name of an early Roman settlement in England.
Linc

LINDELL: (Teutonic) "From the linden tree dell."
Lendell, Lendall

LINUS: (*LYE-nus*) (Latin) "Net." Biblical; a Christian companion to Paul in Rome. Today, Linus has been made familiar by the child character in Schultz's cartoon *Peanuts*.

LIONEL: (Latin) "Young lion."
LEONEL (442) (Spanish), Lionell, Lonell, Lonnell

LLEWELLYN: (*loo-ELL-an*) (Welsh) "Lionlike."
Lewellyn, Lew

LLOYD (474): (Welsh) "Grey."
Loyd

LOCKE: (English) Surname referring to a lock or locksmith.

LOGAN (118): (Gaelic/Scottish) "Low meadow."
Logen

LONNIE (495): An independent name and short form of Lionel and Alonzo. Usage: boys 78%, girls 22%.
Lonny, Lon, Lonne, Londale

LONZO: (Spanish) "Ready, eager." Short form of Alonzo. See also Lanzo.
Lonza, Lonzell

LORCAN: (*LOR-ken*) (Irish) Variant form of Laurence.

LOREN: Variant form of Lorenzo and Lawrence. Usage: boys 53%, girls 47%.
Loran, Lorin

LORENZO (317): (Spanish/Italian) Variant form of Lawrence. Notable name bearer: Lorenzo de Medici, a Renaissance patron of Michelangelo and da Vinci. See also Lawrence and Loren.
Lorenso, Lorenz, Lorence, Lorance

LORNE: (Scottish) Surname; also a variant form of Lawrence.
Lornell

LOUIS (206): (*LOO-iss*) (English) (*loo-WEE*) (French) (Teutonic/French) "Renowned fighter." A name used by eighteen French kings. See also Lewis and Luis.
LOUIE (485), Lou

LOVELL: (*la-VELL*) (French/English) "Young wolf."
Lowell (*LOW-el*)

LOYAL: (French/English) "Faithful, unswerving." A virtue name. See also Lyle.

LUCAS (133): (Latin) "Light, illumination." Variant form of Luke. See also Luke.
Luciano (Italian), Lucio (Spanish), Lucian, Lucien, Luc (French); Lucius (Latin/English); Lucan (Roman)

LUCKY: Nickname literally meaning "fortunate." Lucky is also used as a nickname for Lucas and its variants.

LUIS (55): (*loo-EECE*) (Spanish) Variant form of Louis. See also Lewis.
Luiz, Luigi (Italian)

LUKE (150): (Greek/Latin) "Light-giving." Biblical; a first-century Christian called "the beloved physician," who wrote one of the four Gospel accounts of the life of Christ.
Lukas (Dutch)

LUTHER: (German) "Renowned warrior."
Lothar

LYDELL: (*lih-DELL*) (Scottish) Surname used as a given name.

LYLE: (French) "Islander." The soundalike names Lyell and Lyall are Scottish surnames meaning "loyal." See also Loyal.
Lyell, Lyall

LYNDON: (English) "Place of linden trees."
Lyndell

LYSANDER: (*lye-SAN-der*) (Greek) "Liberator." Lysander is one of the main characters in Shakespeare's *Midsummer Night's Dream*.
Lisandro (Spanish)

M

MAC: (Gaelic) "Son of." Scottish and Irish surname prefix used as a given name or nickname. Mack is an ancient Scottish given name. See also "Mc-" names; Mackenzie and Maxwell.
Mack, Macklin

MACE: Short form of names like Macy and Mason; also an English surname that may be a form of Matthew. Literally, a medieval weapon carried by knights. See Martel.
Macey, Macerio (Spanish)

MACKENZIE: (*ma-KEN-zee*) (Gaelic/Scottish) "Son of Kenzie; fair, favored one." Usage: boys 27%, girls 73%.

MADISON: (English) Surname derived from Matthew, "gift of Jah," or Matilda, "strong fighter." Usage: boys 6%, girls 94%.

MAGNUS: (Latin) "Greatness, nobility." A name favored by Scandinavian royalty.

MAJOR: (Latin) "Greater." Surname that is also a military rank.

MAKANI: (*ma-KAH-nee*) (Hawaiian) "Wind."

MAKOTO: (*ma-KOH-toh*) (Japanese) "Good."

MALACHI: (*MAL-a-kye*) (Hebrew) "Messenger of God." Biblical; a prophet and writer of the final book of the Old Testament.

MALCOLM (394): (*MAL-cum*) (Gaelic/Scottish) "St. Columb's disciple." A name favored by Scottish royalty.
Malcom

MALIK: (*MAL-lik*) (Arabic) "Master."
Malek

MANFRED: (German) "Man of peace."

MANO: (*MAH-no*) (Hawaiian) "Shark." Figuratively, a passionate lover. Mano (Spanish) is a short form of Manuel.

MANU: In Hindu mythology, a creator of mankind. The Hawaiian Manu is the name of a bird.

MANUEL (96): (Spanish) "With us is God." Variant form of Emmanuel.
Manolo, Mano, Manolito, Manny, Mannie

MANZO: (*MAHN-zoh*) (Japanese) "10,000-fold strong third son."

"MAR-" names: Contemporary blends based on Mark. See also Marquis and Mark.
Markaine, Markeith, Marquel, Marsean, Marshawn, Marshon

MARC: See Mark.

MARCEL: (*mar-SELL*) (French) Variant form of the Latin Marcellus, from Marcus.

Marcelo, Marcelino, Marcell, Marcello (Italian), Marcellus, Marciano, Marceau (*mar-SO*) (French)

MARCUS (95): (Latin) "Of Mars." Mythology; Mars, the Roman god of fertility, for whom the spring calendar month March was named, became identified with the Greek Ares, god of war. See also Mark.

MARCOS (215) (Spanish/Portuguese), Marcas, Markus (German/Dutch/Hungarian), Markos, Marcio

MARDEN: (English) Surname used as a given name.
Mardon

MAREO: (*mah-RAY-oh*) (Japanese) "Rare, strong, manly boy; rare, uncommon."

MARIANO: (*mahr-ee-AHN-oh*) (Spanish) Variant form of Marion, a male variant form of Marie. The English Marion (Marian for girls) is very rarely used for American boys today. See also Mario.

MARINO: (*ma-REE-no*) (Latin) "Of the sea."

MARIO (94): (Italian) Masculine form of Mary. A number of male names have been created as variants of names attributed to the Virgin Mary. See also Mariano.
Marius.

MARK (43): (Latin) "Of Mars, the god of war"; (English) Variant form of Marcus. Biblical; the Roman surname of John Mark, missionary companion to Peter and Paul and writer of one of the four Gospel accounts of the life of Jesus. See also Marcus and Marquis.

MARCO (178) (Spanish/Portuguese); MARC (199), Marq, Marque, (French); Marko, Markov (Russian); Marek (Slavic); Marquez (Spanish); Marx, Markel, Markell (German); Marques (Portuguese)

MARLON (448): "Blackbird." Variant form of Merle. Marlin is in rare use for girls.
Marlin

MARLOW: (English) "Marshy meadow." Marlowe and Marley are in rare use as girls' names.
Marlowe, Marley

MARO: (*MAH-roh*) (Japanese) "Myself."

MARQUIS (421): (*mar-KEE*) French title that ranks below a duke and above an earl. The English equivalent is Marquess. See also Mark.
Marquise (Italian), Marques (Portuguese), Markeese, Marqui, Markeece, Markese.

MARSHALL (363): (English) "Military, cavalry officer; caretaker of horses." In America "marshal" is a law enforcement title similar to sheriff.
Marshal, Marsh

MARSTON: (English) "Town near the marsh."
Marsten

MARTEL: (French) (*mar-TEL*) "Mace." The *martel-de-fer* was a medieval iron cudgel carried by knights as an offensive weapon against heavy armor.
Martell

MARTIN (98): (Latin/English) "Warrior of Mars."
Marten (Dutch), Martino (Italian), Marty, Martyn (English), Marton (Hungarian), Marti (Swiss)

MARVIN (244): (English) "Renowned friend."
Marvyn, Marven, Marwin

MASON (235): (English) "Worker in stone; stonemason."

MATTHEW (4): (Hebrew) "Gift of Jehovah." Biblical; the name of one of the twelve apostles, who wrote the first Gospel account of the life of Jesus. The alternate spelling Mathew is an English surname.
MATHEW (163), Matt, Matias, Mateo (Spanish); Matthias, Mathias (Welsh); Matteo (Italian); Mateus (Portuguese); Matthieu, Mathieu (French); Matheson (Scottish)

MAURICE (278): (*maw-REESE/MORE-iss*) (English/French) "Dark-skinned; Moor." See also Morris.
MAURICIO (366) (Spanish), Mauro, Maureo, Maurio, Maurilio, Maury, Maurin, Morino

MAVERICK: (*MAV-rick*) An American Westerner named Maverick refused to brand his calves as other ranchers did, and the name came to signify an independent man who avoids conformity.
Mavrick

MAX (191): (Latin) "The greatest."
Maximo (Italian), Maxim (*max-EEM*) (French), Maxi-mino, Maxx, Maximilian, Maximillian, Maximiliano (Italian)

MAXFIELD: (English) "Field belonging to Mack."

MAXWELL (202): (English/Scottish) "Mack's well." See also Mac.

MAYER: (English/German) "Headman, mayor."
Meyer, Meir (Hebrew) "shining"

MAYNARD: (German/French) "Powerful, strong."
Maynor, Mayne

"Mc-" names: (Scottish/Irish) Surnames occasionally used as given names. See also Mac.
McArthur, McCain, McCarthy, McCormick, Mcgregor, McKay, McKinley, McClain

MEADE: (English/Irish) "Honey-wine" or "meadow."

MELVIN (371): (Gaelic/Irish) "Friend of Michael."
Melvyn, Mel

MERCER: (English/French) "Merchant." Surname in rare use as a given name for both boys and girls.

MERLE: (French) "Blackbird." In rare use for boys and girls. Country-western singer Merle Haggard has made the name familiar today.
Merlin, Merlyn

MERRICK: (Welsh) Variant form of Maurice.
Myrick

MERRILL: (English) "Shining sea."
Merril

MERRITT: (English) "Worthy."

MERVIN: (Welsh) Variant form of Merlin.
Merwyn

MICAH (279): (*MYE-cah*) (Hebrew) Variant form of Michael. Biblical; a prophet and writer of the Book of Micah. Usage: boys 86%, girls 14%.

MICHAEL (1): (Hebrew) "Who is like God?" Michael, the archangel (chief or principal angel), and Gabriel are the only two angels given personal names in the canonical

Bible. Many saints, emperors and kings have borne the name, and there are many variant forms, male and female. In this century, Michael has been among the top fifty names for at least seven decades. (Note: long-standing usage of the spelling variant Micheal may be an accidental transposing of the vowels or an attempt at a phonetic spelling of the French Michel.)

MIGUEL (70) (Spanish/Portuguese), MICHEAL (234), Miquel (French), Michel (French/Dutch); Mikael (Swedish); Mikel, Mikell; Mikhael, Mikhail, Michail, Mikhal (Russian); Mikkel (Scandinavian); Mychal, Mychael; Michal (Czech/Polish); Miko (Slavic)

MICHIO: (*mee-chee-OH*) (Japanese) "Man with strength of threethousand." Michiro (*mee-chee-ROH*) "conducts (or governs) himself well."

MIKE (359): Short form of Michael and Micah, often used as an independent name. The nicknames Mick and Mickey are considered to be particularly Irish. See also Mischa.

Mickey, Mick

MIKI: (*MEE-kee*) (Japanese) "Tree"; "wine for special occasion."

Mikio (*mee-kee-oh*) "three trees together."

MILAN: (*mee-LAHN*) Name of the Italian city used as a given name.

Milano

MILES (232): (German/English) "Merciful." See also Myles.

Milo, Mylo

MILLER: (English) "One who grinds grain." Occupational surname.

Millard, Millen, Milford

MILTON: (English) "Mill town."

MINORU: (*mee-NOH-roo*) (Japanese) "Bear fruit."

MISCHA: (*MEE-sha*) (Slavic) Nickname for Michael. See also Mike. Phonetic forms of Mischa are in rare use for girls.

MITCHELL (105): (English/Scottish/Irish) Variant form of Michael.
Mitchel, Mitch

MODESTO: (*mo-DESS-toh*) (Latin) "Modesty, moderate." A Spanish saint's name.

MOHAMMAD: (Arabic) "Praiseworthy, glorified." Name of the founder of the Islamic religion. Listed here are only a few of the dozens of name variants attributed to Mohammad.
Mohammed, Mohamed, Mohamad, Muhammad, Muhammed, Mahmoud, Mohamet

MONROE: (Gaelic/Scottish) "From the river's mouth."

MONTAGUE: (*MON-tah-gew*) (French) "Steep mountain."

MONTANA: (*mon-TAN-nah*) (Latin) "Mountain." The name of the western state used as a given name. Usage for boys and girls is about equal.
Montaine (*mon-TAYNE*) (French)

MONTARO: (*mon-tah-ROH*) (Japanese) "Design, pattern"; or "big boy."

MONTE: (*MON-tee* or *mon-TAY*) (Italian/Spanish) "Mountain." Short form of names beginning with "Mont-"; also used as a contemporary independent name with variants.
Monty, Montie (English), Montay, Montae, Montel (French), Montrell, Montrel, Montrelle, Montes, Montez

MONTGOMERY: (English/French) "Mountain of the one who rules." A surname of English and Scottish earls.

MORELL: (*moh-REL*) (French) "Dark one; the Moor."

MORGAN (277): (Welsh) "Bright sea." Surname. Usage for girls increased sharply during the eighties, to about 76%, 24% for boys.
Morgen

MORIO: (*mor-ee-OH*) (Japanese) "Forest boy"; or "give good full measure."

MORLAND: (English) "Marsh, wetland."

MORRIS: (English) Variant form of Maurice.

Morrey, Morrie

MOSES (448): (Hebrew) "Saved from the water." Biblical; name of the Hebrew child pulled out of the Nile River and adopted by the Egyptian pharoah's daughter. Moses lived one of the most eventful lives recorded in Scripture (see the Book of Exodus). Moss is an English medieval form of Moses, rarely used today.

MOISES (266) (Spanish), Moshe (Hebrew), Moss

MURRAY: (Celtic) "From the sea." Surname of an ancient Scottish clan, occasionally used as a given name.

MYLES (465): Variant form of Miles.

MYRON: (Aramaic/Arabic) "Myrrh, sweet oil."

N

NAKO: (*NAH-koh*) (Japanese) "How old?" Surname.

NAMIR: (*nah-MEER*) (Arabic) "Leopard."

NAPOLEON: (*na-POH-lee-un*) (French/Italian) "Man from Naples."

NARDO: (German/Latin) "Strong, hardy." A short form of names like Bernardo and Leonardo.

NATHAN (42): (*NAY-than*) (Hebrew) "Given." Biblical; Nathan was God's prophet during the reigns of David and Solomon.

Nate, Nat

NATHANIEL (102): (*na-THAN-yel*) (Hebrew) "God has given." Biblical; one of the twelve apostles.

NATHANAEL (452) (Latin), Nathanial

NAVARRO: (*na-VAR-oh*) (Spanish) "Plains." The name of a medieval kingdom in Spain.

Navarre (French)

NED: Nickname for Edward.

NEHEMIAH: (*nee-ah-MYE-ah*) (Hebrew) "Jah comforts." Biblical; the prophet assigned to lead the Jews on their return to Jerusalem from exile in Babylon.

NEIL (284): (*neel*) (Scandinavian/Gaelic) Variant form of Niall.

NEAL (421) (English), Neale, Neel; Neill, Neilan (Irish/
Scottish); Nils, Niels, Nielsson, Neilson, Nilsen (Scandinavian)

NELSON (297): (Gaelic/English) "Son of Neil."
Nels

NESTOR (390): (Greek) "Remembers." In legend, the learned Greek general who gave counsel in the Trojan War.

NEVADA: (*ne-VAH-dah*) (Spanish) "Snow-clad." The name of the western state, rarely used as a given name.

NEVILLE: (*NEV-il*) (English/French) "New village."

NIALL: (Gaelic) "Champion." See also Neil.
Niles (English), Nyle, Nyles

NICHOLAS (12): (Greek) "Victorious; conqueror of the people." Biblical; one of seven "qualified men" in the first-century Christian congregation. St. Nicholas (fourth century) is known as the patron saint of Russia, children, scholars, sailors and pawnbrokers. Because Nicholas was such a popular name during the Middle Ages, many variant and short forms were created for men and women. Five popes and two emperors of Russia have borne the name. See also Nick.

NICOLAS (169) (Spanish), NICKOLAS (252), NIKOLAS (421) (Slavic); Nikolaus, Nickolaus (German); Nicholaus, Nicolaus, Nicholai; Nikolai (Polish); Nicolai (French/Italian); Nicoli, Nicolo, Niccolo (Italian); Nikita (Russian)

NICK: Short form of Nicholas. Part of the Greek meaning of Nicholas refers to Nike (*NYE-kee*), the Greek goddess of victory. Nikki and Nikko are also Japanese surnames with the potential meanings "two trees" and "daylight."
Nico, Nicky, Nikki, Nikko, Niko, Nikos, Nykko, Nicos, Nickson, Nixon

NIGEL: (*NYE-jel*) (Latin/English) Variant form of Niall.
Niguel (*ni-GEL*) (Spanish)

NILES: Variant form of Niall.

NOAH (260): (Hebrew) "Rest, consolation." Biblical; the

patriarch survivor of the great flood; according to the biblical account, all the world's nations are descended from Noah's three sons.

NOE (368) (Spanish)

NOEL (359): (*NOH-el*) (French) "Birth-day." Commonly used in reference to Christ's birth, Noel is also an alternate name for Christmas. Usage: boys 80%, girls 20%.

NOLAN (348): (Gaelic/Irish) "Renowned, noble."
Nolen, Noland

NORBERT: (*NOR-bert*) (Teutonic) "Shining from the north."
Norberto

NORMAN (477): (English/French) "Man of the north."
Normand, Normando (Spanish)

NORRIS: (Scottish/English) "From the north."

NURI: (Israeli) "Fire."

NYLES: See Niall.

O

"O'-" names: (Irish) "Descendant of." Surnames occasionally used as given names.
O'Brian, O'Brien, Odell, O'Keefe, O'Shea, O'Shay

OCTAVIO (491): (*ahk-TAH-vee-oh*) (Latin) "Eighth." From Octavius.
Octavius, Octavian, Octavianos

OHARA: (*oh-hah-rah*) (Japanese) "Small field." Also an Irish surname.

OLAF: (*OH-loff*) (Scandinavian) "Ancestral heritage."
Olav

OLIVER (398): (English/French) "The olive tree." See historical note under Olivia in the girls' index.
Olivier (*oh-LIV-ee-ay*) (French), Ollie

OMAR (136): (*OH-mar*) (Arabic) "Long-lived"; (Hebrew) "speaker." Biblical; a sheik of Edom and son of Esau. Omar Khayyám (twelfth century) was a Persian poet, as-

tronomer and mathematician. Caliph Omar II made Islam
an imperial power.
Omarr

OREL: (Russian/Slavic) "Eagle."
Orrel, Oriel, Oral, Orell, Orry

OREN: (Hebrew) "Pine tree." See also Orrin.
Orin, Oran

ORION: (*oh-RYE-on*) (Greek) "Rising in the sky; dawning." Greek mythology; Orion was a mighty hunter, the
son of Poseidon. The Orion constellation contains three
of the most conspicuous stars in the nighttime sky.

ORLANDO (326): (*or-LAHN-doh*) (German) "Renowned
in the land"; (Spanish/Italian) Variant form of Roland.
Orland, Orlin

ORRIN: Orrin is the name of a river in England. See also
Oren.
Orran, Orren

ORSON: (Latin) "Bear." Notable name bearer: actor/di-
rector Orson Welles.
Orsino (Italian)

ORVILLE: (French) "Gold town."
Orvelle

OSBORNE: (English) Surname.

OSCAR (103): (English) "God's spear."
Oskar (Scandinavian)

OSMAN: (English/Scandinavian) "Godly protection."
Osmin, Osmond, Osmund, Oswin "God's friend."

OSWALD: (English) "God's power."
Oswaldo (Spanish)

OTTO: (German) "Wealthy."
Otis

OWEN: (Welsh) "Well-born." Variant form of Ewan.
Owynn

OZZIE: Short form of names beginning with "Os-."
Ozzy

P

PALMER: (English/Latin) "Bearing a palm branch."

PANCHO: (Spanish) Nickname for Francisco, Frank.

PARIS: The name of the French capital used as a given name. Greek mythology; Paris was the Prince of Troy whose love affair with Helen led to the Trojan War. Usage: boys 34%, girls 66%.
Parrish

PARKER (346): (English) "Keeper of the forest; forest ranger." A surname made familiar as a given name today by actor Parker Stevenson.

PARNEL: (English/Irish) Surname derived from a medieval given name. Use of Parnell as a given name may be in honor of Charles Parnell, nineteenth-century Irish Nationalist.
Parnell, Pernell

PASCUAL: (*pahs-KWALL*) (Hebrew/Latin) "Passover."
Pasqual, Pasquale (Italian); Pascal, Pascoe

PATRICK (49): (Latin) "Patrician, noble." The Romans once were divided socially and politically into plebeians and patricians, commoners and aristocrats. Patrick, patron saint of Ireland, has given the name its Irish associations.
Patricio (Portuguese); Patric (French); Pat, Paden (Scottish); Padric, Padraic (Irish)

PAUL (53): (Latin) "Little." Biblical; the apostle and evangelist; Paul's letters to early Christians form the majority of the books of the New Testament.
PABLO (246) (Spanish); Paolo (Italian); Paulo (Spanish/Portuguese); Paulino (Portuguese); Paco (Spanish); Poul (Scandinavian); Pauel (Dutch); Paulus (German); Pavel (Czech/Russian); Paulson (English); Paulsen (Dutch/Scandinavian); Pavlov (Russian)

PAYTON: (English) Surname rarely used as a given name. Usage for boys and girls is about equal.
Peyton

PERCY: (French/English) "Pierces."
Percival, Perceval

PERICLES: (*PARE-a-klees*) (Greek) Historical; the name of the Greek statesman who unified the Athenian empire under democratic principles.

PERRY (474): (Latin/English) "Wanderer"; (English) Surname and a short form of Peregrine. The peregrine falcon is the bird most favored in the ancient sport of falconry.
Peregrine (*PARE-a-green*)

PETER (84): (Greek) "A rock." Biblical; one of the twelve apostles, Peter the fisherman is remembered for his impulsive nature as well as for his rocklike faith. In the Catholic faith, the first pope. There are dozens of variants of the name in many languages.
PEDRO (148) (Spanish/Portuguese); Pietro (Italian); Petros (Greek); Pierre (French); Piers (English/French); Peer (German/Scandinavian); Pieter (Dutch); Pyotr (Russian); Pete, Peterson, Pierson (English)

PHILLIP (93): (Greek) "Fond of horses." Biblical; one of the twelve apostles.
PHILIP (142), Philippe (French), Phil

PHILO: (*FYE-loh*) (Greek) "Loves" or "loved."

PIERCE: (English) Variant form of Peter.
Pearce, Pearse, Pierson

PORFIRIO: (*por-FEE-ree-oh*) (Latin) Variant form of Porphyry. (Greek) "Dressed in purple". A saint's name.

PRENTICE: (English) "Apprentice, learner."
Prentiss

PRESCOTT: (*PRESS-kut*) (English) "Priest's cottage."

PRESTON (224): (English) "Priest's town."

PRINCE: (English/Latin) "Principal one; first." The rock musician Prince has made the royal title familiar as a given name today.
Princeton

Q

QUADE: (*kwayde*) (Gaelic/Irish) From McQuade, a Scottish clan name.

QUENTIN (465): (Latin) "Fifth." Related English/French surnames.
QUINTON (461), Quenton, Quintrell, Quentrell, Quint, Quent

QUILLAN: Irish surname.

QUINCY: (English/French) "Fifth," from a Roman clan name. Very rarely used for girls.
Quincey

QUINN (495): (Gaelic/Irish) "Counselor." A Scottish and Irish surname, used as a given name from very ancient times. Usage: boys 77%, girls 23%. Quin (*keen*) is a Spanish short form of Joaquin.
Quinlan, Quinnell, Quin.

R

RADAMES: (*RAH-da-mays*) The name given the Egyptian hero of Puccini's opera *Aida*.

RADFORD: (English) "From the reedy ford." Old English surname.
Redford, Rad

RAFAEL (165): (*rah-fah-EL*) (Hebrew) "God has healed"; (Spanish) Variant form of Raphael. See also Raphael.
Rafe

RAI: (*RYE-ee*) (Japanese) "Come"; "trust"; "lightning, thunder." Surname. Also a Spanish short form of Raimundo.

RAINER: (*RAY-ner*) (English/Scandinavian) "Powerful force." Related surnames in occasional use as given names. See also Raynor.
Rainier, Ranier (French), Reiner

RAJAN: (*rah-JHAN*) (Sanskrit) "King." Raja is an Indian or Malay princely title; raj means "rule."

Raja, Raj (*rahzh*)

RALEIGH: (English) "Deer's meadow."

RALPH (359): (English/Scandinavian) "Wolf counsel." Ralston, "Ralph's town," is an English surname. Rafe is used as a short form of Ralph and Raphael. See also Raul.

Rolf (German); Rafe, Rafer (Scandinavian); Ralston

RAMI: (Arabic) "Loving."

Ramy

RAMIRO (311): (Spanish) "Wise, renowned."

RAMON (187): (*rah-MOHN*) See Raymond.

RAMSEY: (English/Scottish) "Vigorous." Ram, Ramsey and Ramsay are surnames referring to the strength and vigor of a ram. Often confused with Ramses (Egyptian) "begotten by Ra, the sun god."

Ramses, Rameses, Ramzi, Ramzey, Ram, Ramson

RANDALL (204): (English) Randall and the other English surname variants listed here are variant forms of Randolph.

Randal, Randell, Randel, Randale, Rand, Randon, Rendall, Rendell

RANDOLPH: (Teutonic) "Wolf's shield."

Randolf

RANDY (144): Short form of Randall and Randolph, currently used about twice as often as the longer forms.

RAPHAEL: (*rah-fah-EL*) (Hebrew) "God has healed." The name of an archangel in the Apocryphal Book of Tobit and the renowned Italian Renaissance painter. Raphael is also known today as the name of one of the four Teenage Mutant Ninja Turtles. See also Rafael.

RASHAD (495): (Arabic) "Counselor."

Rashaad, Rasheed, Rashid

RASHAUN: (Contemporary) Blend of Ray and Shawn.

Rayshawn, Rayshaun, Rashawn, Raeshawn

RAUL (140): (*rah-OOL*) (English/Scandinavian) "Wisdom of the wolf"; (Spanish) Variant form of Ralph. See also Ralph.

Raoul (French), Ruel

RAVELL: (*ra-VELL*) May be used in reference to the French surname or as a Spanish variant of Rafael.

RAVI: (*RAH-vee*) (Hindi) "Bestowing." A name made familiar by Ravi Shankar, renowned sitar player and composer.

RAY (340): (English/French) "King, royal." A short form of Raymond often used in contemporary blends. See also Raynor.

Rayce, Rayder, Raylen, Raydon, Raynell, Raydell, Rayford

RAYMOND (92): (German/French) "Guards wisely."

RAMON (187) (Spanish), Ramone, Raymon, Raimond, Raymundo, Raimundo, Reymundo, Raymund, Reymond

RAYNOR: (Scandinavian) "Powerful force"; (English) Variant form of Ragnar, an ancient personal name. See also Rainer and Reginald.

Rayner, Rayne, Rane, Ranell, Ragnar

REBEL: (*REB-el*) (Latin) "Opposer, revolutionary." The English word in rare use as a given name.

REDMOND: (Irish/English) Surname and variant form of Raymond.

REECE: (Welsh/English) "Ardent, fiery." Reis is a sound-alike Israeli name meaning "giant."

Reese, Reis

REEVE: (English) Surname. The medieval reeve of a castle or landholding had oversight of all matters of feudal obligations. Reve is the French word "dream."

Reve, Reeves

REGINALD (313): (English) Variant form of Ragnar. See also Raynor.

Reggie, Regino

REGIS: (*REE-jis*) (Latin) "Rules."

REI: (*RAY-ee*) (Japanese) "Law, rule; strive." Reizo can mean "cool, calm; well-governed."

Reizo (*ray-ee-ZOH*)

REID: (English) "Redheaded." English and Scottish surname.
Reed, Reade, Redd

REMINGTON: The character on the TV show *Remington Steele* may have influenced increased use of this English surname as a given name.
Remy, Remi, Remo

RENE (224): (*re-NAY*) (Latin/French) "To rise again."
Renny, Rennie, Renne; Renato (Spanish)

RENJIRO: (*ren-jee-ROH*) (Japanese) "Clean, upright, honest."

RENO: (*REE-noh*) (Spanish) Short form of names ending in "-reno," for example, Moreno. Reno may sometimes be used in reference to the city in Nevada.

RENZO: (Italian) Short form of Lorenzo. The Japanese name can mean "third link" or "third son."

REUBEN: (*ROO-ben*) (Hebrew) "See; a son." Biblical; Reuben was the firstborn of Jacob's twelve sons. See also Ruben.
Reuven

REX: (Latin) "Kings."
Rexford

REYES: (Spanish) "Kings."
Rey

REYNALDO: (Spanish) Variant form of Reynold, from Ragnar. See Raynor.
Renaldo (Spanish), Reinaldo, Reynald, Reynold, Raynaldo

REYNARD: (Teutonic) "Strong counselor."
Reynardo (Spanish); Renard (French); Raynard

RHETT: (Welsh) Variant form of Rhys. Rhett is most familiar as the hero of Margaret Mitchell's *Gone with the Wind*.

RHYS: (*rees*) (Welsh) "Ardent, fiery."

RICH: (English) "Wealthy." Short form of Richard and related surnames like Richmond.

Rico (Spanish); Rique (French); Rikke (Dutch); Richmond

RICHARD (32): (English/German/French) "Powerful; strong ruler." A Teutonic name that developed in several European countries during the Middle Ages, with many variants. England's King Richard Coeur de Lion gave the name lasting impressions of kingliness and the exploits of a crusading knight. See also Ryker.

RICARDO (80) (Spanish/Portuguese), Riccardo (Italian); Ricard, Richardo (French); Rickard (English); RICKY (173), RICK (385), Rickey, Rickie, Ric; Ricco (Italian), Ritchie, Richie; Rikki (Dutch), Rik

RIGEL: (*RYE-jel*) (Arabic) "Foot." In the Orion constellation, Rigel is the blue star of the first magnitude that marks the hunter's left foot.

RIGOBERTO (370): (Spanish/Teutonic) "Rich, bright." Rigo

RILEY (276): (*RYE-lee*) Irish surname, origin uncertain. Usage: boys 83%, girls 17%. See also Ryley.
Reilly

RINJI: (*RIN-jee*) (Japanese) "Peaceful forest."

RIO: (*REE-oh*) (Spanish) "River." An independent name and short form of names ending with "-rio." Rito is a male short form of Margaret.
Rito

RIORDAN: (*REER-den*) (Gaelic) "King's minstrel."

ROALD: (Scandinavian/Teutonic) "Renowned, powerful."

ROBERT (10): (English/French/German) "Famed; bright, shining." One of the all-time favorite names for boys since the Middle Ages. Specially favored by the Scots due to the seventeenth-cenury King Robert the Bruce (see Bruce) and to Robert Burns, the poet. See also Robin and Bobby.

ROBERTO (110) (Spanish/Italian/Portuguese), Robby, Robbie, Rob, Robb

ROBIN (491): (English) Variant form of Robert, in popular

use as a boy's name since the medieval days of Robin Hood. Usage today: boys 25%, girls 75%.
Robbin, Robinson

ROCKY: (English) "Rock." Rocky and the surnames listed here as variants are all based on the literal meaning "rock."
Roque (Portuguese/Spanish); Roel (French); Rocco (Italian); Rock, Rockford, Rockwell

RODERICK: (English/German) "Famous ruler; red." Rodric and Rodrick are often used in Scotland.
RODRIGO (373) (Spanish/Portuguese), Roderic, Rod, Rodd, Roddy, Rodrick, Rodric, Roddric, Roddrick, Roderik; Rodel, Rodell (French)

RODMAN: (English) "Guard wisely." Variant form of Raymond.

RODNEY (208): (English) "Island of reeds."

RODOLFO (240): (Spanish) Variant form of Rudolph.

ROGER (199): (English/German) "Renowned spearman."
ROGELIO (283) (Spanish)

ROHAN: (Gaelic/Irish) "Red-haired; red."
Roane, Royan

ROKA: (*ROH-kah*) (Japanese) "White crest of the wave."

ROLAND: (German) "Renowned in the land." Literary; Roland is celebrated in French and Italian poetic sagas as a hero of the Crusades. See also Orlando.
ROLANDO (431), Rollan, Rolland, Rollo, Rollie, Rolly, Rowland

ROMAN (335): (*roe-MAHN*) (Latin) "Man of Rome."
Rome, Romain (French), Romeo, Romero, Romulo, Romaldo

RONALD (109): (Scandinavian) "Powerful force"; (Scottish) Variant form of Reynold, from the Scandinavian Ragnar.
RONNIE (290), Ron, Ronaldo (Spanish), Ranald (Scottish), Ronny, Ronnell, Ronell, Ronn, Rondell

RORY (461): (Irish) "Red." Variant form of Roderic. Lit-

erary; tales of Rory O'More, sixteenth-century rebel chief, are celebrated in Irish poetry.
Rorry, Rorik

ROSARIO: (*roe-ZAR-ee-oh*) (Spanish/Portuguese) "Rosary." The name refers to devotional prayers honoring Mary. Usage: boys 84%, girls 16%.

ROSCOE: (English/Scandinavian) "Heathland of the roe deer."
Rosco

ROSS (219): (Scottish/German) "Red."
Rossiter, Roth

ROURKE: (Gaelic/Irish) An ancient given name of uncertain origin, adopted as an Irish clan name.
Roarke, Rorke

ROWDY: (English) "Boisterous." Western nickname.

ROY (228): (Gaelic/Scottish) "Red"; (French) "king."
Royal, Royall, Roi

ROYCE: (English/German) "Famous."

RUBEN (126): (Spanish) Variant form of Reuben.
Rubin, Ruven

RUDY (235): Short form of Rudolph.
Rudolph, Rudolpho, Rudolfo, Rudolf

RUFUS: (Latin) "Red-haired."
Rufino

RUPERT: (English/German) Variant form of Robert.

RUSSELL (162): (English/French) Variant form of Rufus.
Russel, Russ

RUSTY: Nickname for a red-haired person; also a short form or nickname for names like Russell and Ruston.
Rustin, Rusten, Rustan, Ruston

RYAN (9): (Irish) "Kingly."
Ryon, Ryne, Rian, Rion

RYDER: (English) "Horseman, rider."
Ryden, Rydell (Scandinavian)

RYKER: (Dutch) Surname form of Richard, now coming into use as a given name, perhaps due to the character

Lieutenant Ryker on the TV show "Star Trek : The Next Generation."

RYLEY: (English/Irish) "Island meadow." Ryley also is in rare use for girls, though usually in variant forms like Rylee and Rylie. See also Riley.
Ryleigh, Rylan, Ryland

S

SABINO: (*sah-BEE-noh*) (Latin) "Of the Sabines"; (Spanish/Italian) Masculine form of Sabina. Saint's name in use at least since the second century.
Savino (Italian)

SACHIO: (*sah-chee-oh*) (Japanese) "Fortunate; fortunately born."

SAGE: (English/French) "Wise one." The similar sounding surnames Sagan (Slavic) and Sagar (English) are in rare use today as given names. Usage for Sage: boys 59%, girls 31%.
Sagar, Sagan

SALEM: (*SAY-lem*) (Hebrew) "Peace." Biblical; name of the ancient city that later was identified with Jerusalem.
Shalom

SALIM: (*sah-LEEM*) (Arabic) "Without flaw."
Saleem

SALVADOR (159): (Latin/Spanish) "Savior."
Salvatore (Italian), Sal, Salvino, Savino

SAMSON: (Hebrew) "The sun." Biblical; a judge of ancient Israel, endowed by God with superhuman strength.
Sampson

SAMUEL (48): (Hebrew) "Name of God." Biblical; the prophet and judge who anointed Saul and David as kings of Israel.
SAM (404), Sammy, Sammie, Samuele

SANDY: Sandy and variant forms listed here are short forms of Alexander. "Defender of mankind." Today Sandy is used more often for girls (97%) than for boys.

Sandro (Italian); Sandor (Hungarian); Sandino, Sanders

SANJIRO: (*sahn-jee-ROH*) (Japanese) "Praise"; "admirable."

SANTIAGO (409): (*sahn-tee-AH-go*) (Spanish) Variant form of James, from "Saint Diego." James the Greater (of the two apostles by that name) is the patron saint of Spain.

SANTOS: (Latin) "Saints."
Santee, Sancho (Spanish), Santino (Italian) "little saint"

SAUL (263): (Hebrew) "Asked; inquired by God." Biblical; the first king of Israel; also the Hebrew name of the apostle Paul.

SAXON: (Teutonic) "Knife." English surname. Saxons were among the Germanic tribes that invaded and settled England in the fifth century, with the eventual result of the term Anglo-Saxon.
Saxton

SCHUYLER: (*SKY-ler*) (Dutch) "Scholar." See also Skyler.
Schyler, Schylar

SCOTT (51): (English/Scottish) "From Scotland, a Gael."
Scotty, Scot, Scottie

SEAMUS: (*SHAY-mus*) (Irish) Variant form of James.

SEAN (37): (SHON) (Irish) Variant form of John, from the French Jean. See also Shawn and Shane.

SEBASTIAN (358): (*se-BASS-tian*) (Latin/Greek) "Revered." Shakespeare gave the name to the twin brother of Viola in *Twelfth Night*. St. Sebastian was a third-century martyred centurion who became a patron saint of soldiers.
Sebastien (French), Sabastian

SEIJI: (*SAY-jee*) (Japanese) "Aright, lawful"; "manages affairs of state."

SERGIO (113): (Latin) "Protector, shepherd." A saint's name.
Serjio, Serge, Sergeo; Sergei (*sehr-GAY*) (Russian); Sarkis (Armenian)

SETH (123): (Hebrew) "Appointed." Biblical; the third named son of Adam and Eve; Eve said Seth had been appointed to take the place of Abel, killed by Cain.

SEVERIN: (French) Variant form of Severus. (Latin) "Strict, restrained". A saint's name.
Severo (Spanish), Severne (English)

SHAAN: (Hebrew) "Peaceful."

SHAD: Short form of the Biblical Shadrach, the Babylonian name of one of the three young Hebrew men who were cast into a fiery furnace and miraculously survived.
Shadd, Shadrach, Shadoe

SHAKA: (*SHAH-kah*) (African) The name of a Zulu tribal leader (sometimes compared to Attila the Hun) who shaped an amalgamation of tribes into the great Zulu nation in the early nineteenth century.

SHANE (85): (Gaelic/Irish) Variant form of Shaun, from John. See also Sean and Shawn.
Shayne, Shain, Shaine, Shan, Shann, Shandon, Shandy

SHANNON (500): (Gaelic/Irish) "Wise." Today this surname is used almost entirely for girls (95%).

SHARIF: (*sha-REEF*) (Arabic) "Illustrious."
Shareef, Shereef

SHAW: (English) "Woods." A surname in rare use as a given name.

SHAWN (79): (Irish) Variant form of John, from Sean. See also Sean and Shane.
SHAUN (223), Shaughn, Shawnn, Shonn

SHEA: (*shay*) (Irish) Surname occasionally used as a given name or middle name for boys (57%) and girls (33%).
Shay, Shaye, Shae, Shai, Shayan

SHELBY: (English/Scandinavian) "Willow farm." English surname used as a given name for girls (84%) and boys (16%).

SHELDON: (English) "Deep valley."
Shelden, Shelton

SHEM: (Hebrew) "Name; renown." Biblical; first-named of the three sons of Noah.

SHERIDAN: (Gaelic/English) "Bright." Usage of Sheridan: boys 39%, girls 61%.

SHERMAN: (English) "Shireman"; (German) "shearman." In medieval times, a shireman served as governor-judge of an English shire or county; a shearman worked as a sheepshearer or finisher of cloth. Sherwood; "Shirewood."
Shermann, Shermon, Sherwood

SHILOH: (*SHYE-loh*) (Hebrew) "The one to whom it belongs." Biblical; a prophetic name for the Messiah. Shiloh is also significant as the site of a crucial battle in the American Civil War. Rare usage for boys and girls.
Shilo

SHODA: (*SHOH-dah*) (Japanese) "Flat, level field." Surname.

SIDNEY: (English/French) "From St. Denis." In current usage Sidney is favored for boys (boys 56%, girls 44%) and Sydney is favored for girls (girls 93%, boys 7%).
Sydney

SIGMUND: (German) "Victory, protection." A name made famous by the Austrian psychologist Sigmund Freud.

SILAS: (*SYE-las*) (Greek/English) Variant form of Sylvanus. (Latin) "Forest, woods". Biblical; Silas was a missionary companion to Paul and Timothy. See also Silvano.

SILVANO: (Spanish) Variant form of the Latin Sylvanus, referring to the mythological Greek god of trees. A number of saints bore the name, and variants were formed in several language groups. See also Silas and Silvester.
Silverio (Spanish/Portuguese); Silvino (Spanish); Selwyn, Selvyn (English)

SILVESTER: (Latin/German) "Trees, sylvan." See also Sylvester and Silvano.
Silvestre (French)

SIMON (328): (Greek) Variant form of a Hebrew name meaning "hear, listen." Biblical; Simon was the name of two of the apostles, including Simon Peter.

Simeon, Symon

SINCLAIR: (English/French) "St. Clair." Through long usage, some saints' names have been blurred into a single name. Sinjin is a blurred form of St. John.
Sinclaire, Sinjin

SKYE: Name used in reference to the Isle of Skye in Scotland, as nicknames for the Skyler variants, or as nature names referring to the sky. Usage: boys 15%, girls 85%.
Sky

SKYLER (249): Phonetic spelling of Schuyler. Usage: boys 85%, girls 15%. See also Schuyler.
SKYLAR (499), Skylor

SLADE: (English) "Valley."

SLOAN: (Gaelic/Scottish) "Fighter, warrior." Surname in rare use as a given name; Sloane is the feminine form.

SOLOMON: (Greek) Variant form of a Hebrew name related to Shalom; "peace." Biblical; Solomon, son of David and Bathsheba, succeeded his father as king of Israel. He wrote the Book of Proverbs, Ecclesiastes and the Song of Solomon.
Salomon (Spanish), Soloman, Sol

SONNY (420): (English) "Son." A nickname in steady use as a given name for boys.
Sonnie

SOREN: (English/Yiddish) Surname, variant form of Sarah.

SPENCER (99): (English) "Dispenser, provider."
Spenser, Spence

STACY: (English) "Productive." Short form of Eustace. Today Stacy is used almost entirely as a girl's name (96%).
Stacey

STAFFORD: (English) "Stony ford."

STANLEY (359): (English) "Stony meadow."
Stanford, Stanton, Stan

STEELE: (English) "Hard, durable."

STERLING (453): (English/German) Variant form of a name meaning "easterner," given to pre-medieval refiners of silver. Today Sterling means "of high quality; pure."

Stirling

STEVE (214): Short form of Steven and Stephen used as an independent name. Usage of Stevie: boys 23%, girls 77%.

Stevie

STEVEN (23): (Greek) "Crown, wreath." Biblical; Stephen was the first Christian martyr.

STEPHEN (52) (English), Stephenson, Stevenson, STEPHAN (282) (French), Stephon (Contemporary), STEFAN (373) (Slavic), Steffen, Steffan, Steffon, Stevan, Stevon, Stevyn, Stephano, Stefano (Italian); Stephanos (Greek)

STEWART: (Scottish) "Steward." A medieval steward was charged with the care of castle and estate affairs. See also Stuart.

STONEY: Nickname and surname based on the word stone. Stone, Stoner (English), Steiner (German)

STORM: (English/Teutonic) English surname with the literal meaning of a storm.

STUART (308): (Gaelic/Scottish) Stuart and Stewart are clan names of the royal house of Scotland; Stuart is the family name of many kings of England. See also Stewart.

SULLIVAN: (Gaelic/Irish) "Dark eyes."

SUMNER: (English) "Court official."

SUNNY: Nature name. Occasional usage is about equal for boys and girls.

SUTTON: (English) "South town."

SVEN: (Scandinavian) "Youth, boy."

SYDNEY: See Sidney.

SYLVESTER: See Silvester.

T

TABOR: *(TAY-bor)* (Hebrew) Biblical; Mt. Tabor, a landmark mountain near Nazareth.

Tab, Taber

TAD: Short form of Thaddeus.

Tadd, Tadeo (Spanish)

TADAO: *(tah-dah-oh)* (Japanese) "Complacent, satisfied."

TADASHI: *(tah-dah-shee)* (Japanese) "Serves the master faithfully."

TAJ: *(tahzh)* (Hindi) "Crown." Taji *(TAH-jee)* is a Japanese surname with the potential meaning "silver and yellow color."

Taji, Tahj

TAKEO: *(Tah-kay-oh)* (Japanese) "Strong like bamboo."

TAL: (English) "Tall, fierce." With related surnames. Tal is also an Israeli name meaning "dew."

Talbot, Talbert, Talford, Talmadge, Tallon

TANJIRO: *(tahn-jee-ROH)* (Japanese) "High-valued second son."

TANNER (209): (English/Latin) "Worker in leather."

TARIQ: (Arabic) A name of Moorish kings.

Tarik, Tarek, Tarick, Tarique, Tareq

TARO: *(tah-ROH)* (Japanese) "Big boy."

TATE: (Scandinavian) "Cheerful." Rare usage for boys and girls.

Tait

TAU: (African) "Lion."

TAUREAN: *(TAH-ree-an)* (Latin) "Bull-like." From Taurinus, a saint's name. Taurus is a constellation picturing the forequarters of a bull and is the second sign of the astrological zodiac.

Tauro, Taurino, Taurus, Toro (Spanish)

TAVIS: *(TA-viss)* (Scottish) Variant form of Thomas. Tavio is a Spanish short form of Octavio; Tavin is a nickname for Gustav. The contemporary variants listed below are probably adaptations of favored rhyming patterns of Travis, Trevin and Devon.

Taveon, Tavion, Tavon, Tavin, Tavio, Tevis, Tevin

TAYLOR (71): (English) "Tailor." Surname frequently

used today as a given name for girls and boys. Usage: boys 57%, girls 43%.

Tayler, Tayson, Taylan

TEAGUE: *(teeg)* (English/Irish) "Handsome." Taggart is a similar sounding Scottish surname in rare use as a given name.

Tighe, Tag, Taggart

TED: Short form of Theodore. Tedrick is a variant of the old German name Theodoric, "ruler of the people." Tedman refers to St. Edmund.

Teddy, Tedd, Teddie, Tedman, Tedrick

TEIJI: *(tay-EE-jee)* (Japanese) "Righteous second son"; "righteous, well governed." Teijo *(TAY-joh)* "established," "regulated."

TEMPLETON: (English) "Temple-town." This surname refers to the medieval priories and settlements of the Knights-Templar, a military religious order. Temple is in rare use today as a name for boys and girls.

Temple

TEO: *(TAY-oh)* (Spanish) "God." Short form of names like Mateo and Teodor.

Teyo

TERRAN: (English) "Earthman." Variants are contemporary rhyming blends of Ter- plus Darin.

Terron, Terrin, Terren, Tarrin, Taron

TERRANCE (338): (English/Latin) Roman clan name; Terence is the older English form.

TERRENCE (354), Terence

TERRELL (429): (English/German) "Strength." English and Irish surname. See also Tyrell.

Terrel, Terell, Terrelle, Terrall, Terrill, Terryl

TERRY (209): Short form of names like Terrance; Terry is also an anglicized phonetic form of the French given name Thierry, from an older Germanic name meaning "powerful; ruler of the people." Usage: boys 80%, girls 20%.

THADDEUS: *(THAD-dee-us)* (Greek) Biblical; one of the twelve apostles. See also Tad.
Thadeus, Thad, Tadeo (Spanish)

THANE: (English/Scottish) Title of an Anglo-Saxon feudal baron or a Scottish feudal lord. Shakespeare's *Macbeth* was Thane of Cawdor and Glamis.

THEODORE (244): (Greek) "God-given."
Teodoro (Italian/Portuguese), Theo, Theodor, Teodor (Spanish)

THERON: *(THER-on)* (Greek/French) "Untamed."
Theon, Tharon

THOMAS (31): (Aramaic) "Twin." Biblical; one of the twelve apostles.
TOMMY (268), TOMAS (387) (Spanish), Tom, Thompson, Thom

THOR: (Scandinavian) Mythology; Thor was the god of thunder, one of the sons of Odin. Thursday was named for Thor.
Thurman, Thorin, Thorsson

THORNTON: (Gaelic/English) "Town of thorns." Thorn variants are English surnames used as given names.
Thorn, Thorne

TIMOTHY (33): (Greek) "One who honors God." Biblical; Timothy was an energetic, well-trained young Christian to whom Paul wrote, "Let no man look down on your youth."
Timmy, Tim, Timoteo (Spanish), Timon

TITUS: *(TITE-us)* (Latin) Biblical; a Greek Christian missionary, to whom Paul wrote the canonical letter Titus.
Tito

TOBY: (Hebrew) "Jah is good"; (English) Short form of Tobiah.
Tobias (Spanish), Tobin, Tobey, Tobie, Tobyn

TODD (182): (English) "Fox." Tod is a Scottish nickname meaning a clever or wily person.
Tod

TOMEO: *(toh-MAY-oh)* (Japanese) "Stop; stand still"; "cautious man."

TONY (147): Short form of Anthony and its variants, frequently used since medieval times as an independent name.
Tonio (Spanish)

TORIO: *(toh-ree-OH)* (Japanese) "Bird's tail." Torrio is a Spanish short form.
Torrio

TORRENCE: (Scottish/Irish) "From the craggy hills." Tor is a name for a craggy hilltop and also may refer to a watchtower. Torrance, Torence, Tor, Torin, Toren, Torran, Torren.

TORU: *(toh-roo)* (Japanese) "Sea."

TORY: (Scottish/English) Surname based on Tor, Torrence or Tower. Tory variants may also be short forms of Victor and Victoria. Usage of Tory: boys 62%, girls 38%. The rarer usage of Torey and Torrey is about equal for boys and girls.
Torey, Torrey; Torre (Italian); Torrie, Torry (Scottish); Torrian, Torian, Toriano

TOSHIRO: *(toh-shee-ROH)* (Japanese) "Talented, intelligent; sincerity."

TRACY: English and French surname dating from before the Norman Conquest. Usage today: boys 15%, girls 85%.
Trace

TRAVIS (40): (English/French) "Crossing, crossroads."

TREMAYNE: *(tre-MAYNE)* (English/Welsh) "From the big town."
Tremaine, Tramaine, Tremain

TRENT (249): (English) Refers to the river Trent in England.
TRENTON (235), Trenten, Trentin

TREVIN: (English/Welsh) "Fair town." Trevin and the variants are based on combinations of Trevor and Devon, Travis and Davion.

Travon, Trevon, Trevonn *(tre-VON)*, Trevan, Treven, Trevyn, Travion, Traveon, Trevion, Trevian

TREVIS: Variant form of Treves, French surname and place name. Contemporary usage is probably due to its sounding like Travis.

TREVOR (74): (Welsh) "Goodly town."

TREY (421): *(tray)* (English) "Three." A recently popular, similar sounding variant of Troy.

TRISTAN (335): *(TRISS-tan)* (French/English) "Tumult, outcry." Based on an older Celtic name. In Arthurian legend, Tristan was a Knight of the Round Table and the tragic hero of the medieval tale *Tristan and Iseult*. Usage of Tristan: boys 84%, girls 16%.

Tristin, Tristen, Triston, Tristian, Trystan, Tristyn

TROY (145): As a given name, Troy may derive from the ancient Greek city of Troy or from an Irish surname meaning "soldier."

Troye

TUCKER (485): (English) "Cloth-maker."

TY: Short form of names beginning with "Ty-."

Tye

● TYLER (26): (English) "Tile-layer" or a variant form of Taylor. An English surname very frequently used today as a given name.

Tylor

TYRELL: *(tye-RELL* or *TER-ell)* (English/Irish/Teutonic) Derivative of Tyr, the name of the Scandinavian god of battle. Tuesday was named for Tyr. See also Terrell.

Tyrel, Tyrelle, Tyrrell, Tyree (Scottish)

TYRONE (380): *(TY-rone* or *ter-RONE)* (Irish) County Tyrone in Ireland has been made familiar today as a boy's given name primarily due to the late actor Tyrone Power.

Tyronne

TYRUS: (Contemporary) Blend of Tyrone and Cyrus, or a reference to the ancient Phoenician city of Tyre.

TYSON (248): (English/French) "Fiery."

Tyce

U

UGO: (Nigerian) "Eagle."

ULYSSES: *(you-LISS-ees)* (Latin) Variant form of the Greek name Odysseus. Ulysses was the clever and resourceful hero of Homer's epic tale *Odyssey*.
ULISES (Spanish)

URIEL: *(OOR-ee-el)* (Hebrew) "Angel of light." In the Apocrypha, Uriel is one of seven archangels. In Muslim tradition, he is the angel of music who will sound the trumpet on Judgment Day.

V

VALENTINE: (English) Variant form of Valentinus. (Latin) "Strong". The name of more than fifty saints and three Roman emperors.
Val, Valentin (Spanish), Valentino (Italian), Valente (Italian/Portuguese), Valen

VAN: (Dutch) "Of." Equivalent of "de" in French names, Van was sometimes converted from a surname prefix to a given name by early immigrants to America, and today is in use for both boys (55%) and girls (45%).
Vann

VANCE: (English) "Marshland."

VAUGHN: (Welsh) "Little." The soundalike name Von is the German equivalent of Van.
Vaughan, Von, Vonn

VERDELL: *(ver-DELL)* (Latin/French) "Green, flourishing."
Vernell

VERNON: (French/English) "Place of alder trees." Aristrocratic surname brought to England at the time of the Norman Conquest. Vern and Verne are related French/English surnames today often used as short forms of Vernon or Lavern.
Vern, Verne

VICTOR (68): (Latin) "Conqueror." A very popular saint's name. At one time more than two hundred were listed in the *Catholic Dictionary of Saints*.
Vittorio (Italian); Victoriano; Viktor (Czech); Vic, Victorino, Victorio

VIDAL: *(vee-DAL)* (Latin) "Life." Several language groups (French, English, Spanish and Portuguese) use Vidal as a surname or given name. See also Vito.
Videl

VINCENT (81): (Latin) "Conquering."
VICENTE (373) (Spanish/Portuguese), Vincenzo (Italian), Vince, Vinson, Vinnie

VIRGIL: *(VER-jil)* (Latin) "Flourishing." The writings of Virgil, the Roman poet-philosopher, have provided classic texts for the study of Roman history and the Latin language for the past two thousand years.

VITO: *(VEE-toh)* (Latin) "Life." See also Vidal.

VLADIMIR: (Russian) "Princely ruler."

W

WADE (310): (English/Scandinavian) Medieval given name taken from Scandinavian mythology. Also an English surname referring to a water crossing.
Wayde

WALDO: (English/German) "Powerful." Short form of Oswald.

WALKER: (English) "Worker in cloth."

WALLACE: (English/Scottish) "Welshman, stranger."
Wally

WALTER (218): (German) "Rules, conquers."
Walt, Walton

WARD: (English) "Protector."
Wardell

WARNER: (German/English) "Defender."

WARREN (380): (German/English) "Defender."

WAYLON: (English/Scandinavian) Scandinavian mythol-

ogy; Wayland was a blacksmith with supernatural powers, corresponding to the Roman Vulcan. A notable name bearer today is singer Waylon Jennings.
Wayland, Waylan

WAYNE (284): (English) "Wagon-driver."

WEBSTER: (English) "Weaver." (Note: the "-ster" ending on English occupational surnames like Webster and Brewster is an indication that the work was originally a female occupation. When the occupations were taken over by males, the names were adopted as well.)

WENDELL: (Teutonic) "Traveler, wanderer."
Wendall

WESLEY (119): (English) "West meadow." Wesley is a variant of the English surname Westley.
Westley, Wes

WESTON (340): (English) "West town."
Westin, Westen, West

WILBERT: (English/German) "Willful, bright."
Wilbur, Wilber, Wilburn

WILEY: *(WYE-lee)* (English) Short form of William.
Wylie

WILFRED: (English/German) "Desires peace."
Wilfredo, Wilford

WILLARD: (English/German) "Bold, resolute." Saxon given name of great antiquity.

WILLIAM (20): (Teutonic) "Resolute protector." For a long time after the Norman Conquest in 1060, three out of four English boys were given some form of the conqueror's name, William. Great numbers of short forms and variants came into being with a common basic meaning of "will," "determined" or "resolute." The firstborn son of the current Prince of Wales is named William.
Williams, Willis; Wilhelm (German); Willem (Dutch)

WILLIE (328): Short form of names beginning with "Wil-."
Willy, Will, Wil

WILMER: (English/German) "Resolute, famous."

WILSON: (English) "Son of Will."

WINSTON: (English) "Friend; stone; marker of friendship." In occasional use as a given name.
Winslow, "friend's hill"; Winfield, "friend's field"; Wynston

WOODROW: (English) "From the cottages in the wood."
Woody

WYATT (380): (English) "Lively." Variant form of the French name Guy.

WYNN: (English) "Friend." Variants are English surnames in rare use as given names for boys.
Wynton, Wyndell

X

XAVIER (271): (ecks-ZAY-vee-er) (Basque/Spanish) "Bright, splendid." See also Javier.

XIOMAR: (zhoh-MAR) "Famous in battle." Variant form of Geomar.

Y

YALE: (Welsh) "Heights, upland."

YANCY: Variant form of John.

YORK: (English) Place name and surname.

YURI: (Russian) Short form of George.

YVES: (eeve) (French) Variant form of Ivo; (Teutonic) "archer's bow." See also Ives.

Z

ZACCHAEUS: (zah-KAY-us) (Hebrew) "Clean, pure." Biblical; a tax collector who became one of the disciples of Jesus.

ZACHARIAH (328): (zak-a-RYE-ah) (Hebrew) "Jehovah has remembered"; (Latin) Variant form of Zechariah. Biblical; the name of thirty-one persons including the prophet who wrote the Book of Zechariah.

Zacharias, Zackariah, Zacharia, Zacarias (Spanish), Zechariah

ZACHARY (27): *(ZAK-a-ree)* (English) Variant form of Zachariah. Zachary is one of several names from the Bible that are enjoying a revival. See Jacob, Jared and Joshua.

ZACHERY (331), ZACKARY (355), ZACKERY (431), Zakary, Zack, Zach, Zak, Zakari

ZADOK: *(ZAY-dok)* (Israeli) "Just."

ZANDER: Short form of Alexander. Also a German Yiddish name.

ZANE: Possibly a variant form of John. The most notable name bearer was Western writer Zane Grey.

Zain, Zaine, Zayne.

ZAREK: (Slavic) "God protects."

ZEKE: Short form of Ezekiel, in rare use as an independent name.

GIRLS' INDEX

A

ABIGAIL (115): (Hebrew) "My father rejoices."
ABBY (287), Abbey, Abbie, Avagail

ABRIANA: (*ay-bree-AHN-ah*) (Italian) Feminine form of Abraham.
Abrianna, Abrienne, Abra, Abri, Abree, Abrielle

ACACIA: (*a-KAY-sha*) (Spanish/Greek) "Honorable." Biblical; acacia wood was used to build the wilderness Tabernacle.

ADA: (Hebrew) "Ornament"; (Nigerian) "first daughter."
Adah, Ayda

ADAIR: (Scottish) "From the oak tree ford." In rare use today for both boys and girls.

ADALIA: (*ah-dah-LEE-ah* or *a-DALE-yah*) (Spanish) Variant form of Adela.
Adalie (French)

ADANNA: (Nigerian) "Her father's daughter." Adana is a Spanish feminine form of Adam.
Adana

ADARA: (Arab) "Virgin."

ADDIE: Short form of names beginning with "Ad-."
Addy

ADELA: (Spanish/Teutonic) "Of the nobility; noble."
Adelle, Adele (French), Adella, Adelita (Spanish), Adelia, Adelaide (French)

ADELINE: Variant form of Adela.

Adilene, Adalene, Adelynn, Adalyn, Adelina

ADELISA: (*ah-da-LEES-ah*) (French/Teutonic) Forerunner of Alice.

Adelise (French), Adaliz, Adalicia

ADINAH: (*ah-DEEN-ah*) (Israeli) "Ornament, pleasure." Variant form of Ada.

Adina (Spanish)

ADIRA: (*ah-DEER-ah*) (Arab) "Strong."

ADONIA: (*ah-DON-ya*) (Greek/Spanish) "Beautiful lady." Also feminine form of Adonis.

ADRIANA (79): (*ay-dree-AHN-ah*) (Latin) From Adria, the Adriatic sea region; also means "dark."

ADRIANNA (266), Adreanna, Adrianne; Adriane (French); Adriene, ADRIENNE (277) (French), Adrienna, Adra, Adrea, Adria, Adrina, Adrielle

AGATHA: (Latin/Greek) "Good."

AGNES: (Latin/Greek) "Chaste."

AIDA: (*ah-EE-dah*) (Italian) The name of the Ethiopian princess in Verdi's opera *Aida*. Also a Japanese surname (*ah-ee-DAH*) "runs across the field."

AIDEE: (Greek) "Modest." Variant form of Haidee.

Aydee

AILANI: (*ah-ee-LAH-nee*) (Hawaiian paraphrase) "High chief."

AILEEN: (*eye-LEEN*) (Irish) Variant form of Helen; (Greek) "light-bearer."

Aileene

AIMEE (280): (*ay-MEE*) (Latin/French) "Loved"; Variant form of Amy. See also Amy.

AISHA: (Arabic) "Woman, life." Aisha was the name of the favorite wife of the prophet Mohammad. See also Asha, Asia and Isha.

Aishah, Aysha, Ayesha, Ayeisha

AKIKO: (*ah-KEE-koh*) (Japanese) "Iris"; "autumn"; "light, bright."

AKILAH: (*ah-KEE-lah*) (Arabic) "Bright, smart."

Akili (Tanzanian)

AKIMA: (*ah-kee-mah*) (Japanese) "Autumn space." Most commonly used as a surname in Japan.

ALAIR: (Latin/Greek) "Cheerful, glad"; (French) Variant form of Hilary

Allaire

ALANA (392): (*ah-LAH-nah*) (Irish) "fair, good-looking," feminine form of Alan; (Hawaiian) "awakening."

Alanna, Alannah; Allana, Alani, Alona, Alonna, Alaine (French), Alaina, Alayna, Alayne, Alynna

ALANDRA: (Spanish) Variant form of Alexandra.

Alondra, Alandria

ALANZA: (*ah-LAHN-zah*) "Ready for battle." Feminine form of Alonzo.

ALARICE: (*AL-a-riss*) "Rules all." Feminine form of Alaric.

Allaryce

ALBERTA: (English/German) "Noble, bright." Feminine form of Albert.

Albertina, Albertine, Alba

ALCINE: (Italian) Literary; in the Orlando poems, Alcina is a mistress of alluring enchantments and sensual pleasures.

Alcina, Alcinia, Alcee

ALDA: (Spanish/Italian) "Wise, elder." Variant form of Aldo.

Aldene, Aldona (Spanish)

ALETHA: (Greek) "Truthful."

Alethea, Alethia, Alathea, Alithea, Aleta

ALEXANDRA (37): (Greek) "Defender of mankind." Feminine form of Alexander.

ALEXANDRIA (97), Alexandrea, Alexandrina, ALEJANDRA (151) (Spanish); Allessandra (Italian); Alyssandra, Alixandra (French); Allessondra

ALEXIS (87): (*a-LEX-iss*) (Greek) "Helper, defender." Short form of Alexandra. Use of Alexis: boys 20%, girls 80%.

ALEXA (203): Alexia, Alyx, Alix, Alexi, Alexina, Alexine

ALFREDA: Feminine form of Alfred.

ALI: (*AL-ee*) (Arabic) "Greatest." A variant form of Allah, title of the Supreme Being in the Muslim faith. Allie is a short form of names beginning with "Al-." Usage of Ali: boys 80%, girls 20%.
Allie, Alli

ALIA: (Israeli) "Immigrant to a new home."
Aleah, Alea, Aliyah, Aleana

ALICE (345): (English) "Of the nobility." Variant form of the old French name Adeliz.
Alyce, Alise, Aleece, Allyce, Alyss, Alliss, Alys

ALICIA (52): (Latin) Variant form of Alice. See also Alisha.
Alycia, Alecia, Aleecia, Aleesha, Alishia, Alisia

ALIDA: (*ah-LEE-da*) (Latin) "With wings."

ALIKA: (*ah-LYE-ka* or *a-LEE-ka*) (African) "Most beautiful."

ALIMA: (*ah-LEE-mah*) (Arabic) "Sea maiden."

ALINA: (Latin) "Of the nobility." Variant form of Adelina.
Aline, Allina, Alyna

ALISHA (132): Variant form of Alicia. See also Alicia.
ALISA (392) (Spanish), ALYSHA (423), Aleesha, Alyssha

ALISSA (342): Variant form of Alice. See also Alyssa.
Alisse, Alessa, Aleeza

ALITA: (*ah-LEE-tah*) (Spanish) Short form of Adelita.

ALIX: (French) "Helper of mankind." Short form of Alexandra.

ALIZAH: (*a-LYE-zah*) (Hebrew) "Joy, joyful."
Aliza

ALLEGRA: (*ah-LAY-grah*) (Italian) "Lively, happy."

ALLENA: (Celtic) "Fair, good-looking." Feminine form of Allen or variant form of Helen. Alena is a Russian diminutive and a variant of Adelina.

Alena, Allene, Alene, Aleena, Aleen, Aline

ALLISON (55): (French/English) Diminutive form of Alice.

ALISON (142) (Scottish), ALLYSON (306), Alyson, Alisanne

ALMA (210): (Latin) "The soul."

ALMIRA: (*al-MEER-ah*) (Arabic) "Truthful."

ALOISE: (*AL-oh-eez*) (Spanish) Feminine form of Aloysius. (German) "Famous in battle".

ALOMA: Short form of Paloma, meaning "dove."

ALPHA: (*AL-fah*) (Greek) The first letter of the Greek alphabet.

ALSATIA: (*al-SAY-sha*) From Alsace, a region in France.

ALTA: (Spanish) "High." Short form of Altagracia, a reference to the "high grace" of Mary the mother of Jesus.
Altagracia

ALTAIRA: (*al-TARE-ah*) (Arabic) "High-flying." In astronomy, Altair is a star of the first magnitude.

ALTHEA: (Greek) "Wholesome."

ALVA: (Hebrew) "Sublime." The similar sounding names Alvarita and Alvera are Spanish feminine forms of Alvaro, meaning "speaker of truth." Alvina is the feminine form of Alvin, meaning "wise friend."
Alvarita, Alvera, Alverna, Alvina

ALYSSA (33): (*ah-LISS-ah*) Variant form of Alice. See also Alissa.
Alysse (*ah-LISS*), Alyssia, Alyse (*ah-LEESE*), Alysa, Allysa, Allyse

AMA: (*AH-ma*) (Ghanese) "Saturday's child."

AMABEL: (Latin) "Lovable."

AMADA: (*ah-MAH-dah*) (Spanish) "Beloved." Variant form of Amy.
Amadia, Amadea, Amadita

AMALA: (Arabic) "Beloved."

AMANDA (3): (Latin) "Worthy of being loved."

AMANTHA: (*ah-MAN-thah*) (Greek) Variant form of Amarantha, a flower name, or a short form of Samantha.

AMAPOLA: (*ah-mah-POH-lah*) (Arabic) "Poppy."

AMARA: (*ah-MAHR-ah*) (Spanish) "Imperishable."

AMARIS: "Child of the moon." Astrological name for Cancer.
Amarissa

AMARYLLIS: (*am-ah-RILL-iss*) (Latin) Flower name; poetically, a simple shepherdess or country girl.

AMAYA: (*ah-MAH-yah*) (Japanese) "Night rain." Surname.

AMBER (15): (French/Arabic) A jewel-quality hardened resin; as a color, the name refers to a warm honey shade. Contemporary variants may be rhyming variants based on Kimberly.
Amberly, Amberlee, Amberli, Amberlyn, Amberlynn, Ambria

AMELIA (226): (Latin) "Industrious, striving."
Amalia (Spanish/Portuguese), Amalie, Amelie (French)

AMETHYST: (Greek) "Against intoxication." A purple or violet gemstone. According to ancient Greek superstition, an amethyst protected its owner against the effects of strong drink.

AMINA: (*ah-MEEN-ah*) (Arabic/Swahili) "Trustworthy."
Amineh, Aminah, Ameena, Ameenah

AMIRA: (*ah-MEE-rah*) (Hebrew) "Princess; one who speaks."
Amirah (Arabic), Ameera

AMITA: (*ah-MEE-tah*) (Israeli) "Truth."

AMITY: (*AM-a-tee*) (English/French) "Friendship." One of the virtue names.

AMY (36): (Latin) "Beloved." The soundalike Ami is a name from Ghana, meaning "born on Saturday." See also Aimee.
Amie, Amia, Ami

ANA (81): (*AHN-ah*) (Spanish) "Grace, favor." Variant form of Anna. Ana is often used in blended names like Anabel "beautiful, graceful" or Anarosa "rose of grace."

ANABEL (485), Annabel, Annabelle, Anabelle, Anna-
bella, Analena, Anarosa, Analee, Analeigh, Anamarie

ANAIS: (*ah-NAY-us*) (Greek) Meaning uncertain.

ANASTASIA (375): (*ahn-a-STAH-shah* or *ahn-a-STAY-
shah*) (Greek) "Resurrection."
Annastasia (*an-a-STAY-zhah*), Anastacia, Anastasha,
Anastashia, Anastassia, Anastazia

ANDA: (*awn-dah*) (Japanese) "Meet at the field." Surname. Also a short form of Andrea.

ANDEE: Feminine short form of Andrea.
Andi, Andie, Andena

ANDREA (32): "Womanly, brave." Feminine form of
Andrew.
Andria (Spanish); Aundrea, Andreya, Andreana, An-
driana, Andreanna, Andrianna, Andrianne, Andrienne,
Andrena, Andrina, Andra; Andree (French); Andranetta

ANDROMEDA: (*an-DRAH-ma-dah*) (Greek) Mythology;
Ethiopian princess, the wife of Perseus. Also a northern
constellation.

ANEKO: (*ah-NAY-koh*) (Japanese) "Older sister."

ANGEL (200): (Greek) "Messenger." Usage: boys 82%,
girls 18%. See also Angela.
Angele, Angell, Angelle

ANGELA (41): (Greek/Latin) "Messenger." Angie is a
short form often used as an independent name. See also
Angel.
ANGIE, Angelee, Angeli, Anjali (Contemporary);
ANGELINA (200), Angeline, Angelene, Angelena, An-
gelita, Angelia, Angelyn, Angelynn, Angelisa

ANGELICA (77): (Latin) "Like an angel."
Angelika (Greek); Anjelica (Spanish); Angelique
(French); Anjelique, Angelicia

ANISSA: Variant form of Anne.
Annissa, Anyssa, Annice, Annis, Anisha, Aneisha,
Anessa

ANITA (399): (Spanish) Diminutive form of Ann.
Anitra (Scandinavian)

ANJANETTE: "Gift of God's favor." Blend of Ann and Janet.

Anjeanette, Annjeanette, Anjanique (*ahn-ja-NEEK*)

ANNA (58): (Latin) Variant form of Anne. Biblical; a devout woman who saw the infant Jesus presented at the temple in Jerusalem. Anna is often used in combination with other names. See also Anne and Ana.

Annabeth, Annalee, Annamarie, Anne-Marie (French)

ANNALISA: "Graced with God's bounty." Combination of Anna and Lisa.

Annalise, Annelise, Anneliese, Annelisa, Annalissa, Analisa, Analise, Analiese, Analissa, Analicia, Analisia

ANNE (180): (English/French) Variant form of Hannah. (Hebrew) "Favor, grace." See also Anna.

ANNIE (298), Ann (318), Anya

ANNETTE (424): (French) Diminutive form of Anne.

Annetta, Annika, Anneka, Anneke (Scandinavian), Anneli (Finnish)

ANNORA: (*an-NOR-ah*) (Latin) English variant form of Honora.

ANTHEA: (*ANN-thee-ah*) (Greek) "Lady of flowers." Anthia

ANTOINETTE (392): (*ann-twa-NET*) (French) "Highly praiseworthy." Feminine form of Anthony.

ANTONIA: (Spanish) Feminine form of Anthony, with contemporary variants.

Antonina, Antonette, Antonetta, Antonique, Antonella

APHRA: (*AFF-ra*) (Hebrew) "Dust." Biblical place name.

APHRODITE: (*aff-roh-DYE-tee*) (Greek) Mythology; goddess of physical love and beauty, equivalent to the Roman goddess Venus.

APOLLONIA: (*ah-poh-LONE-yah*) (Latin) "Belonging to Apollo." Mythology; Apollo was the Greek god of sunlight, music and poetry.

APRIL (80): (Latin) The month as a given name; often used to symbolize spring. See also Averil.

Apryl, Apryll, Aprille, Abril (Spanish)

AQUANETTA: (Contemporary) Created name based on Aqua, the blue-green color of the sea.

AQUILINA: (*ah-kee-LEE-nah*) (Spanish) "An eagle; sharp-eyed." Feminine form of Aquila.

ARABELLE: (Latin) "Calling to prayer."
Arabella

ARACELI (274): (*ar-ah-SAY-lee*) (Latin/Spanish) "Altar of heaven."
Aracely, Aracelia, Aricela, Arcelia, Arcilla

ARCADIA: (*ar-KAY-dee-ah*) (Greek) "Pastoral simplicity and happiness."

ARDEL: (Latin) "Eager, industrious." Rare usage for boys and girls.
Ardelle, Ardella

ARDEN: (Celtic) "Lofty, eager." In rare use for boys and girls.
Ardena, Ardene, Arda

ARDIS: (Scottish/Irish) Variant form of Allardyce, of uncertain meaning.
Ardys, Ardyce, Ardiss

ARETHA: (*a-REE-tha*) (Greek/Arabic) "Virtuous, excellent."
Areta

ARGENE: (*ar-JEEN*) (Latin/French) "Silvery."
Arjean

ARIA: (*ARE-ee-yah*) Operatic solo; also an astrological name.
Arietta "little song"

ARIADNE: (*ar-ee-AD-nee*) (Greek) "Chaste, holy." Mythology; Ariadne aided Theseus to escape from the Cretan Labyrinth.

ARIANA (194): (Latin) Variant form of Ariadne.
ARIANNA (360), Ariane (French); Arianne, Arriana

ARIEL (227): (Hebrew) "Lion of God." Biblical; a name for Jerusalem. Shakespeare gave the name to a prankish spirit in *The Tempest*. Usage: boys 29%, girls 71%.

ARIELLE (282), Ariela (Spanish); Ariella, Arrielle; Ariele (French)

ARLEIGH: (Teutonic/English) "Meadow of the hare."

ARLENE (424): (Latin) "Strong, Womanly"; (English) Feminine form of Charles.
Arleen, Arlena, Arleene, Arleena, Arline, Arlina, Arlyne, Arlana, Arleana, Arla, Arlyn, Arlenna, Arlette, Arletta, Arleta

ARLINDA: "Strength and wisdom." Blend of Arlene and Linda.

ARLISS: "Womanly strength." Feminine form of Arlo, from Carl.

ARMANDA: "Of the army; soldier." Feminine form of Armando.

ARNELLE: "The eagle rules." Feminine form of Arnold.
Arnette, Arnetta

ARSENIA: (ar-SEE-nee-ah) "Potent." Feminine form of Arsenio.
Arcenia

ARTEMIS: (AR-te-miss) (Greek) "Virgin goddess of the moon; huntress." Mythology; the equivalent of the Romans' Diana.

ARTHURINE: "Noble, courageous." Feminine form of Arthur.

ASENATH: (a-SEE-nath) (Egyptian) Biblical; Joseph's Egyptian wife.
Acenath

ASHA: (Swahili) "Life." Variant form of Aisha.
Ashia (Somali)

ASHLEY (2): (English) "Meadow of ash trees." Formerly an English surname used as a given name for boys or girls, Ashley is now almost entirely used for girls.
ASHLEE (141), ASHLEIGH (266), ASHLIE (399), ASHLY (410), Ashlyn, Ashlynn, Ashlynne, Ashlin, Ashlinn, Ashlen, Ashleen, Ashleena, Ashleah, Ashla

ASHTON (368): (English) "Town of ash trees." Usage: boys 54%, girls 46%.

Ashten, Ashtyn

ASIA (485): "The rising sun." The name of the continent
used as a given name. According to the Koran, Asia was
the name of the pharaoh's wife who raised the infant Moses. Asia is also a variant form of Aisha ("life"), the
name of Mohammad's favorite wife, one of the four "perfect women." See also Fatima, Khadija and Mary.
Azia, Asianne

ASTRA: (Latin) "Star."

ASTRID: (Scandinavian) "Godly strength."

ATHENA: (*a-THEE-nah*) (Latin) Variant form of Athene,
the mythological goddess of wisdom and war.
Athene

AUBERTA: (*oh-BEHR-ta*) (French) "Noble, bright."
Feminine variant of Albert.

AUBREY (319): (English/French) "Rules with elf-wisdom."
Usage of Aubrey: boys 13%, girls 87%.
Aubree, Aubrie, Aubry, Aubriana, Aubrianne

AUDREY (183): (English) "Nobility, strength." Audelia is
a Spanish form of Adela.
Audra; Audree (French); Audrie, Audri, Audrea, Audria,
Audriana, Audrianna, Audreana, Audreanna, Audrielle,
Audrina, Audris; Audene, Audelia

AUGUSTA: (Latin) "Majestic, grand." Feminine form of
August.
Augustina, Agustina

AURELIA: (Latin) "Golden." Aurielle is a blend with Arielle.
Aurene, Auriel, Aurielle; Arela, Arella (Spanish)

AURORA: (*oh-ROHR-ah*) (Latin) Roman mythology; Aurora was the goddess of dawn.
Aurore (French)

AUSTEN: (French/English) Variant form of Augustine.
Usage of Austen: boys 83%, girls 17%.
Austine (*aws-TEEN*), Austina

AUTUMN: (Latin) The fall season used as a given name.

AVA: (*AH-vah* or *AY-vah*) (Hebrew) "Alive; living one."
Variant form of Eve.
Avah, Avalee, Avelyn, Avlynn, Avelina

AVALON: Mythological; the island paradise to which King
Arthur was carried after his death.
Avilene

AVERIL: (Latin) "Opening buds of spring; born in April."
See also April.
Avril (French), Avrill, Avriel, Averill

AVIANA: (*ah-vee-AHN-ah*) "Living grace." Contemporary) Blend of Ava and Ana. Aviance is the name of a
popular perfume.
Avianna, Avia, Aviance (*AH-vee-AHNSE*)

AVIS: (*AY-viss*) (English) Variant form of the medieval
name Avice; (French) "refuge."

AVIVA: (*a-VEE-vah*) (Hebrew) "Springtime."
Avivah

AYA: (*ah-YAH*) (Japanese) "Figured cloth; damask."

AYLA: (*AY-la*) (Hebrew) "Oak tree." Literary; Ayla is the
Cro-Magnon heroine of Jean Auel's *Clan of the Cave
Bear*.
Ayala (Hebrew) "Doe"

AZALEA: (*a-ZAYL-yah*) (Latin/Greek) "Dry." A flower
name.
Azalia

AZIZA: (*ah-ZEE-zah*) (Arabic) "Beloved"; (Swahili) "very
beautiful."

AZURE: (English/French) The color used as a given name;
a clear sky blue.
Azura, Azurine

AZUSENA: (*ah-zoo-SAY-nah*) (Arabic) "Lily."
Azucena, Asucena, Azusa

B

BAHIRA: (*ba-HEE-rah*) (Arabic) ''Dazzling.''

BAILEY (263): (English/French) A steward or public official; a magistrate. Usage of Bailey: boys 8%, girls 92%.
Baylee, Bailie (Irish), Bayley, Baylie, Bailee, Baylee

BAMBI: (Italian) ''Little child, bambino.'' Pet name.

BARBARA (236): (Greek) ''Stranger, foreigner.'' Used since medieval times as a given name for girls. In Catholic custom, St. Barbara is invoked as a protectress against fire and lightning.
Barbra, Barbie, Barbi; Babette (*ba-BET*) (French); Barbarita, Barbarella

BEATA: (*bee-AH-ta*) (Latin) ''Happy.''

BEATRICE: (*BEE-a-triss*) (Latin) ''Brings joy.''
BEATRIZ (323) (Spanish); Beatrix (Italian); Beatriss, Bea, Bee

BECKY: Short form of Rebecca.
Becki, Becca

BELEN: (*bay-LEN*) Spanish word for ''Bethlehem'' used as a given name.

BELINDA: (Spanish) ''Very beautiful.''

BELLA: (Latin) ''Fair, lovely one.''
Belle, Bel (French); Bellissa, (Italian); Belva

BENECIA: (*ba-NEE-sha*) (Latin) ''Blessed one.''
Benicia

BENITA: (Latin) ''Blessed.'' Feminine form of Ben.

BERNADETTE: ''Little bear cub.'' Feminine form of Bernard. Most famous name bearer was St. Bernadette, canonized in 1933. See also Lourdes.
Bernadina, Bernadine, Bernarda, Bernadea, Bernette, Bernetta, Bernita, Berdine, Bernelle

BERNICE: (*ber-NEECE*) (Greek) ''One who brings victory''; (Latin) Variant form of Berenice. Berry and variants are short forms.
Bernyce, Berniss (*BER-niss*), Bernicia (Spanish), Ber-

nisha, Berenice (*BARE-a-neece*), Berenise, Berenisa, Berrie, Berry

BERONICA: (Spanish) "True image." Variant form of Veronica.

BERTHA: (German) "Bright."
Berta (Spanish), Bertina, Berthe (French)

BERYL: (Greek) A gemstone of varying colors, most often yellow-green. Biblical; the eighth foundation stone of the wall of New Jerusalem is described as being made of beryl.

BETH: (Hebrew) Short form of Elizabeth.

BETHANY (135): (Hebrew) The name of a village near Jerusalem where Jesus often visited Mary, Martha and Lazarus.
Bethanie, Bethani, Bethanee, Bethann

BETHEA: (*BETH-ee-ah*) (Hebrew) "Maidservant of Jehovah."
Bethia

BETHEL: (Hebrew) "House of God."

BETTY: Short form of Elizabeth.
Betsy, Betsey; Bettine (French); Bettina, Bette, Bessie, Bessy, Bess

BEULAH: (*BEW-lah*) (Hebrew) "Claimed as a wife." Biblical; a name symbolic of the heavenly Zion.

BEVERLY: (English) "Beaver stream."
Beverley, Beverlee

BIANCA (93): (Italian) Variant form of Blanche. (French) "White, shining".
BLANCA (253) (Spanish), Blanche, Bianka, Byanca

BIBI: (Arabic) "Lady." Bibiana is a Spanish form of Vivian.
Bibiana

BILLIE: "Determination, strength." Nickname for William used as a feminine name, often combined with other names. Usage: boys 38%, girls 62%.
Billie-jean, Billie-Jo

BIRDENA: (Contemporary) "Little bird."

Birdine, Byrdene

BIRGITTA: (*ber-GIT-ah*) Scandinavian form of Bridget.
Birgit, Birgitte, Brita

BLAINE: (Scottish/English) "Thin, lean." Mostly used as
a boy's name; in rare use for girls.

BLAIR: (Scottish/Gaelic) "Field of battle." Usage: boys
39%, girls 61%.
Blaire

BLAKE: (English/Scottish) "Dark, dark-haired." Can also
mean the reverse, "fair, pale." Very rarely used for girls.
Blakelee

BLISS: (English) "Joy, cheer." Bliss and its variants are
surnames that date from medieval times, rarely used today as given names.
Blyss, Blysse, Blisse; Blix (Swedish)

BLONDELL: (English/French) "Fair-haired, blond." The
similar sounding Blandina is a Spanish name meaning
"coaxing, flattering."
Blondelle, Blondene, Blandina

BLYTHE: (English) "Merry." Variant spelling of the English word "blithe," meaning "lighthearted, happy."

BO: Nickname and short form. Bo is used as an independent name for boys and, due to actress Bo Derek, for
girls. Also a Chinese name meaning "precious." Usage:
boys 85%, girls 15%.

BOBBI: Pet form of Roberta and Barbara. Usage of Bobbie: boys 27%, girls 73%. Bobbi is often combined with
other names, with or without a hyphen.
Bobbie, Bobbiejo, Bobbijo, Bobbiejean

BONITA: (*boh-NEE-tah*) (Spanish) "Pretty little one."

BONNIE (347): (Scottish) Diminutive of the French word
bon; "good." In Scottish usage, "bonnie" means
"pretty, charming."
Bonny, Bonni, Bonnibelle, Bonny-Jo, Bonny-Jean,
Bonny-Lee

BRANDY (143): (Contemporary) The name of the bever-
age used as a given name, with contemporary variants.

Brandi is also an Italian surname form of Brand, "fiery beacon."

BRANDI (106), Brandee, Brandie, Brandice, Brandyce, Branda, Brandelyn, Brandilyn, Brandyn

BREANNA (120): See also Brianna, Bryanna and Briona.

BREANNE (435), Breann, Breeann, Breeanne, Breeanna, BREANA (491), Breeana, Breonna, Breona, Breonda

BRECK: (Irish/Gaelic) "Freckled."

BREE: (Contemporary) Short form of names like Brina and Breanna.

Bria, Brea, Brielle

BRENDA (76): "Beacon on the hill." Feminine form of Brendan.

Brendalynn, Brendolyn

BRENNA (450): Variant form of Brenda.

BRETT: (English/French) "Brit." A native of Britain (England) or Brittany (France). Very rarely used for girls.

Bret, Brette, Bretta, Brettany

BRIANNA (67): (Celtic/Contemporary) "She ascends." Feminine form of Brian. See also Breanna, Bryanna and Briona.

BRIANA (109), BRIANNE (333), Briannah, Brianna, Briann, Briannon, Brienna, Brienne

BRIDGET (218): (Irish) "Strength." Mythology; the Celtic goddess of fire and poetry. See also Birgitta.

Bridgette, Bridgett, Brigette; Brigitte (French); Brigid, Brigida (Scandinavian)

BRINA: (*BREE-na*) Short form of Sabrina.

Breena, Brena

BRIONA: (*bree-OH-na*) Variant form of Brianna.

Brione, Brionna (*bree-AHN-ah*), Brionne (*bree-AHN*), Briony (*BRY-o-nee*), Brioni

BRISA: (*BREE-sah*) Short form of the Spanish name Briseida, from Briseis, the Greek name of the woman loved by Achilles in Homer's *Iliad*.

Brissa, Bryssa, Briza, Breezy, Brisha, Brisia

BRITT: (English) "From Britain." Rare usage of Britt is about equal for boys and girls.
Britta, Brit, Brita (*BREE-ta*)

BRITTANIA: (*bri-TAHN-yah*) (Latin) A poetic name for Great Britain.
Britania, Brittanya

BRITTANY (4): (*BRIT-'n-ee*) (English) From the name of an ancient duchy (Bretagne) in France. Celtic Bretons emigrated from France and became the Bretons of England; later the name "Britain" came to signify the entire country.
BRITTANI (288), Brittaney, Britani, Brittanie

BRITTNEY (43): (*BRITT-nee*) Very popular modern variant of Brittany; the phonetic spelling ensures a two-syllable pronunciation.
BRITNEY (152), Brittnee, Brittni

BRONWYN: (*BRON-win*) (Welsh) "White-breasted."
Branwyn, Bronwen

BROOKE (75): (English) "Water, stream." Actress Brooke Shields has made the English surname familiar as a girl's given name today. Usage of Brook: boys 37%, girls 63%.
Brook, Brooklyn, Brooklynn, Brooklynne

BRYANNA: Feminine form of Bryan. See also Brianna and Briona.
Bryana, Bryann, Bryanne, Bryani

BRYNN: (Celtic/Irish) "The heights."
Bryn, Brynne, Bren, Brenne, Brynna, Brynnan, Bryna, Brynda, Brynelle

BURGUNDY: In contemporary usage, Burgundy is probably a spin-off of Brandy, taking the name of a wine as a given name.

C

CADY: (*KAY-dee*) "Pastoral simplicity and happiness." Short form of Arcadia. Cadence literally means "a rhythmic flow of sounds." See also Kady.

Cadi, Cadee, Cadie, Cadence

CAILIN: (*KAY-lin*) (Irish/Gaelic) Meaning uncertain; may be a variant form of Cayley. See also Kaylyn.
Caylin, Cailyn, Caelan, Calynn, Caileen, Cayleen

CAITLIN (59): (*KATE-lin*) (Irish) Variant form of Katherine. (Greek) "Pure". See also Catherine, Kaitlin, Katherine and Katelyn.
CAITLYN (317) (English), Caitlynn, Caitlan, Catelyn, Caitlinn; Cateline (French); Cait, Caitrin, Caitland, Catlin, Catline, Catlyn

CALANDRA: (*ka-LAHN-drah*) (Greek/Italian) "Lark." Calinda and Calynda are contemporary variants or blends with Linda.
Calendre, Calinda, Calynda

CALISTA: (*ka-LEES-ta*) (Greek) "Beautiful." A saint's name. Mythology; an Arcadian nymph who metamorphosed into a she-bear, then into the Great Bear constellation. See also Kallista.
Calisto, Callista, Calysta, Calissa, Cali

CALLAN: (Gaelic) "Powerful in battle." See also Kallan.
Callen, Calynn

CALLIE (463): Variant form of Cayley, also short form of names beginning with "Cal-." See also Kallie.
Calli, Callee, Cali, Calley

CALLIOPE: (*ka-LIE-ah-pee*) (Greek) "Beautiful voice." Mythology; the muse of epic poetry.

CALVINNA: (Latin) "Bald." Feminine form of Calvin.

CALYPSO: (*ka-LIP-so*) (Greek) Mythology; a nymph who beguiled Odysseus for seven years. Music; a West Indies style of extemporaneous singing.

CAMELIA: (*ka-MEEL-yah*) (Latin) A flower name often associated with the name Camille. See also Kamelia.
Camella, Camellia

CAMEO: (*KAM-ee-o*) (Italian) A gem portrait carved in relief. See also Kamea.

CAMERON: (Gaelic) "Bent nose"; (Scottish) Clan surname based on the nickname given a valorous ancestor. Usage: boys 97%, girls 3%. See also Kameron.

Camryn

CAMILLE (232): (*ka-MEEL*) (Latin/French) "Freeborn, noble." Literary; in Virgil's *Aeneid*, Camilla was a swift-running warrior maiden. See also Kamille.

Camilla, Camile, Camila, Cammi

CANDICE (145): (*KAN-diss*) (English) Variant form of Candace, an ancient hereditary title used by Ethiopian queens, as Caesar was used by Roman emperors. See also Kandace.

CANDACE (160), Candyce, Candiss

CANDIDA: (*kan-DEE-dah*) (French/Latin) "Bright, glowing white."

Candide

CANDY: Short form of Candace, also used as an independent name meaning "sweet." Candi and Canda are Spanish diminutive forms of Candida.

Candi, Candie, Canda, Candra

CAPRICE: (*ka-PREESE*) (French) "Whimsical, unpredictable." Capri, as in the Isle of Capri, is rarely used today as a given name. See also Kaprice.

Capricia (*ka-PREE-sha*), Capri, Capriana

CARA (277): (Latin) "Beloved." Cari is a Spanish short form of Caridad, "dear, darling," and is also the name of a star in the Orion constellation. See also Kara and Caroline.

Cari, Carita, Carella, Caralea, Caralee, Carillie, Caralisa

CARESSE: (*ka-RESS*) (French) "Tender touch." See also Charis.

Caress, Caressa, Carressa

CAREY: (Welsh/English) "Loving." See also Carrie. Usage: boys 63%, girls 37%.

Caree, Carree

CARINA (343): (*ka-REEN-a*) (Spanish/Italian) "Little darling." See also Karina.

Carrina, Carena, Carine, Carin, Carinna, Cariana

CARISSA (246): (*ka-RISS-a*) (Greek) "Very dear." See also Karissa.

Carrissa, Carrisa, Carisa (Spanish), Carisse

CARLA (215): Feminine form of Charles, which means "manly." In the feminine form, the meaning is "womanly" or "strength." See also Carol, Charla and Karla.

CARLY (218), Carley, Carlie, Carli, Carlee, Carleigh, Carlene; Carleen (Irish); Carlyn, Carlynne, Carlisa, Carletta; Carlena, Carlina, Carlita (Spanish)

CARLOTTA: (Spanish/Italian) Variant form of Charlotte.

Carlota (Spanish)

CARMELA: (*car-MAY-lah*) (Latin) "Fruitful orchard," a reference to Mount Carmel in Palestine. See also Karmel.

Carmel, Carmelle, Carmelita, Carmella

CARMEN (215): (Spanish) Variant form of Carmel. See also Karmen.

Carmina (Italian), Carmencita

CAROL (370): (Latin) Feminine form of Carl. See also Carla.

Carole (French); Caryl; Carola, Carrola (Spanish); Carroll (Irish)

CAROLINE (158): (English) Variant form of Carol. Carolan is an Irish surname. See also Cara.

CAROLYN (192), Carolynn, Carolann, Carolanne, Carolan, CAROLINA (206) (Latin), Caroliana (Spanish); Carolyne, Caro, Caralyn, Caralynn, Carilyn, Carilynne

CARRIE (186): Short form of Carol and Caroline often used as a given name. See also Carey.

CARSON: (Scottish) Surname in rare use as a given name for girls.

CARYN: See also Karen.

Carynn

CASEY (137): (Irish) "Vigilant." Usage: boys 66%, girls 34%. Caycee and Cacia are short forms of Acacia. See also Kasey.

Cacey, Casee, Caycee, Cacia

CASSANDRA (46): (*ka-SAN-dra* or *ka-SAHN-dra*) (Greek)

"Unheeded prophetess." Literary; in Homer's *Illiad*, Cassandra foretold the fall of Troy but was unheeded. See also Kassandra.

CASANDRA (428) (Spanish), Cassondra, Cassaundra, Cassandrea

CASSIA: (*KASH-ah*) (Greek) "Spicy cinnamon." See also Kassia.

CASSIDY: (Irish) "Curly-headed." Usage: boys 22%, girls 78%. See also Kassidy.

CASSIE (234): Short form of Cassandra frequently used as an independent name. See also Kassie.
Cassi, Cassy

CATHERINE (86): (Latin/Greek) "Pure." One of the great traditional names for women, with variations in many languages. Historical; the name of several saints and queens including Catherine the Great, Empress of Russia. See also Katherine and Caitlin.
Catriona (Gaelic); Caitrin; Catarina (Italian/Portuguese); Cathryn, Catharine, Cathleen, Cathrine (*kath-REEN*), Catheryn; Catalina, Catrina, Caterina (Spanish)

CATHY: Short form of Catherine. See also Katherine.
Cathie, Cathi, Cathia

CATRICE: (*ka-TREECE*) (Contemporary) Blend of Catrina and Patrice.

CAYLEY: (Scottish/English/French) Variant form of Caley; (Gaelic) "slender" or Cailley; (French) "from the forest." Caela is also a short form of Micaela. See also Kayla and Kaylee.
Cailley, Cailee, Caleigh, Caylee, Caylie, Caileigh, Carley, Caela, Caila, Cayla

CECILIA (213): (*sess-SEEL-ya*) (Latin) "Blind." The blind St. Cecilie, patron saint of music, was herself a talented musician.
Cecelia, Cicilia (*siss-SEEL-ya*), Cecily, Cecilie, Cecilee (*SESS-a-lee*), Cicely (*SISS-a-lee*) (English); Cicily; Cecile (*sess-SEEL*) (French); Cecille, C'Ceal, Ceci (*see-see*), Cecia

CEDRICA: *(sed-REE-kah)* Feminine form of Cedric.
Cedrika, Cedrina, Cedra *(SED-rah)*

CELESTE (431): *(seh-LEST)* (Latin/French) "Heavenly."
Celesta, Celestina (Spanish), Celestine, Celestyna, Celestia, Celestiel, Celesse, Celisse

CELIA: *(SEEL-yah)* Variant form of Cecilia.
Celie (French), Ceil, Cele

CELINA: "Goddess of the moon." Variant form of Celia
or Selena. Mythology; Celena was one of the seven
daughters of Atlas who were transformed by Zeus into
the stars of the Pleiades constellation. See also Selena.
Celena, Celene; Celine (French); Celinda, Celinna, Celenia, Celicia, Celenne

CERES: *(SEHR-ees)* (Latin) "Of the spring." The Roman
goddess of agriculture and fertility.

CERISE: *(ser-REESE)* (French) "Cherry; cherry red."

"CHA-" names: (Contemporary) With pronunciation emphasis on the second syllable. See also Charis, Cherie
and "Sha-" names.
Chalia, Chalise, Chalon, Chalonn, Chalonne, Chalyse,
Chanae, Chanee, Chenay, Chanice, Chanise, Chaquita,
Charita, Charelle, Charice, Chevelle, Chavonne, Chevonne, Chevon

CHALINA: *(sha-LEEN-ah)* Spanish diminutive form of
Rosa.

CHANA: (Hebrew) Variant form of Hannah. Chana is also
a feminine Spanish diminutive of names ending in
"-iana."
Channa, Channah

CHANDELLE: *(shan-DELL)* (French) "Candle."
Chandel

CHANDLER: (English/French) "Candlemaker." Usage:
boys 79%, girls 21%.

CHANDRA: *(SHAN-dra)* (Hindi) "Of the moon." Chanda
means "foe of evil."
Chanda, Chandy, Chandara, Chandria, Chaundra

CHANEL (455): *(sha-NELL)* (French) "Canal, channel."

Recent popularity is probably influenced by the perfume Chanel and the "Sha-" name pattern.

Chanelle, Channelle, Chanell, Chenelle

CHANTEL (344): (*shahn-TELL*) (French) "Singer." See also Shantel.

Chantelle, Chantell, Chauntel, Chantal, Chantalle, Chantrell, Chante (*shawn-TAY*) "to sing," Chantay, Chantae, Chanta (Spanish); Chaunte

CHANTILLY: (*shahn-TEE* or *shan-TILL-ee*) (French) A delicate lace from Chantilly, France.

CHARIS: (*KARE-iss*) (Greek) "Grace." Charisma is the related English word used as a given name. See also Caresse, Cherise, "Cha-" names and Karisma.

Charissa (*sha-RISS-a* or *ka-RISS-ah*), Chariss (*ka-RISS*), Charisse, Charise (*sha-REESE*), Charice, Charisa, Charisma, Carisma (*ka-RIZ-mah*)

CHARITY: (Latin) "Benevolent goodwill and love." A virtue name.

CHARLA: (*SHAR-la* or *CHAR-la*) Feminine form of Charles. Charlie as a name for girls may be influenced by the perfume Charlie. Usage: (Charley) boys 71%, girls 29%; (Charly) boys 64%, girls 36%. See also Carla and Sharlene.

Charlee, Charli, Charlie, Charly, Charlyn, Charlynn

CHARLENE (329): (*shar-LEEN*) Diminutive feminine form of Charles. "Char-" is also used as a blend prefix. See also Sharlene.

Charleen, Charleene, Charline, Charlena, Charleena, Charlaine, Charlayne, Charlita, Charlisa, Chardae

CHARLOTTE (325): (French) Feminine form of Charles. See also Carlotta.

Charlotta, Charlette

CHARMAINE: (*shar-MAYNE*) (French) "Fruitful orchard." Variant form of Carmel. Charmian is the name of one of Cleopatra's attendants in Shakespeare's *Antony and Cleopatra*.

Charmayne, Charmian, Charmine

CHARO: (*CHAR-oh*) (Spanish) Pet name for Rosa.

CHASTITY: (*CHASS-ta-tee*) (Latin/French) "Purity, innocence." A virtue name

Chasity, Chasta (*CHASS-ta*), Chastine (*chass-TEEN*), Chastina

CHAVELA: (*sha-VAY-lah*) (Spanish) Variant form of Isabel.

Chavelle

CHAYA: (*CHYE-ah*) (Spanish) Short form for names ending in "-aria."

CHELSEA (28): (*CHELL-see*) Place name, especially in reference to the district in London, well-favored today as a given name for girls.

CHELSEY (147), CHELSIE (290), Chelsi, Chelsee, Chelsy, Chelsa

CHERIE: (*sha-REE*) (French) "Dear one, darling." Contemporary variants of Cherie follow the "sha-" name pattern. See also "Cha-" and "Sha-" names, Cheryl and Sherry.

Cher, Chere, Cheri, Cheree, Cherree, Charee, Chereen, Cherina, Cherine, Cherita, Cherrelle, Cherelle, Cherell (*sher-RELL*)

CHERISE: (*sha-REESE*) (Contemporary) Blend of Cherie and Cerise. See also Charis.

Cherisse, Cherice, Cherese, Cherisa, Cheresse (*sha-RESS*)

CHERRY: (English) Fruit-bearing tree of the rose family.

Cherrie, Cherri

CHERYL (392): (*CHARE-el* or *SHAR-el*) Rhyming variant of names like Meryl and Beryl, developed early this century. Cherilyn is a further variant based on Marilyn. See also Cherie and Sheryl.

Cheryll, Cherrell, Cherrill, Cherilyn, Cherilynn

CHESSA: (Slavic) "At peace."

Chessie

CHEYENNE: (*shy-ANN*) (French/American Indian) Name

of an Algonkin tribe of the Great Plains and of the capital city of Wyoming. Usage: boys 14%, girls 86%.
Cheyanne, Cheyanna, Chiana, Chianna

CHIKA: (*CHEE-kah*) (Nigerian) "God is supreme." The Spanish pet names Chica and Chiquita mean "little girl." Chiko (*CHEE-koh*) is a Japanese name with the potential meanings "arrow; arrow shaft"; "promise, pledge."
Chica, Chiquita, Chiko

CHINA: Place name used as a given name. Chynna Phillips is a popular singer today.
Chynna, Chyna

CHINARA: (Nigerian) "God receives."

CHIYO: (*chee-yoh*) (Japanese) "Thousand years"; "eternal." Surname.

CHLOE (313): (*KLO-ee*) (Greek) "Fresh-blooming."

CHRISANN: (*kriss-ANN*) (Greek/English) "Golden flower." Variant form of Chrysantus, a saint's name. Chrysandra is a contemporary blend using Sandra. See also Krisandra.
Chrisanne, Chrisanna, Chrysann, Crisann; Crisanna (Spanish); Chrysantha, Chrysandra

CHRISTA (410): (Greek) "Anointed one; a Christian." See also Chrysta and Kristal.
Chrysta, Crista (Spanish), Crysta

CHRISTABEL: (Latin) "Beautiful Christian."
Cristabel, Cristabell, Christabella

CHRISTEL: Variant form of Christa or Crystal. See also Crystal and Kristal.
Christelle, Christella, Cristela, Cristella

CHRISTEN: Variant form of Christian. Spanish and Italian forms begin with "Cr-." See also Khristina and Kristen.
Christin, Christyn, Christan, Christanne, Christana, Christaine, Cristin, Cristen, Cristyn

CHRISTIAN (377): (Greek) "Follower of Christ." Spanish and Italian forms begin with "Cr-." Usage of Christian: boys 91%, girls 9%.
Christiana, Christianna, Christiane (French), Chris-

tianne, Chrystian, Cristian, Cristianne, Cristiana, Cristianna

CHRISTINA (18): Variant form of Christiana. See also Khristina and Kristina.

CRISTINA (128), Cristine (Spanish/Italian), Christena, Chrystina, Christeena

CHRISTINE (61): (French) Variant form of Christiana. Christene, Christeen

CHRISTY (349): Short form of "Chris-" names. "Cr-" spellings are Spanish. See also Krista.

Christie (Scottish), Christi, Cristy, Cristie, Chrissy, Chrissie, Chrissa, Crissa, Crissie, Crissy

CHRYSTA: (Greek) "Golden one." These names may also be variants of Christa or Crystal. See also Christa and Krista.

Crysta, Chrystie, Chryssa.

CIANA: (*see-AHNA* or *chee-AHNA*) (Italian) Feminine variant form of John.

Ciandra

CIARA (399): (*chee-ARR-ah* or *see-ARR-ah*) (Italian) Variant form of Clare. Ciaran is the name of two major Irish saints. See also Sierra.

Chiara (*chee-ARR-ah*), Ciarra, Ciaran, Cierra, Ciera

CINDY (112): Short form of Cynthia and Lucinda.

Cindi, Cyndi, Cyndy, Cyndee, Cinda, Cindia, Cindel

CIRA: (*SEE-rah*) Spanish variant form of Cyril. See also Cyrilla and Cyrah.

Ciri, Ceri, Ceria

CIRCE: (*SIR-see*) (Latin) Mythology; a sorceress who tempted Perseus and changed his men into swine and back again.

CLAIRE (187): (English) "Bright, shining and gentle; famous." Also French form of Clare.

Clara, Clare, Clair; Clarita, Clarisa (Spanish); CLARISSA (360), Claressa, Clairessa, Clarrisa; Clarisse (French); Clarice, Clarinda

CLARIBEL: "Bright, beautiful." Blend of Clare and Bella. A literary name used by Shakespeare in *The Tempest*.

CLAUDIA (116): Feminine form of Claude.
Claudine, Claudette, Claudelle

CLEMENCE: (*klem-awnse*) (French/Latin) "Clemency, mercy." Mythology; the Roman goddess of pity.
Clementina, Clementine

CLEO: (*KLEE-oh*) (Greek) Short form of names like Clotilde and Cleopatra. Clio (*KLY-o*) is the mythological Muse of historic poetry.
Clea, Clio

CLEONE: (*KLEE-a-nee*) (Greek) "Glorious."
Cleonie

CLEOPATRA: (Greek) "Glory of her father." Historical; the queen of Egypt who was immortalized by Shakespeare in *Antony and Cleopatra*.

CLETA: (*KLEE-tah*) "Illustrious." Feminine form of Cletus.

CLORIS: (Greek) "Blooming." Mythology; the goddess of flowers.
Chloris

CLYTIE: (*KLY-tee*) (Greek) Mythology; a nymph who loved Helios, god of the sun. Clytie was changed into a sunflower, which always turns its face toward the sun.

COCO: (Spanish) Diminutive form of Soccoro. Also a French pet name.

CODY: (Irish/Gaelic) "Helpful." Very rarely used for girls. See also Kodi.
Codi, Codee

COLBY: (English) "Dark-skinned." Rare usage is about equal for boys and girls. See also Kolby.

COLETTE: (French) "Victorious." Variant form of Nicolette.
Collette, Coletta, Colletta, Coleta (Spanish)

COLLEEN (250): (Irish) "Girl."
Collene, Collena, Colene

COLOMBIA: (Latin) "Dove-like, gentle."

CONCETTA: (Latin) Italian form of Concepcion, referring to the doctrine of the Immaculate Conception of Mary.
Concepcion, Conchita (Spanish)

CONNIE (407): Short form of names beginning with "Con-."

CONSTANCE: (Latin) "Constancy, steadfastness." A virtue name.
Constancia (Spanish); Constantina (Italian); Constantia (Latin)

CONSUELO: (Spanish) "Consolation."

CONTESSA: (Italian) Title, the feminine equivalent of Count.
Countess (English)

CORA: (Greek) "Maiden." Possibly a variant form of Kore. See also Kora.
Coralee, Coralyn, Corlene, Corella, Coretta, Corissa, Corrissa

CORAL: (Latin/Greek) A semiprecious natural sea growth, often deep pink to red in color, from which jewelry is made.
Coraline, Coralie, Coralia

CORAZON: (*kor-a-SOHN*) (Spanish) "Heart."
Corazana

CORBY: (English) Place name.

CORDELIA: Literary; in *King Lear*, Shakespeare portrays Cordelia as a woman of sincerity and honesty.
Cordella

CORINA (443): (*ko-REE-nah*) (Latin) Variant form of Corrinne. The "-een" spellings are Irish endings.
Corrina, Corrine (French), Corine, Coreen, Correen, Coreene, Correena.

CORINNE (485): (*ko-RINN*) (French) Variant form of Cora.
Corinna, Corynne, Corryn (*KOR-in*), Coryn, Corynn, Corrin

CORINTHIA: (*ko-RIN-thee-ah*) (Greek) "Woman of Corinth."

CORLISS: (English) "Carefree."

CORNELIA: (*kor-NEEL-yah*) (Latin) Feminine form of Cornelius.
Cornella

CORY: (English/Irish) Cory and variants are in rare use as girls' names. Corrie and Corry are Scottish surnames. Cori is also used as a prefix in contemporary blended names. See also Kori.
Cori, Corey, Corie, Corri, Corrie, Corry, Coriann, Corianne, Corrianne, Corrianna, Coretta, Corisa

COURTNEY (26): (English/French) Place name and surname, used today as a given name for girls. Courtlyn is a contemporary variant. See also Kourtney.
CORTNEY (323), Courtlyn

COZETTE: (French) "Little pet." Literary; in Victor Hugo's *Les Miserables*, Cosette is Jean Valjean's beloved adopted daughter.
Cosette

CRECIA: (*KREE-sha*) (Latin) Short form of Lucrecia.

CRYSTAL (34): A transparent quartz, usually colorless, that can be cut to reflect brilliant light. The character played by Linda Evans on the TV series "Dynasty" undoubtedly influenced Crystal's sudden rise in popularity. See also Christel and Krystal.
CRISTAL (381), Chrystal, Christal, Crystall, Cristalle, Christelle, Crystell, Christella, Cristella, Chrystalann, Crystalann, Cristalyn, Chrystalyn, Crystalynn, Crystalina

CYBELE: (*si-BELL*) (Greek/Roman/Oriental) Mythology; an ancient nature goddess worshipped as the Great Mother in Asia Minor. The mother of all gods, men and wild nature, lions were her faithful companions. She was identified with Rhea by the Greeks, with Maia and Ceres by the Romans.

CYBIL: (Latin) Variant form of Sibyl, the name given in Greek mythology to a prophetess or fortune-teller.
Cybill

CYDNEY: Variant form of Sydney.
Cydnee, Cidney

CYNTHIA (57): (Greek) Mythology; one of the names of Artemis, the goddess of the moon, referring to her birthplace on Mount Cynthus.
Cinthia, Cyntia (Spanish)

CYRAH: (*SEER-ah* or *SYE-rah*) "Enthroned." Feminine form of Cyrus. Cyrene is the name of an ancient city on the north coast of Africa. See also Cira and Kyra.
Cyra, Cyrena, Cyrina, Cyrene

CYRILLA: "Mistress, ruler." Feminine form of Cyril. See also Cira.
Cirilla, Cerella, Cerelia

CZARINA: (*zar-REEN-ah*) (Latin/Russian) Feminine form of Czar, the Russian equivalent of a female Caesar or Empress.

D

"DA-"names: (Contemporary) Blends of "Da-" plus various endings, with pronunciation emphasis on the second syllable. See also Dale and "De-" names.
Dalynn, Dameshia, Danessa, Danisha, Daniesha, Danille, Daneille, Dashay, Davisha, Davonne

DAGMAR: (Scandinavian) "Glorious."

DAHLIA: (*DAL-yah*) (Swedish) "Valley." The flower was named for botanist Anders Dahl. Dalia is a Tanzanian name meaning "gentle."
Daliah (Israeli), Dalia

DAISY (107): (English) A flower name. Dacia is Spanish meaning "from Dacia."
Daizy, Daysi, Daisey, Daisie, Daisi, Deysi, Daisha, Dacia, Dacey, Dacy, Deyci

DAKOTA: (American Indian) "Friend, ally." Tribal name. Usage: boys 86%, girls 14%.

DALE: (English) "Small valley." Very rarely used for girls. The Dalena and Dalenna variants are also short forms of Madeline. See also "Da-" names.

Dayle, Dalene, Dalena, Dalina, Dalenna, Dael (Dutch), Daly, Daelyn, Dahl (Scandinavian), Dallana

DALLAS: (Scottish) "From the dales, the valley meadows." Name of the Texas city used as a given name. Usage: boys 87%, girls 13%.
Dallis

DAMARIS: (*DAM-a-riss*) (Latin) "Gentle." Biblical; an educated woman of Athens who heard Paul speak at the Areopagus.
Damara, Damariss, Damaress

DAMIANA: (*day-mee-AHN-a*) (Greek) "One who tames, subdues." Feminine form of Damian.

DANA (156): (*DAY-nah*) (Scandinavian) "From Denmark." Also a variant form of Daniel. Usage: boys 15%, girls 85%.
Dayna, Danah, Daena, Daina

DANAE: (*da-NAY*) (Greek) Mythology; the mother of Perseus by Zeus. Variants follow the "De-" name pattern.
Danay, Danaye, Danee, Denae, Denay

DANE: (Scandinavian) "From Denmark."
Dayne, Danea, Daney, Dania

DANICA: (*DAN-i-kah*) (Slavic) "Morning star."
Dannica, Danika, Dannika

DANIELLE (22): (*dan-YELL*) (French) "God is my Judge." Feminine form of Daniel.
DANIELA (326) (Spanish), DANIELLA (485), Daniele, Danyelle, Dhanielle, Donielle

DANNA: Feminine variant form of Danny and Daniel. Dannah is a Biblical place name.
Dani (Spanish/Italian), Dannee, Danni, Dany, Danelle, Dannell, Dannelle, Dannon, Danitza, Danice, Danise, Danette, Danita, Dannia, Danya, Dania, Dannalee, Dantina, D'Anna, Dannah

DAPHNE: (*DAFF-nee*) (Greek) "The laurel tree." Mythology; virtuous Daphne was transformed into a laurel tree to protect her from Apollo.
Daphney, Dafne (Israeli), Daphna

DARA: (Hebrew) "Wise." Biblical; the name of a descendant of Judah noted for his wisdom. Also a Gaelic name meaning "strong, stouthearted."

Darah, Darra, Darrah, Dareen, Darissa, Darice

DARBY: (English) Place name and surname. Rare usage is about equal for boys and girls.

DARCY: (Irish/French) "Dark." Very rarely used for boys. See also Dorcey.

Darcie, Darci, Darcey, D'Arcy, Darcia, Darcel, Darcell, Darcelle, Darchelle

DARIA: Feminine form of Darius, a Persian royal name. Variants may also be feminine forms of names like Daryl and Darin.

Darielle, Dariele, Darrelle, Darian, Darienne, Darianna

DARLENE (370): (English) Contemporary form of the Old English "dearling, darling."

Darla, Darline, Darleen, Darlena, Darlina, Darleena, Darleane

DARNELL: (English) "Hidden." Place name and surname. Very rarely used for girls.

Darnelle, Darnae, Darnisha, Darnetta

DARYL: Actress Daryl Hannah has probably influenced the occasional use of Daryl and variants as names for girls. Usage: boys 88%, girls 12%. See also Daria.

Daryll, Darryll, Darrill, Darylene, Darylyn, Darolyn, Darrellyn, Darrylynn

DARYN: (Greek) "Gift." Contemporary feminine form of Darin.

Darynn, Darynne

DAVENEY: (*DAV-nee* or *DAV-a-nee*) (French) Name of a town and castle in Flanders. May also be used as a rhyming variant of Daphne.

DAVIDA: (*da-VEE-dah*) "Beloved." Feminine form of David.

Davita, Davina, Davia, Davonna, Davy, Davynn, Daveen, Davine, Davianna

DAWN (389): (English) "The first appearance of light; daybreak."

Dawna, Dawne, Dawnika, Dawnette, Dawnetta, Dawnelle, Dawnielle

"DE-"names: (Contemporary) With pronunciation emphasis on the second syllable. See also "Da-" names, Delicia, Deandra and Danae.

DeAngela, Dejana, Dejanee, Dejeanee, Delana, Delaree, Delena, Deleena, Delise, Deloise, Delyse, Delinda, Delyn, DeLynden, Demeisha, Denell, Denesha, Deneisha, Denitia, DeShay, DeShawna

DEANDRA: (*dee-AN-dra*) (Contemporary) Blend of Deanne plus variants of Andrea and Sandra.

Deandrea, Deandria, Deeandra, Diandra, Diandre, Dianda, Deanda

DEANNA (217): Variant form of Diana. See also Dionna.

Deanne, Deann, Deeana, Deeann, Deeanna, Deana, Deena, Deane, Deonna, Deonne, Deona, Deondra

DEBORAH (295): (Hebrew) "Bee." Biblical; a prophetess who summoned Barak to battle against an invading army. The victory song she wrote after the battle is part of the Book of Judges. See also Devora.

DEBRA (471), DEBBIE (491), Debrah, Debby, Debora (Spanish), Debralee

DEE: Short form of names beginning with "De."

DeeDee, Dede, DiDi

DEIDRE: (*DEE-dra*) (Gaelic) "Melancholy." Phonetic spelling of the older form "Deirdre" (*DEER-dra*).

Deirdre, Deidra, Deedra, Diedra, Diedre

DEITRA: (*DEE-tra*) Variant form of Demetria.

Deetra, Detria

DEJA: (*DAY-hah*) (Spanish) Short form of Dejanira, from the Greek name Deianeira, the wife of Hercules. Sometimes a use of the French "déjà vu" (*day-zhah*) "remembrance."

Dejah, Deija, Daija

DEKA: (*DEE-kah*) (African/Somali) "Pleasing."

DELANEY: (*de-LAY-nee*) Irish surname. Very rarely used for boys.

Delaina, Delaine (*de-LAIN*) (French), Delayne, Delayna

DELFINA: (*del-FEEN-ah*) (Latin) "Dolphin." (Spanish) Variant form of Delphine, the name of a thirteenth-century French saint. See also Delphi.

DELIA: (Greek) "From Delos." Mythology; the island of Delos was Artemis's birthplace. Delia is also used as a short form of Cordelia and Adelia.

DELICIA: (*de-LEE-sha*) (Latin) "Gives pleasure." Variant forms follow the "De-" name pattern.

Delisa, Delisha, Dalisha, Delissa, Delyssa, Deliza, Delight

DELILAH: (*dee-LYE-lah*) (Hebrew) "Languishing." Biblical; the woman who beguiled Samson into revealing the secret of his superhuman strength. Dalila (Tanzanian) "gentle."

Delila, Dalila

DELLA: Variant form of Adele meaning "of the nobility." Dell

DELMA: (*DEL-mah*) (German) "Noble protector." Short form of Adelma from Aldhelm.

Delmy, Delmi, Delmira

DELORES: See also Dolores.

Deloris, Delora

DELPHI: (*DELL-fee* or *DELL-fye*) (Greek) "Dolphin." Refers to the Oracle of Delphi on Mount Parnassus. See also Delfina.

Delphia, Delphene, Delphine (French)

DELTA: (*DEL-tah*) (Greek) Fourth letter of the Greek alphabet.

DEMELZA: (*de-MELL-zah*) (English) "Fortified." Place name in Cornwall.

DEMETRIA: (Greek) "Of Demeter." Feminine form of Demetrius. Mythology; Demeter was the goddess of corn and harvest. See also Deitra.

Demetra, Demitra, Dimetria, Demitras, Demeter

DEMI: Short form of Demetria.

DENA: (*DEE-na*) Variant form of Deana and Dina.
Dene, Denia, Deneen, Denni, Denica

DENISE (114): (*de-NEES*) (French) Feminine form of
Denis, from the Greek name "Dionysius."
Denice, Deniece, Denisse, Denisha, Denisa (Spanish),
Dennise, Denyse, Denissa

DERICA: (Contemporary) "Gifted ruler." Feminine form
of Derek.
Dereka, Derrica, Dericka

DERRY: (Irish) Surname also used as a short form of names
like Derica. Very rarely used for girls.

DESIREE (109): (*dez-a-RAY*) (French) "The one desired."
Often spelled phonetically to ensure the French pronun-
ciation.
DESIRAE (481), Desiraye, Desarae, Desaree, Deziree,
Dezarae, Dezirae, Desire (English), Desyre

DESSA: From the Greek name Odysseus, meaning "wandering."

DESTINY (246): (English/French) Literally "one's certain
fortune; fate."
Destina (Spanish), Destinee, Destinie, Destini, Desta-
nee, Destine (*dess-TEEN*)

DEVA: (*DEE-vah*) (Hindi) "Divine." Name of the Hindu
goddess of the moon.

DEVANY: (*DEV-a-nee*) (Gaelic/Irish) "Dark-haired."
Devenny, Devaney, Devanie, Devinee, Devony

DEVON: (English) The name of a county in England noted
for beautiful farmland. Usage: (Devon) boys 72%, girls
28%; (Devin) boys 85%, girls 15%; (Devan) boys 68%,
girls 32%.
DEVIN (429) (English/French) "divine," Devan, Devyn, Devynn, Devana, Devanna, Devonna, Devonne,
Devona, Devondra, Devonette

DEVORA: (*DEV-or-ah*) (Hebrew) "Bee." Variant form of
Deborah.
Devorah, Devra, Devri, Devery, Devi

DEXTRA: (Latin) "Adroit, skillful."

DHANA: (*DONN-ah*) (Hindi) "Wealthy."
Dhanna

DIAMOND: (Greek/English) "Of high value; brilliant."
The gemstone used as a given name. Usage: boys 25%,
girls 75%.
Diamonique, Diamante, Diamanda, Diamontina

DIANA (62): (Latin) "Divine." Mythology; Diana was an
ancient Roman divinity who came to be associated with
the Greek Artemis. Noted for her beauty and fleetness,
Diana is often depicted as a huntress. See also Deanna
and Dionna.
DIANE (303) (*dee-AHN*) (French), Dianna, Dianne,
Diahna, Diannah, Diahann, Di, Dian, Diandra, DiAnne,
Dyanna, Dyann, Dyana

DIANTHA: (*di-ANN-tha*) (Contemporary) Blend of Diana
and Anthea.

DILYS: (*de-LEES*) (Welsh) "Perfection."

DIMETRIA: See Demetria.

DINAH: (*DYE-nah*) (Hebrew) "Judged and vindicated."
Biblical; Jacob's only daughter. Dina (*DEE-nah*) and Di-
nora are Spanish forms of Dinah.
Dina, Dynah, Dinora, Dinorah, Dena

DIONNA: (French) "From the sacred spring." Mythol-
ogy; Dione was the wife of Zeus and the mother of
Aphrodite. See also Diana and Deanna.
Dionne, Diona, Dione, Diondra

DIOR: (*dee-ORR*) French surname in rare use as a given
name. D'Or is a soundalike French variant meaning
"golden."
D'Or

DITA: (*DEE-tah*) (Spanish) Short form of Edith.

DIVINA: (*dih-VEEN-a*) (Latin) "Divine one."
Devina

DIXIE: In England, a surname and short form of Dick. The
American name refers to the French word for "ten" or

to the region of the southern states below the Mason-Dixon line.

DOLORES: (Latin/Spanish) "Sorrows." A devotional name that refers to the Virgin Mary as "Mary of the sorrows." See also Delores.
Doloris

DOMINGA: (*do-MEEN-gah*) (Spanish) "Of the Lord." Feminine form of Domingo.

DOMINIQUE (227): (*dom-min-NEEK*) (Latin/French) "Of the Lord." French spelling of Dominic primarily used in America for girls (71%). Boy's usage: 29%.
Dominica, Domenica, (Spanish); Domenique, Dominee

DONNA (269): (Latin/Italian) "Lady." A title of respect, equivalent to "Don" for men. See also Madonna.
Dona (Spanish); Donni, Donnie, Donielle, Donelle, Donella, Donnella, Donisha, Donetta; Donya, Dahnya, Dahna, Donnalee, Donnalyn, Donna-Marie

DORA: (Greek) "Gift." Short form of Dorothy. Also used as a prefix in blended names.
Dorah, Doria, Dorae, Doreina; Dorlisa (German); Doreen (Irish); Dorene, Dorena, Dorina, Dorine, Doralee, Doralyn, Dorinda, Dorelia, Dodie, Dodi

DORCAS: (*DOR-kuss*) (Greek) "Gazelle." Biblical; a woman who "abounded in good deeds and gifts of mercy."

DORCEY: (English) Variant form of Darcy.
Dorsey

DORIAN: (Greek) "Gift." Usage: boys 81%, girls 19%. Also a variant form of Dora.
Dorianna, Dorianne, Dorrian, Dorienne, Doriana

DORIS: (Greek) Mythology; a daughter of the sea god Oceanus.
Dorris, Dorice, Dorisa, Dorit

DOROTHY: (Greek) "Gift of God."
Dorothea; Dorotea (Spanish); Dorothee, Dorotha, Dortha, Doro, Dottie, Dolly, Dollie

DORRIE: Short form of names beginning with "Dor-."

Dorri, Dorry, Dori, Dorie, Doree

DREW: "Manly (womanly), brave." Short form of Andrew. Usage: boys 92%, girls 8%.
Drue

DRINA: (*DREE-nah*) (Spanish) Short form of Alexandra.
Dreena

DRUSILLA: (*drew-SILL-a*) (Latin) "Strong."
Drucilla, Dru

DUANA: (*D'WAY-na*) (Irish) "Dark." Feminine form of Duane.
Duayna

DULCE: (*DOOL-cee*) (Latin) "Sweet, sweetness." Dulcinea was a name created by Cervantes's *Don Quixote* for his idealized lady.
Dulcie, Dulcy, Dulcea, Dulcia, Dulcine, Dulcina, Dulcinea (*dul-see-NAY-ah*)

DUSTY: Nickname used occasionally as a given name for girls as well as boys.
Dusti, Dustee

E

EARLINE: (*er-LEEN*) A title of nobility, feminine form of Earl. Erlina is the Spanish form of Herlinde (German) "shield."
Earlene, Earlina, Earlena, Erlene, Erlina

EARTHA: (*ER-tha*) (German) "The earth."
Ertha

EBONY (302): (*EBB-o-nee*) (Greek/Egyptian) "Black."
Eboni, Ebonee, Ebonique (*ebb-o-NEEK*)

ECHO: (*EK-ko*) (Greek) "Sound." Mythology; a nymph who faded away until only her voice was left behind.
Ekko

EDDA: (German) "Strives." Variant form of Hedda or Hedwig.
Eda

EDEN: *(EE-den)* (Hebrew) "Pleasure." Biblical; the name of the gardenlike first home of Adam and Eve.
Edenia (Spanish), Edana

EDITH (407): (English) "Spoils of war."
Edythe, Edytha, Edie, Edee, Edelina, Edita (Spanish)

EDLIN: (German) Diminutive form of Ed. Edlyn and Edelina are contemporary blends of Ed and Adeline.
Edlyn, Edelina, Edrica

EDNA: (Hebrew) "Pleasure."

EDWINA: *(ed-WEEN-a)* "Rich in friendship." Feminine form of Edwin.
Edwinna *(ed-WIN-a)*

EFFIE: (Greek) "Well spoken." Short form of Euphemia.

EGYPT: *(EE-jipt)* The name of the country as a given name.

EILEEN (392): (Irish) "Shining light." Variant form of Helen. See also Ilene.
Eilene, Eilena, Eileene, Eila

ELAINE (326): *(ee-LAYNE)* (French) Variant form of Helen.
Elaina, Elina (Spanish), Elayna, Ellaine, Ellayne *(ell-ayne)*, Eleana (Contemporary)

ELANA: *(ee-LANN-a)* (Israeli) "Tree." See also Ilana.
Elanna, Elanah, Elanie *(ELL-a-nee)*

ELDORA: (Spanish) Variant form of Heliodorus. (Greek) "Gift of the sun". The name of many saints.
Eleadora

ELEANOR: *(ELL-a-nor)* (French) "Shining light." Variant form of Helen. See also Leonora.
Eleonora, Eleanora, Eleanore, Elinor (English)

ELEKTRA: (Greek) "The fiery sun." The daughter of Agamemnon; a central character in three Greek tragedies and the inspiration for a character (Lavinia) in Eugene O'Neill's trilogy of plays, *Mourning Becomes Electra*.
Electra

ELENA (262): *(eh-LAYN-a)* (Spanish) Variant form of Helen.
Eleni (Russian), Elina, Eleena

ELFRIDA: *(el-FREE-dah)* (German) "Peaceful ruler." Variant form of Frieda.

ELIANA: Variant form of Elena.
Elianna, Elianne, Eliane (French)

ELISE (249): *(ell-EESE)* (French) Short form of Elisabeth. See also Elyse and Ellyce.
ELISA (249), Elissa, Elisse, Elisha, Ellisha, Elliisa, Elysha, Elisia, Ellecia, Elicia, Elishia, Elisamarie

ELITA: *(el-LEE-ta)* (Latin) "Chosen one."

ELIZABETH (9): (Hebrew) "My God is bountiful; God of plenty." Biblical; the mother of John the Baptist. Since the reign of Queen Elizabeth I, Elizabeth has been one of the most frequently used names for girls, with variants and short forms still being created today.
ELISABETH (331), Elisabet, Elizabet, Elisabetta, Elizabel, Eliza, Elyza.

ELKE: (Scandinavian) "Helper of mankind." Short form of Alexandra.

ELLA: Short form of Eleanor and Ellen. Also a French medieval given name meaning "all."
Ellie, Elly, Elle, Ellee, Ellia, Ellesse

ELLEN (245): (English) Variant form of Helen.
Ellyn, Elynn, Elleen (Irish), Ellena, Ellene

ELLYCE: *(ell-EESE)* (English) Variant form of Elias, the Greek form of Elijah. See also Elise and Elyse.
Elyce, Ellice, Ellison

ELMA: (German) "God's protection."

ELNORA: *(el-NOR-ah)* Variant form of Eleanor.

ELOISA: *(ell-o-WEE-sa)* (Spanish/Italian) "Renowned fighter." Variant form of Louise. See also Heloise.
Eloise (English), Eloiza

ELORA: *(eh-LOR-a)* Blend of "El-" and Lora, "God gives the Laurel, the crown of victory." Ellora is a name given to the cave temples of India.
Ellora

ELSA: (German) Short form of Elisabeth.
Elsie, Elsy, Elza

ELSPETH: *(ELLS-peth)* (Scottish) Variant form of Elisabeth.
Elsbeth

ELVIRA: *(ell-VYE-ra* or *ell-VEER-a)* (Teutonic/Spanish) "Elfin."
Elva, Elvia, Elvera, Elvie, Elvina, Elvinia, Elvita

ELYSE (358): *(ell-LEESE)* Variant form of Elise and Elissa. See also Ellyce.
Elysa, Elyssa, Elysse, Elysia

EMANUELE: *(ee-MAN-you-ELL)* (Hebrew) "With us is God"; (Latin) Feminine form of Immanuel. Biblical; a name-title applied to the Messiah.
Emmanuelle, Emanuelle

EMBER: (English) "Anniversary." Usage today may be as a rhyming variant of Amber, or refer to "Ember day," a day in Lent devoted to fasting and prayer.

EMILY (14): (Latin) "Industrious, striving."
Emilia, Emilie, Emilee, Emelia, Emalee, Emmalee, Emmalei

EMMA (174): (English/German) "Whole, complete."

EMMALINE: (German/French) "Hardworking."
Emmeline, Emeline (French), Emmalyn, Emmy

ENID: (Welsh) "Life."

ENRICA: *(ahn-REE-ka)* (Spanish) "Rules her household." Feminine form of Henry.

ERICA (38): (Scandinavian) "Ever kingly." Feminine form of Eric.
ERIKA (63), ERICKA (455), Erikka, Eryka

ERIKO: *(air-EE-koh)* (Japanese) "Child with a collar." "-ko," meaning child, is a frequently used ending in Japanese girls' names.

ERIN (46): (Gaelic) Poetic name for Ireland. Usage as a boys' name has become very rare.
Erinn, Eryn, Erynn, Erinne, Erienne, Erina, Erinna

ERMA: (German) "Complete." See also Irma.

ERNESTINA: "Serious, determined." Feminine form of Ernest.

Ernestine, Erna, Ernesha

ESME: (French) "Esteemed."

ESMERALDA (221): *(ez-mer-AHL-da)* (Spanish) Variant form of emerald, the prized green gemstone.

Ezmeralda, Emerald

ESPERANZA: *(ess-per-AHN-za)* (Spanish) "Hope."

ESTEFANY: *(ess-STEFF-a-nee)* (Spanish) "Crown, wreath." Feminine form of Stephan.

Estefania, Estephanie, Estefani

ESTELLA: *(ess-STEL-a)* (Latin) "Star."

Estelle (French); Estee, Estela, Estelita, Estrella, Estrellita

ESTHER (285): *(ESS-ter)* (Persian) "Myrtle leaf." Biblical; a young Hebrew woman who became the wife of the Persian ruler Xerxes and risked her life to save her people.

Ester (Spanish)

ETHEL: (Teutonic) "Noble."

ETTA: (Teutonic) "Happy." Also a short form of names ending in "-ette" or "-etta," especially Harriette.

Ettie, Etty

EUGENIA: *(you-GEEN-ya)* (Greek) "Well born." Feminine form of Eugene.

Eugenie *(you-ZHAY-nee)* (French), Eugena, Eugina

EULALIE: *(you-LAY-lee)* (Greek) "Sweet-spoken."

Eulalia, Eula, Eulah *(YOU-la)*, Eulia

EUNICE: *(YOU-niss)* (Greek) "She conquers." Biblical; a woman who was noted for being "without hypocrisy."

EUSTACIA: *(you-STAY-sha)* "Productive." Feminine form of Eustace.

EVA (283): *(AY-va* or *EE-va)* (Hebrew) "Living one"; (Latin) Variant form of Eve. Biblical; the first woman. See also Ava.

Eve, Evette, Evetta, Evie, Evita, Evia, Eviana, Evin, Evanna, Evania, Evanee

EVANGELINA: (Greek) "Brings good news."

Evangeline, Evangelyn, Evangela, Evangelia

EVELYN (153): (English/French) Meaning uncertain; a male surname used in this century as a given name for girls.

Evelin, Evalyn, Evelina, Eveline, Evaline, Evalina, Evaleen, Evelyne, Evelynn, Evelynne

EVERLEY: (English) Place name and surname rarely used as a girl's name.

Everly

EVONNE: (Teutonic/French) "Archer's bow." Variant form of Yvonne, from Yves. See also Ivonne.

Evon, Evonna, Evony *(EV-ah-nee)*

F

FABIOLA (463): *(fah-bee-OH-lah)* (Latin) Feminine variant of Fabian, from the Roman family clan name Fabius.

Fabianna, Fabienne (French), Fabianne, Favianna, Faviola, Fabia, Fabra

FAITH (444): (Latin/Greek) "Confidence, trust; belief." A virtue name.

Faythe

FALLON: (Gaelic/Irish) "In charge."

Falon, Fallyn, Falyn, Falynn, Faline

FANNY: Nickname and variant of Frances.

Fannie, Fanni, Fannia, Fanceen, Fantine

FARRAH: (English) "Fair-haired"; (Arabic) "happy."

Farah, Fara (English) "traveler."

FARREN: (English) "Adventurous." Farren and Farrin are in rare use for boys or girls.

Faryn, Farrin, Farryn, Farran, Farron, Faren, Farin, Ferran, Ferryn

FATIMA: *(FAH-tee-mah)* (Arabic) The name of a daughter of the prophet Muhammad; one of the four "perfect women" mentioned in the Koran. See also Aisha, Khadijah and Mary.

Fatimah

FAUSTINE: *(foss-TEEN)* (Latin) "Fortunate one." Feminine form of Faustus. The name of many saints.

FAWN: (English) Literally "young deer." A name from nature.
Fawna, Fawne

FAYE: (English/French) Variant form of Faith.
Fay, Fae, Fayanna

FELICIA (129): *(feh-LEE-shah)* (Latin) "Happy." Feminine form of Felix. Felicity is one of the "virtue" names.
Felisha, Felecia, Felicity, Felicitas, Felicita, Felice, Felisa, Falisha, Feliciona

FERN: A green shade-loving plant. A name from nature.
Ferne

FERNANDA: *(fer-NAHN-dah)* "Adventurous." Feminine form of Fernando.

FIALA: *(fee-AH-lah)* (Czech) "Violet."

FIAMMETTA: *(FEE-a-MET-tah)* (Italian) "A flickering fire."
Fia *(FEE-ah)*

FIDELIA: *(fee-DAYL-yah)* (Latin) "Faithful."
Fidelina, Fidessa

FILOMENA: *(fee-lo-MAY-nah)* (Italian) "Beloved." Variant form of Philomena.

FIONA: *(fee-OWN-nah)* (Gaelic) "Fair."
Fionna *(fee-AHN-nah)*

FLAIR: (French/English) Literally, "style, verve."

FLAVIA: *(FLAH-vee-ah)* (Latin) "Yellow-haired." Feminine form of Flavius, a Roman clan name.

FLOR: (Latin) "Flower"; (Spanish) Variant form of Flora. Roman mythology; Flora was the goddess of flowers.
Flora, Florita, Florinda, Floressa, Floriana, Florida, Floretta, Flori, Florrie, Floria, Fleur (French)

FLORENCE: (Latin) "Flowering." The name of the Italian city.
Florencia (Spanish), Florentina, Florenza (Italian)

FONTANNE: *(fawn-TAN)* (French) "Fountain, spring."

FORTUNA: *(for-TOON-na)* (Latin) Mythology; the Roman goddess of fortune, chance. Also a saint's name.

FRANCES (407): (Latin) "From France." Feminine form of Francis.
Frankie, Franki, Francie, Franci, France, Francia; Francoise (French); Fran

FRANCESCA (491): *(fran-CHESS-ka)* (Italian) Variant form of Frances.
Francisca (Spanish), Franchesca, Franchesa, Franceska, Francheska

FRANCINE: (French) Variant form of Frances.
Francene, Francina, Francena, Francille *(fran-SEEL)*

FREDERICA: (German) "Peaceful ruler." Feminine form of Frederick.
Frederika, Fredrika, Frederica, Fredda, Freddi, Frieda, Freda, Frida

FREYA: *(FREE-ya or FRAY-ah)* Scandinavian mythology; Freya, wife of Odin, was the goddess of love and fertility. Friday is named for Freya.

FRITZI: *(FRIT-zee)* Feminine form of Fritz, a nickname for Frederick.

G

GABRIELA (125): (Hebrew) "God's able-bodied one"; (Latin) Feminine form of Gabriel.
GABRIELLE (148) (French), GABRIELLA (438), Gabriell, Gabriele, Gavrielle, Gabi, Gaby

GAEA: *(GYE-ah)* (Greek) "The earth." The womanly personification of the earth; a Greek earth deity.
Gaia

GAIL: "Joyful." Short form and variant of Abigail. See also Gayle. Gael is a descendant of the ancient Celts, especially in Scotland, Ireland and the Isle of Man.
Gale, Gaila, Gala, Gael, Gaylene

GALATEA: *(gal-ah-TEE-ah)* Greek mythology; Galatea

was a statue loved by Pygmalion and brought to life by Aphrodite.

GALIANA: *(gah-lee-AHN-ah)* (Arabic) The name of a Moorish princess for whom a splendid palace was built in Spain.

GALINA: *(ga-LEEN-ah)* (Russian) Variant form of Helen.

GARDENIA: The flower; a name from nature.

GARNET: (English/French) A dark red gemstone named for the pomegranate that the garnet crystals resemble. Also a surname. See also boys' index.

GAVINA: *(gah-VEE-nah)* (Latin) "From Gabio"; (Spanish) Variant form of Gabinus. A saint's name.

GAYLE: Variant form of Gail. Gala literally means "festive party." See also Gail, and Galen in boys' index.
Gayla, Gala, Galea, Gaylen, Galen, Galena

GEMMA: (Latin) "Gem; a jewel." See also Jemma.
Gemmalyn, Gemmalynn, Gem

GENA: *(JEE-nah)* Variant form of Gina. Other variants listed here are contemporary creations. See also Gina and Genna.
Geena, Genelle *(je-NELL)*, Geneene, Genina, Genie, Genalyn, Genae *(je-NAY)*, Genaya, Geana, Geanndra, Genelle, Genette

GENESIS (480): *(JEN-eh-siss)* (Hebrew) "Origin, birth." Biblical; name of the first book in the Bible. In Catholic tradition, Genisia, Virgin Mary of Turin, is invoked as a protectress against drought.
Genessa, Genisa, Genisia, Genisis

GENEVIEVE (476): *(JEN-a-veeve, ZHAN-vee-ev)* (German/French) "Of the race of women"; (Celtic) "fair, white."
Geneva *(je-NEE-va)*, Geneve, Genevie, Genivee

GENEVRA: *(je-NEV-ra)* (English) Variant form of Guinevere.
Ginevra (Italian)

GENNA: Short form. See also Ginny, Jenna and Jenny.

GEORGIA: *(JOR-jah)* "Farmer." Feminine form of George.

GEORGINA: Diminutive and variant form of Georgia.
Georgiana, Georgianna, Georgeanne, Georgegina, Georgette (French); Georjette

GERALDINE: "Rules by the spear." Feminine form of Gerald.
Geraldina, Geralyn, Geralynn

GERANIA: *(jer-RANE-yah)* (Contemporary) Variant form of Geranium, the flower.

GERI: Feminine form of Gerry. Variant forms listed here are contemporary blends of Geri plus Erica and Marilyn.
Gerri, Gerica, Gerika, Gericka, Geralyn, Geralynn, Gerrilyn

GERMAINE: *(jer-MAYNE)* (French) "People of the spear." Feminine form of German.

GERTRUDE: (German/French) "Spear's strength."

GHISLAINE: *(zhee-LAYNE)* (German/French) "Pledge."

GIANNA: *(jee-AHN-a)* (Italian) Feminine form of Jane, from John.
Gia, Giana, Gianina, Giannina, Gianella, Gianara, Gionna, Geonna

GIGI: *(JEE-jee* or *zhee-ZHEE)* (French) Nickname for Gabrielle.

GILANA: *(je-LAHN-ah* or *gil-ann-ah)* (Hebrew) "Joy."

GILDA: *(JILL-da* or *GEEL-da)* (English) "Golden." Also a short form of Teutonic names containing "gilde."

GILLIAN: *(GILL-ee-an* or *JILL-ee-an)* (Latin) "Jove's child." Variant form of Juliana. See also Jillian.

GINA (153): *(GEE-nah)* Short form of names ending in "-gina." Often used as a prefix in blended names. See also Gena and Jina.
Ginamarie, Gini

GINGER: (English) Nickname for Virginia. Literally "pep, liveliness," referring to the pungent root used as a spice.

GINNY: Short form, usually of Virginia. See also Genna.

Ginnie, Genny, Ginnette, Ginnelle, Ginna, Ginnilee, Ginelle, Gineen

GIORDANA: (Italian) Feminine form of Jordan. From the Jordan River. See also Jordan.

GIOVANNA: *(jo-VAHN-ah)* (Italian) Feminine form of John.
Giovana, Giavanna, Geovana, Geovanna

GISELLE: *(je-ZELL)* (French) "Pledge."
Gisela (Spanish); Gisell, Gisele, Gizelle, Gisella, Giselda

GITA: *(JEE-ta or GE-ta)* (Slavic) Short form of Margaret.

GIULIANA: *(JOO-lee-AHN-na)* (Italian) "Jove's child." Feminine form of Julian.
Giulia

GLADYS (463): *(GLAD-iss)* (Welsh) Variant form of Claudia.
Gladis

GLENDA: (Welsh) "Fair, good."
Glinda, Glynda

GLENNA: (Gaelic) "Valley." Use of Glenn for girls is probably due to actress Glenn Close. See also Glynnis.
Glenn, Glenne, Glyn, Glynn, Gleniesha

GLORIA (182): (Latin) "Glory."
Glorianne, Gloriana, Glorianna, Glory, Gloribel, Gloribell

GLYNNIS: (Welsh) "Valley girl." See also Glenna.
Glynis, Glenys, Glynice, Glynae *(glen-NAY)*, Glennis

GOLDIE: The precious metal as a given name or nickname. Golda is a variant made prominent by Golda Meir, the late premier of Israel.
Golda

GRACE (164): (Latin) "Favor; blessing." One of the virtue names referring to God's grace. Mythology; the Three Graces were goddesses of nature: Aglaia (Brilliance), Thalia (Flowering) and Euphrosyne (Joy).
Graciela, Gracielle, Gracella, Gracelynn, Gracelynne, Grecia *(GRAY-sha)* (Spanish), Gracia, Gracie, Gracee, Grayce

GREER: (Scottish/Irish) "Watchful." Variant form of Gregory.

GRETA: (German/Scandinavian) "Pearl." Short form of Margaret.
Gretta, Gretel (German/Dutch)

GRETCHEN: (German) Variant form of Margaret.

GRISELDA (424): (gri-ZELL-da) (Latin/German) "Gray, gray-haired." Boccaccio's use of the name in a tale about an exceptionally patient wife has made the expression "patience of Griselda" proverbial.
Gricelda, Grizelda, Gryselda, Griselle, Grisella; Grizel (Scottish)

GUADALUPE (162): (gwah-da-LOO-pay) (Spanish/Arabic) "Wolf valley." Refers to Mary as Mexico's "Our Lady of Guadalupe." Usage: boys 15%, girls 85%.

GUINEVERE: (GWIN-a-veer) (Welsh) "Fair one." The name of King Arthur's queen; an early form of Jennifer.
Guenevere, Gwenevere, Genevra (je-NEV-ra) (Italian)

GWEN: (Welsh) "Fair, blessed."
Gwyn, Gwenna, Gwenda, Gwendi, Gweneth, Gwenyth, Gwyneth, Gwynne, Gwynn, Gwinn

GWENDOLYN: (Welsh) "Fair-haired."
Gwendolynn, Gwyndolyn, Gwyndolynne, Gwendelyn

GYPSY: Nickname derived from "Egyptian," used to describe migratory tribes of dark Caucasians who came from India to Europe in the fifteenth century.
Gipsy, Gitana (gui-TAH-na) (Spanish)

H

HADARA: (Hebrew) "Adorned with beauty."
Hadarah

HADASSAH: (ha-DAHS-sa) (Hebrew) "Myrtle tree." Biblical; the Persian Queen Esther's Hebrew name.

HADLEY: (English) "Field of heather." Surname in rare use as a girl's name. It was the name of Hemingway's first wife.

HAIDEE: *(HAY-dee)* (Greek) "Well-behaved."
Haydee, Hadiya (Swahili) "gift"

HALEY (150): *(HAY-lee)* (English) "Field of hay." The surnames listed here as variants undoubtedly came into popular use as girls' names due to actress Hayley Mills. HAYLEY (299), HAILEY (349), Haylee, Haylie, Hailee, Haleigh

HALIA: *(hah-LEE-ah)* (Hawaiian paraphrase) "Remembrance of a loved one."

HALIMA: (Swahili) "Gentle."
Haleema

HALLIE: *(HAL-lee)* "From the Hall."
Halli, Halley

HANA: (Japanese) *(ha-NAH)* "Flower"; (Hawaiian) *(HAH-nah)* "work." Also the Hawaiian form of Hannah. See also Hannah.

HANAKO: *(han-NAH-koh)* (Japanese) "Flower child."

HANNAH (40): (Hebrew) "Favor, grace." Biblical; mother of the prophet Samuel. See also Hana.
HANNA (414), Hanah (Israeli), Hannalee, Hanalise

HARLENE: (English) "Meadow of the hares." Feminine form of Harley.
Harleen, Harlee, Harlie

HARMONY: (Latin/Greek) "Unity, concord; musically in tune." Mythology; Harmonia was the daughter of Aphrodite.
Harmonie, Harmoni, Harmonee, Harmonia

HARRIET: "Rules her household." Feminine form of Harry, from Henry.
Harriett, Hattie

HASINA: *(hah-SEE-nah)* (Swahili) "Good."

HAYLEY: See Haley.

HAZEL: *(HAY-zel)* "The hazel tree." A name from nature.
Hazell

HEATHER (17): The English name for an evergreen flowering plant that thrives on peaty barren lands, as in Scotland. Heather was one of the flower names that first came into use in the late 19th century. By the mid-20th century Heather became increasingly popular, first in England, then in the US. Since the 70's it has been one of the most popular girls' names.

HEDDA: (German) "Warfare." Variant form of Hedwig.
Hedy *(HED-ee)*

HEIDI (175): *(HYE-dee)* (German/Swiss) "Noble." Short form of Adelheid.
Heide, Heidie

HELEN (299): (Greek) "Shining light." Greek mythology; the abduction of Zeus's mortal daughter Helen resulted in the Trojan War. Ellen, Elaine, Eleanor, Eileen and Aileen are among the many variant forms of Helen.
Helena *(HEL-e-nah)*, Helene *(heh-LAYNE)* (French); Helaine, Helaina *(heh-LAYNE-ah)*, Heleena, Helana; Halina (Polish); Helenna

HELGA: *(HEL-gah)* (Scandinavian) "Holy, devout."

HELOISE: *(HEL-oh-ees)* (French) "Renowned fighter." Variant form of Eloise, a feminine form of Louis. See also Eloisa.

HENRIETTA: "Rules her household." Feminine form of Henry.
Hetta

HERA: *(HARE-ah)* Greek mythology; Hera (Juno to the Romans) was the Queen of Heaven, wife of Zeus and the goddess of marriage.

HERMINIA: *(air-MEEN-ee-ah)* (Latin) Feminine form of Herman. A saint's name.
Hermine, Hermione *(her-MY-oh-nee)*

HESPER: *(HESS-per)* (Greek) "Evening star."

HESTER: "Myrtle leaf." Variant form of Esther.
Hettie, Hetta

HILDA: (German) "Warfare." Scandinavian mythology; Hildegard was a Valkyrie, sent by Odin to escort battle heroes to Valhalla.
Hildagarde, Hildegard, Hilde, Hulda

HILLARY (274): *(HILL-a-ree)* (Latin/Greek) "Joyful, glad."
HILARY (288), Hilaire *(hih-LARE)* (French)

HOLLIS: (English) "The holly tree." Very rare usage for boys or girls.
Hollace

HOLLY (96): (English) "The holly tree." A name often used for a daughter born on or near Christmas.
Hollie, Holli, Hollee, Hollyann

HONEY: (English) "Nectar." Nickname and name of endearment.

HONOR: *(AHN-er)* (Latin) Literally, one's good name and integrity. A virtue name.
Honora *(ah-NORE-ah)*, Honore *(ah-NORE)* (French), Honour (English)

HOPE (384): (English) "Expectation, belief." A virtue name.

HORTENCIA: *(or-TEHN-see-ah)* (Latin) "Garden"; (Spanish) Variant form of Hortense. Very rarely used today.
Hortensia, Hortense

HOSANNA: *(ho-ZAN-ah)* (Greek/Hebrew) A prayer of acclamation and praise for salvation.

HYACINTH: *(HYE-a-cinth)* (Greek) "Alas." Name of a flower and a color that ranges from sapphire to violet. A saint's name. See also Jacinda.

I

IANTHE: (Greek) "Violet flower." Mythology; sea nymph, a daughter of Oceanus. Poetry; a name for delicate, fairy-like girls.
Iantha

IDA: (Scandinavian/English) "Diligent."

IDALIA: *(eye-DAYL-yah)* (Greek) "Behold the sun."

IDELLE: *(eye-DELL)* (Celtic/Welsh) "Bountiful."
Idella, Idelisa

IGRAYNE: *(ee-GRAYNE)* Mythology; in Arthurian legend, the mother of Arthur.
Igraine, Ygraine

ILANA: *(ee-LAHN-ah)* (Hebrew) "Tree." See also Elana.

ILENE: *(eye-LEEN)* Variant form of Eileen (Helen).
Ileen, Ilena, Ila

ILIANA (491): *(ee-lee-AHN-ah)* (Spanish) Variant form of Elena.
Ileana, Ileanna, Ileane

ILIMA: *(eye-LEE-mah)* (Hawaiian) "The flower of Oahu."

ILONA: (Hungarian) "Shining light." Variant of Helen.

ILSE: *(ILL-sah)* (German) Short form of Elizabeth.
Ilsa

IMELDA: *(ee-MEL-dah)* (Teutonic/Spanish) "Powerful fighter." The name of a fourteenth-century Spanish saint.

IMOGENE: *(EYE-mah-jeen)* or *(IM-ah-jeen)* (Latin) "Blameless, innocent."
Imogen

INA: *(EYE-nah* or *EE-nah)* Diminutive ending of many names, used as an independent name.

INDIA: *(IN-dee-ah)* The name of the country and the state (Indiana) used as given names.
Indiana, Indee, Inda

INDIGO: *(IN-dee-go)* The dark blue color used as a given name.

INDIRA: *(in-DEER-ah)* (Hindi) Hindu mythology; Indra is the god of heaven and thunderstorms.
Indra, Indria

INEZ: *(ee-NEZ)* (Spanish) "Chaste." Variant form of Agnes. See also Ynes.
Ines (Italian), Inessa (Russian), Inetta

INGA: (Scandinavian) "Ing's abundance." Feminine form of Ing. See also Ingrid.
Inge

INGRID: (Scandinavian) "Ing rides." Norse mythology; Ing, god of the earth's fertility, rides the land each year to prepare it for spring planting. See also Inga.

IOLA: *(eye-OH-lah)* (Greek) "Violet-colored dawn."

IOLANA: *(ee-oh-LAH-nah)* (Hawaiian) "To soar like the hawk."

IONE: (Greek) "Violet."
Iona

IRENE (238): *(eye-REEN* or *eye-REE-nee)* (Greek) "Peace." The three-syllable pronunciation is mostly British.
Irena (Slavic); Irayna, Irenee; Irina (Russian); Iriana

IRIS (476): (Greek) "Rainbow." A flower name. Greek mythology; Iris was a messenger-goddess who rode rainbows between heaven and earth. See also Rainbow.
Irisa (Russian), Irisha *(eye-REE-sha)*

IRMA (449): (German) "Complete." Short form of names like Ermintrude. See also Erma.

ISABEL (264): (Latin/English) Variant form of Elizabeth.
Isabelle, Isabeau (French); Isabell (English); Isobel (Scottish); Isabela, Isabelita, Isabella (Spanish/Portuguese); Izabel (Portuguese)

ISADORA: *(iz-a-DOR-ah)* (Greek) "Gift of Isis." Feminine form of Isadore; Notable name bearer: Isadora Duncan, acclaimed American dancer in the 1920s.

ISHA: *(ee-sha)* (Hebrew) "Woman." See also Aisha.

ISIS: *(EYE-siss)* (Egyptian) Mythology; the most powerful of all the female goddesses; sister to Osiris.

ISMAELA: *(ees-mah-AY-la)* (Hebrew) "God listens"; (Spanish) Feminine form of Ishmael.

ITALIA: *(ee-TAL-ya)* (Latin) "From Italy."

IVANA: *(ee-VAH-na)* Feminine form of Ivan, from John.
Ivanna, Ivania, Ivannia

IVETTE: (Spanish) Variant form of Yvette.

IVONNE: *(ee-VON)* Variant form of Yvonne. See also Evonne.
Ivonna

IVORY: *(EYE-vree)* Literally, a reference to the creamy-white color, or to the hard tusk used for carving fine art and jewelry.

IVY: *(EYE-vee)* (English) Name from nature; an evergreen climbing ornamental plant.
Ivey, Ivie, Iva, Ivalyn, Ivyanne

J

"JA-"names: (Contemporary) With pronunciation emphasis on the second syllable. The second syllable may or may not begin with a capital. See also "Je-" and "Jo-" names, Janae, Janessa and Jameelah.
Jacodi, Jaconda, JaCoya, JaDeana, Jadine, Jakeisha, Jakisha, Jakiya, Jakira, Jalaine, Jalaina, Jalayna, Jalena, Jaleese, Jaleesa, Jalicia, Jalisa, Jalissa, Jalessa, Jamaine, Jamari, Jamesha, Jamisha, Jameisha, Jamiesha, Jamika, Jameka, Janika, Janique, Janecia, Janeesa, Janeese, Janeil, Janeille, Janielle, Janisa, Janisha, Janora, Jacquese, Jacquetta, Jarae, Jarai, Javonna

JACEY: Phonetic form based on the initial "J.C."
Jaci, Jacee, Jacie, Jacy, Jaicee, Jaycee, Jaycie, Jacelyn, Jacilyn

JACINDA: (Greek) "Hyacinth." See also Hyacinth.
Jacinta (Spanish/Portuguese), Jacenia.

JACKIE (444): Short form of Jacqueline and its variants.
Usage of Jackie: boys 25%, girls 75%.
Jacque, Jackee, Jacqui, Jacquie, Jacki, Jacquetta

JACLYN (172): *(JAK-lin)* (Contemporary) Two-syllable phonetic form of Jacqueline.
JACKLYN (454), Jacklynn, Jaclynn, Jackleen, Jakleen, Jaklyn

JACQUELINE (49): *(JAK-kwa-lin; jak-LEEN; zhak-leen; ZHAK-ah-leen; JAK-ah-lin; JAK-lin)* (French) Feminine form of James and Jacob. See also Jackie and Jaclyn.
JACQUELYN (209), Jaqueline, Jacquelyne, Jacquelynn, Jacqualine, Jacqualyn, Jacquelynne, Jacquelina, Jacqueleen, Jaquelyn, Jaquelin, Jaquelynn, Jacalyn, Jacalynn

JADE (250): The gemstone and the color (green) used as a given name, and contemporary variants.

Jada, Jadira, Jadee, Jady, Jaeda, Jaida, Jaide, Jayde, Jaydra

JAE: Feminine variant form of Jay; some variants follow the pattern of "Ja-" names.

Jaelana, Jaeleah, Jaeleen, Jaena, Jaenelle, Jaenette, Jaya, Jayleen, Jaylene, Jaylee, Jaylynn

JAIRA: (Spanish) "Jehovah enlightens." Feminine form of Jairus.

JAMAICA: (ja-MAY-ka) The name of the West Indies island as a given name.

JAMEELAH: (Arabic) "Beautiful." See also "Ja-" names.

Jameela, Jamila (Somali), Jamilah, Jamilla, Jamilia, Jemila, Jahmila, Jamelia, Jamille

JAMIE (50): (Scottish/Spanish) Variant form of James. Jamie and Jaime are frequently used for both boys and girls. Usage: (Jamie) boys 12%, girls 88%; (Jaime) boys 82%, girls 18%.

JAIME (334) (Spanish/Scottish), Jaimee, Jaimi, Jaimelynn, JAIMIE (450), Jami, Jamee, Jamey, Jaymie, Jaymee, Jamia, Jamielee, Jamilyn, Jamison

JAN: (Dutch/Slavic) Variant form of John. Usage: boys 71%, girls 29%.

JANA: (Polish/Czech) Feminine form of Jan, from John, with contemporary variant forms.

Janna, Jannie, Janny, Janah, Jannah, Janne, Janica, Janceena, Janalee, Jannalee, Janalyn, Janalynn

JANAE (463): (ja-NAY) An especially favored "Ja-" name with contemporary variations based on Jane or Jean. Janai is a biblical male name with the meaning "God has answered."

Janay, Janai, Janaye, Jannae, Jeanae, Jeanay, Jenae, Jenay, Jenee, Jenai, Jennae, Jennay, Jenaya, Janaya, Janais

JANE (349): (Hebrew) "Jehovah has been gracious, has shown favor"; (English) Variant form of Joan, from John. This classic name has produced many variant forms, and new blends and compounds are still being formed. See also Joan.

Janie, Jayne, Janee, Janey, Jaina, Jayna, Jaynie, Jayni; Jenica (Rumanian); Jenika

JANELLE (242): (Contemporary) Variant form of Jane. See also Jeanelle.

Janel, Janell, Jannelle, Janella

JANESSA: (Contemporary) Blend of Jan and Vanessa. See also "Ja-" names.

Janesse, Jannessa, Janissa

JANET (149): (Scottish) Variant form of Jane, from the French Jeanette.

JANETTE (378), Jannet, Janett, Janetta, Janeth, Janneth

JANICE (463): Variant form of Jane.

Janiece, Jannice, Janise, Janeece, Janicia, Janis, Jannis

JANINE: Variant form of Jane. See also Jeannine.

Janina, Janeen, Janene, Jannine, Jannina

JASMINE (38): *(JAZ-min* or *jaz-MEEN)* (Arabic/French) A flower name, from the earlier form Jessamine. See also Yasmin and Jazlyn.

JASMIN (198), Jasmyn, Jasmyne, Jasmina, Jasmeen, **JAZMIN** (241), **JAZMINE** (299), Jazmyn, Jazzmyn, Jazmyne, Jazzmine, Jessamine, Jessamyn

JAVIERA: *(HA-vee-ER-ah)* (Spanish) "Bright." Feminine form of Xavier.

JAXINE: Variant form of Jacinta. May also be a contemporary blend of Jack and Maxine.

JAZLYN: (Contemporary) Variant form of Jasmine, influenced by Jocelyn and the musical term jazz. See also Jasmine.

Jazzlyn, Jazlynn, Jaslyn, Jaslynn, Jasleen, Jazzalyn, Jasmaine, Jazmaine, Jasminique, Jazmina, Jazma, Jazzy.

"JE-" names: (Contemporary) With pronunciation emphasis on the second syllable. The second syllable may or may not begin with a capital. See also "Ja-" and "Jo-" names.

Jelani, Jelisa, Jelissa, Jemelle, Jenessa, Jeondra, JeRae, JeRaine, Jeree, Jeressa, Jerona

JEAN: (French) Variant form of John. Usage: boys 43%, girls 57%.

Jeanne, Jeana, Jeane, Jeanna, Jeanice, Jeena, Jeannie, Jeanie, Jeanee

JEANELLE: (Contemporary) Variant form of Jean. See also Janelle.

Jeannell, Jeannelle, Jenelle, Jenell, Jenneil, Jenella

JEANETTE (166): *(je-NET)* Diminutive form of Jean. A favorite name in France and Scotland, frequently used today in America. See also Janet.

JEANNETTE (431), Jeanetta, Jenette; Jennet (Scottish)

JEANNINE: (French) Variant form of Jane or Jean. See also Janine.

Jeanine, Jeanina, Jenine, Jenina, Jennine

JELENA: *(ya-LAY-na* or *je-LEE-na)* (Russian) "Shining light." Variant form of Helena.

JEMIMA: *(je-MYE-mah)* (Hebrew/Arabic) "Little dove." Biblical; one of the three daughters of Job (see also Keziah and Keren), renowned as the most beautiful women of their time.

Jemimah

JEMMA: Feminine variant form of James, also a short form of Jemima. See also Gemma.

JENEVIEVE: *(JEN-nah-veeve)* Phonetic form of Genevieve and Geneva.

Jennavieve, Jenavieve, Jenneva, Jeneva

JENNA (85): (Contemporary) Variant form of Jenny and Jennifer, used in blends and compound names. See also Jenny and Genna.

Jennah, Jennabel, Jennalee, Jennalyn, Jennarae, Jennasee, Jenesi

JENNIFER (6): (Welsh) "Fair one"; (English) Form of Guinevere. In Arthurian tales, Guinevere was Arthur's queen. Jenifer is a spelling variant used especially in Cornwall. See also Jenna.

Jenifer

JENNY (169): Diminutive and variant form of Jane and Jennifer. See also Genna and Jenna.

Jennie, Jenni, Jeni, Jinny, Jinni, Jen, Jennyann, Jennylee, Jennilee, Jenalee, Jennilyn, Jenilynn, Jenalyn, Jenalynn, Jena, Jeneen, Jenene, Jenetta, Jenita, Jennis, Jenice, Jeniece, Jenise, Jenarae, Jennessa, Jennika.

JEORJIA: Phonetic variant form of Georgia.

Jorja

JEOVANA: *(joe-VAH-nah)* (Contemporary) Feminine form of Giovanni or variant of Jovana. See also Jovita.

Jeovanna *(joe-VAN-ah)*

JERALDINE: Variant form of Geraldine.

JERALYN: (Contemporary) Blend of Jerry and Marilyn.

Jerelyn, Jerilyn, Jerilynn, Jerralyn, Jerrilyn

JERI: Feminine form of Jerry.

Jerri, Jeralee

JERICA: *(JARE-ah-ka)* (Contemporary) "Strong, gifted ruler." Blend of Jeri and Erica.

Jerrica, Jerika, Jerrika

JERUSHA *(je-ROO-sha)* (Hebrew) "He has taken possession." A biblical name that James Michener used for the missionary heroine in his novel *Hawaii*.

JESSENIA: *(jes-SEE-nee-ah or ya-SEE-nee-ah)* (Spanish) Meaning uncertain; may be variant form of Esenia (Latin) meaning "of the Essenes." See also Yesenia and Llessenia.

Jesenia, Jasenia

JESSICA (1): (English/Hebrew) Feminine form of Jesse. In *The Merchant of Venice*, Shakespeare is said to have devised this name for Shylock's daughter, a young Jewish woman who elopes with Lorenzo and converts to Christianity. See also Jessie.

Jessika

JESSIE (270): Short form of names beginning with "Jess-." Also an English variant form of the male name Jesse. Usage: boys 61%, girls 29%. "Jess-" is a popular prefix in contemporary girls' names, especially blends that sound like Jocelyn. See also Jessica.

Jessi, Jessye, Jessa, Jessalyn, Jessalynn, Jesselyn, Jessilyn, Jesslyn, Jesslynn, Jessamae, Jessina, Jessana, Jessandra, Jeslyn, Jesirae, Jessarae, Jeziree

JETTA: (English) Refers to jet, an intensely black, shiny gemstone.

JEWEL: (English/French) ''Playful.'' Literally, a precious gem.

Jewell, Jewelle, Jewelene, Jewelissa, Jewelyn

JEZEBEL: *(JEZ-a-bel)* (Hebrew) ''Where is the prince?'' Rarely used as a given name, due to the notoriety of the biblical Jezebel, a queen of Israel condemned by God.

JIANA: *(jee-AHN-ah)* (Contemporary) Phonetic form of Gianna, an Italian form of Jane.

Jianna

JILL (319): Short form of Jillian. See also Gillian.

Jyl, Jyll, Jilly

JILLIAN (157): *(JIL-ee-an)* (English) ''Jove's child.'' Variant form of Gillian, from Julian. See also Gillian.

Jillianne, Jilliann, Jilliane, Jillianna, Jilian, Jillanne, Jillayne *(jil-LANE)*, Jillesa, Jillene, Jyllina

JIMI: Feminine form of Jimmy, the short form of James.

Jimmi

JINA: *(JEEN-ah)* (African) ''Named child.'' See also Gina.

Jineen

JISELLE: *(ji-ZELL)* (Contemporary) ''Pledge.'' Phonetic form of Giselle.

JO and ''JO-'' names: (Contemporary) With emphasis on the second syllable. Jo is an independent name and short form of names like Joanna and Josephine, frequently used as a prefix in blends and compound names. See also ''Ja-'' and ''Je-'' names, Jolene and Jodelle.

Jobeth, Jobelle, Jodean, Joetta, Joette, Joleesa, Jolisa, Jolise, Jolissa, Jolynn, Jolyn, JoLyn, Jolinda, JoMarie, Jonelle, Jonell, Jonetia, Jonessa, Joniece, Jonique, Jonisa, Joquise, Jorene, Josanna, Josanne, Joselle, Jozelle, Jozette, Jovelle

JOAN: (English) Feminine form of John. See also Jane.

JOANNA (119): (Latin/English) Variant form of Joan. Biblical; the name of several woman who were disciples of Christ.

JOANNE (496), Joana, Joann, Joan, Joanie, JOHANNA (334) (Hebrew/German), Johannah, Joeanna, Joeanne.

JOAQUINA: (wah-KEE-na) (Spanish) Feminine form of Joaquin.

JOCELYN: (JOSS-lin or JOS-sa-lyn) (English/French) Medieval male name adopted as a feminine name. Josalind is a contemporary blend of Jocelyn and Rosalind.

Jocelynn, Jocelyne, Joceline, Jocelina, Joscelyn, Josalyn, Josalynn, Josilyn, Joslyn, Joslin, Jozlyn, Josalind

JODELLE: (jo-DELL) (French) Surname used as a given name. See also "Jo-" names.

Jodell, Jo Dell

JODI: Feminine form of nicknames for Joseph and Jude. Usage of Jody: boys 37%, girls 63%. The similar sounding Joda is the Hebrew name of an ancestor of Christ.

Jody, Jodie, Jodee, Joda

JOELLE: (jo-EL) (French) "Jehovah is God." Feminine form of Joel.

Joella, Joellen, Joellyn, Joell

JOHNNA: (Contemporary) Feminine form of John and Jon. Johnnie is rarely used as a girl's name.

Johnette, Johnetta, Johnelle, Johnnie, Jonette, Jonetta, Jonalyn, Jonalynn, Jonna, Jonnie, Joni, Jonni, Jonita, Jonay, Jonell, Jonnelle

JOLENE: A well-established "Jo-" name.

Joleen, Joline, Jolena, Jolina, Jolleen, Jollene

JOLIE: (zho-LEE) (English/French) "Cheerful, pretty."

Joli, Jolee, Joleigh (joe-LEE)

JONINA: (yo-NEE-na) (Israeli) "Little dove."

JORDAN (84): (JOR-dan) (Hebrew) "Downflowing." The river in Palestine where Jesus was baptized, used as a given name since the time of the Crusades. Usage: boys 78%, girls 22%. See also Giordana.

Jordana (Spanish), Jordyn, Jourdan, Jordane, Jordaine (French), Jordanne, Jordann, Jordanna *(jor-DAN* or *jor-DAN-ah)*, Jordyn, Jori, Jorry

JORGINA: Either a phonetic spelling *(jor-GEEN-ah)* or the Spanish form *(hor-HEE-nah)* of Georgina, with contemporary variants.

Jorgeanne, Jorgelina (Spanish), Jorjana *(jor-JAN-ah)*, Jorga

JOSEPHINE (382): (French) Feminine form of Joseph.

Josephina, Josefina (Spanish), Josefa (German)

JOSIE: Diminutive form of Josephine.

Josette (French), Josina, Josey

JOVITA: *(hoe-VEE-tah)* (Spanish) Feminine form of Jovian, from Jove, the Roman Jupiter, "father of the sky." A saint's name; see Jovan in the boy's index. See also Jeovana.

Jovena, Jovina, Jovana, Jovanna

JOY (419): (Greek/French) "Rejoicing." A virtue name.

Joya; Joie (French); Joi, Joia, Joyanna, Joyann, Joyanne, Joyelle

JOYCE (455): (Latin) "Cheerful, merry."

Joycelyn, Joycelynn, Joyceanne.

JUANITA (442): *(wah-NEE-tah)* (Spanish) Diminutive form of Juana, from John.

Juana *(WAH-na)*, Juanetta, Juanisha

JUDITH (399): (Hebrew) "The praised one"; (English) Feminine form of Judah.

Judy (462), Judi, Judie, Judeana, Juditha

JULIANA (319): (Latin) "Jove's child." Feminine form of Julius.

JULIANNE (427), Julieann, Juliann, Julieanne, Juliane, Julianna, Julieanna

JULIE (92): (French) Feminine form of Julian. Julie and Julia are popular today and have numerous contemporary variants.

⌐ JULIA (101), Julee, Juli, Juleen, Julena, Julina (Spanish), Julisa, Julissa, Julyssa, Julisha, Julita, Julayna, Juliza

JULIET: *(joo-lee-ET)* (English/French) Variant form of Julia. Shakespeare used the name Juliet twice, in *Romeo and Juliet* and *Measure for Measure*.
Julieta (Spanish); Juliette (French); Julietta (Italian)

JUNE: (Latin) "Young." Roman mythology; Juno was the protectress of women and of marriage, hence June is known as the bridal month.
Junel, Junelle, Junette, Junae

JUSTINE (171): *(juss-TEEN)* (French) "Just, upright." Feminine form of Justin.
Justina (Latin); Justyne, Justene, Justeen, Justeene; Jestine, Jestina (Welsh)

K

"KA-" names: (Contemporary) Blends of "Ka-" plus various endings, with pronunciation emphasis on the second syllable. See also "Ke-" and "Ki-" names.
Kalana, Kalania, Kalea, Kaleah, Kaleila, Kalia, Kalisha, Kaleesha, Kalisa, Kalissa, Kalyssa, Kamara, Kamari, Kamesha, Kaneisha, Kanisha, Karaina, Karisa, Karisha, Karysa, Kasaundra, Kashana, Kashonna, Katana, Katasha, Katisha, Katiya, Katessa, Katrice, Katrisa, Kavonna

KACIE: (Contemporary) Kacie and its variants are probably phonetic forms of the initials "K.C." or variants of the Irish name Casey, meaning "alert, vigorous." In rare use for boys and girls. See also Kasey.
Kacey, Kaci, Kaycee, Kaycie, Kayci, Kacy, Kacee, K.C., Kayce, Kacia, Kaesha

KADY: *(KAY-dee)* Rhyming variant of Katy or Cady.
Kadie, Kadi, Kadee, Kaedee, Kadia, Kadian, Kadienne

KAI: *(kye)* (Hawaiian) "The sea." Usage: boys 82%, girls 18%. See also Kay.

Kaia

KAILA (455): (Israeli) "The laurel crown"; (Hawaiian) *(kye-EE-lah)* "style." See also Kayla and Kylie.

Kaela, Kaylah, Kailah, Kaelah, Kayle

KAITLIN (118): Phonetic form of the Irish name Caitlin, from Catherine. See also Katelyn, Katherine and Caitlin.

KAITLYN (123), Kaitlynn, Kaitlan, Kaytlyn, Kaitleen

KALANI: *(kah-LAH-nee)* (Hawaiian paraphrase) "The sky; chieftain." See also Keilani.

Kaloni, Kalanie, Kailani *(kye-LAH-nee)* "sea and sky"

KALEI: *(kah-LAY-ee)* (Hawaiian) "The flower wreath; the beloved."

KALI: *(KAH-lee)* (Hawaiian) "Hesitation." The Hindu Kali, wife of Shiva, is a goddess symbolizing the essence of destruction. See also Kallie.

KALIFA: *(kah-LEE-fah)* (Somali) "Chaste; holy."

KALILAH: *(kah-LEE-lah)* (Arabic) "Darling, sweetheart."

KALINA: *(ka-LEE-na)* (Polish/Czech) A flower name and place name. Kalena is the Hawaiian equivalent of Karen.

Kalena, Kaleen, Kalene, Kaleena

KALINDA: *(ka-LEEN-da)* (Sanskrit) "The sun." Hindu mythology; a reference to the mountains of Kalinda or the sacred Kalindi River.

Kalynda, Kalindi

KALLAN: (Scandinavian) "Flowing water." See also Callan.

KALLIE: Short form of names beginnng wth "Kal-." Kalle is a Finnish variant form of Carol, "strength." See also Kali and Callie.

Kalli, Kalle, Kally, Kahli, Kallita

KALLISTA: *(ka-LISS-ta)* (Greek) "Beautiful." See also Calista.

KAMBRIA: *(KAM-bree-a)* Variant form of Cambria, referring to Wales.

KAMEA: *(kah-MAY-ah)* (Hawaiian) "The one (and only)."

Kameo (see also Cameo)

KAMELIA: *(ka-MEEL-ya)* See Camelia.
Kamella

KAMERON: Usage: boys 85%, girls 15%. See also Cameron.
Kamryn, Kamron, Kamrin, Kamren

KAMI: (Japanese) "Lord." Also short form variant of names beginning with "Kam-."
Kammi, Kammie, Kamlyn, Kamia, Kamielle

KAMILLE: (Arabic) "Perfection." Also a variant form of Camille.
Kamilah, Kamila, Kamilla, Kamillia

KANANI: *(kah-NAH-nee)* (Hawaiian) "The beautiful one."

KANDACE: See also Candice.
Kandice, Kandis, Kandyce, Kandiss, Kandy, Kandi, Kandee

KANI: *(KAH-nee)* (Hawaiian) "Sound." Also the Hawaiian equivalent of Sandy.

KAPRI: See also Caprice.
Kaprice, Kapricia, Kaprisha

KARA (127): (Scandinavian) Short form of Katherine. See also Cara and Keri.
Karah, Karrah, Karalyn, Karalynn, Karalee, Karalie, Kaira, KARI (236), Karie, Karrie, Karri, Karee, Kary, Karianne, Kariann, Karianna, Kariana, Karielle

KAREN (88): (Danish) Short form of Katharine. See also Karina, Keren and Caryn.
Karin (Norwegian); Karyn, Karon, Karren, Karrin, Karryn, Karan

KARIDA: (Arabic) "Virgin."

KARIMA: *(ka-REE-mah)* (Arabic) "Generous; a friend." Feminine form of Karim.

KARINA (108): *(ka-REE-na)* Variant form of Katherine. See also Karen and Carina.
Karena (Scandinavian), Karyna, Kareena, Kareina, Karenah, Karene, Kareen, Karine, Karinna, Karinne

KARIS: *(KARE-iss)* (Greek) "Grace." Phonetic form of Charis.

KARISMA: *(ka-RIZ-ma)* "Favor, gift." See also Charis.

KARISSA (313): (Greek) "Very dear." See also Carissa.
Karessa, Karyssa, Karisa, Karess

KARLA (190): (German) "Womanly, strength." Feminine form of Karl. See also Carla.
Karly, Karli, Karlie, Karlee, Karley, Karleigh, Karlesha, Karleen, Karlene, Karline, Karlina, Karlyn, Karlen, Karlin

KARMA: (Sanskrit) "Actions are fate." In Buddhism and Hinduism, Karma is the inevitable effect of actions during life.

KARMEL: "Fruitful orchard." See also Carmela.
Karmelle

KARMEN: Variant form of Carmen.
Karmina

KAROL: (Hungarian) "Womanly." Variant form of Carol.
Karole, Karolyn, Karoline, Karolina

KASEY (295): (Irish) "Alert, vigorous." Contemporary variant form of Casey. Usage: boys 22%, girls 78%. See also Casey and Kacie.
Kasie, Kasi, Kasia

KASHMIR: *(kazh-meer)* The name of a state in India.
Kasmira, Kazhmir, Kasha

KASSANDRA (339): (Greek) "Unheeded prophetess." Contemporary variants are based on some of the preferred pronunciations of Sandra. See also Cassandra.
Kasandra (Spanish), Kassondra, Kasondra, Kasaundra, Kazandra

KASSIA: *(ka-SEE-ah)* (Polish) Short form of Katharine. Also a variant form of Cassia *(KASH-ah)*.

KASSIDY: "Curly-headed." Usage: boys 20%, girls 80%. See also Cassidy.

KASSIE: Short form of names that begin with "Kas-," especially Kassandra. See also Cassie.
Kassi, Kassy, Kassie

KATELYN (100): Phonetic form of Caitlin, an Irish form of Katherine. Kateline is a medieval English form. See also Kaitlin and Caitlin.

Katelynn, Katelin, Kateline, Katelinn, Katlin, Katlyn, Katlynn, Katlynne, Kitlyn.

KATHERINE (27): (Latin/Greek) "Pure." A name in use at least since the third century A.D. The early Latin forms Katerina and Caterina became Katharine and Catherine. The French Cateline and English Catlyn came into wider use during the medieval period, and variant forms multiplied. Preference in modern times is for the "K" spelling, which is closest to the original Greek versions. See also Katie, Kathy, Kaitlin, Katelyn, Catherine, Cathy and Caitlin.

KATHRYN (65), Kathrine, Kathryne, Kathrynn, Kathrina, KATHLEEN (103) (Irish); Kathlene, Kathlena, Kathleena, KATRINA (117) (Scottish/German); Katrin (Iceland); Katrine, KATHARINE (384), Katheryn, Katharyn, Katherina; Katarina (Hungarian); Katerina (Russian); Katriane (French); Katriana; Katrya (Russian); Katria, Katalina; Katina (Greek); Katreena, Katrice

KATHY (375): Short form of Katherine.

Kathie, Kathia, Kathi; Kathe (German); Kathlyn, Kathlynn

KATIE (54): The most popular English short form of Katherine.

KATE (337), KATY (431), Kati (Hungarian); Katee, Katey; Katya (Russian); Katia (Spanish); Katianne, Kaydee, Kaydi; Kata (Czech); Kat, Katilyn

KATRIEL: *(ka-tree-ELL).* (Hebrew) "My crown is God."

KAY: (English/Scandinavian) "Keeper of the keys." Kay is not a short form of Katherine. Once a name for boys, Kay is now used in America almost exclusively for girls, often as a middle name. See also Kayla, Kai, Kaylee and Kaylyn.

Kaye, Kayanna, Kayana

KAYA: *(KAH-yah)* (Japanese) "Adds a place of resting."
Also an African name of uncertain meaning.

KAYLA (21): (Contemporary) Variant form of Kay. Popularity of the name in recent times may be influenced by
the character Kayla on the daytime TV drama "Days of
Our Lives." See also Kaila, Kaylee, Kaylyn and Cayley.

KAYLEE (306): (Contemporary) Variant form of Kay and
Kayla. See also Cayley.
Kayleigh, Kaylie, Kayley, Kayli, Kaylei, Kaylea, Kayleen, Kaylene, Kailee, Kailey, Kaley, Kalie, Kaleigh, Ka-
lee, Kaeley, Kaeli, Kaeleigh, Kaelee, Kaelie

KAYLYN: Variant form of Kay and Kayla. See also Cailin,
and in the boys' index, Kaelan.
Kaylin, Kaylen, Kaylynn, Kaylan, Kalyn, Kalynn, Kalin,
Kalen, Kalan, Kaelyn, Kaelin, Kaelynn, Kailyn, Kai-
lynne, Kailin, Kailan, Kayleen, Kaelene, Kaileen,
Kailene, Kayleena

"KE-"names: Contemporary, with pronunciation emphasis on the second syllable. See also "Ka-" and "Ki-"
names.
Keandra, Keaundra, Keona, Keonna, Keosha, Kevonda,
Keana, Keeana

KEALA: *(kay-AH-lah)* (Hawaiian) "The pathway."

KEELY: (Irish) "Lively; agressive." Variant form of Kelly.
Keeley, Keelie, Keelyn, Keila, Keilah

KEENA: Possibly a contemporary feminine variant form of
Keane (Irish/English), meaning "quick, brave."

KEIKI: *(kay-EE-kee)* (Hawaiian) "Child."

KEIKO: *(KAY-koh)* (Japanese) "Be glad"; "rejoicing
child."

KEILANI: *(kay-ee-LAH-nee)* (Hawaiian) "Glorious chief."
Keilana; "glory, calmness." See also Kalani.
Keilana

KEISHA (410): *(KEE-sha)* Short form of Lakeisha, developed from Leticia, a variant form of the eighteenth-
century name Letitia. See also Leticia.
Keshia, Kisha, Kesha, Keesha, Kiesha, Kecia

KEITHA: "Woodland." Feminine form of Keith.

KELBY: (Scandinavian/Gaelic) "Place by the fountain; spring." Very rarely used for girls.

KELLEN: (German) Habitation name that may derive from the name Charles. Kellen and its variants may also be variants of Kelly. Usage: boys 86%, girls 14%.
Kellyn, Kellan

KELLY (42): (Gaelic/Irish) "Lively, aggressive." Usage: boys 8%, girls 92%.
KELLI (178), KELLIE (297), KELLEY (331), Kellee, Kellye, Kelleen, Kelleigh, Kellyann, Kellyanne, Kelianne.

KELSEY (313): (English/Irish) "Brave." Popular preference for Kelsey and its variants may have been influenced by names like Chelsea and Casey.
KELSIE (291), Kelsi, Kelsy, Kelsee, Kelsa, Kellsey, Kellsie, Kelcie, Kelcey, Kelcy

KENDALL (414): (English) "Royal valley." Surname referring to Kent, England. Usage: boys 27%, girlsl 73%.
Kendal, Kendahl, Kendyl, Kindall, Kyndall, Kyndal

KENDRA (120): (Contemporary) "Royal defender." Blend of Ken and Sandra or Andrea.
Kenna, Kindra, Kenndrea, Kendria, Kyndra

KENISHA: *(ken-NEE-sha)* (Contemporary) "Beautiful woman." Blend of Ken and Iesha.
Kennesha, Keneisha, Keneshia

KENYA: Name of the mountain and country in Africa, used as a given name.

KENZIE: "The fair one." Short form of McKenzie.
Kenza, Kenzy, Kinzie

KEREN: (Hebrew) Biblical; one of the three daughters of Job. See also Karen.
Kerrin, Keryn

KERRY: (Irish/Gaelic) "Dusky, dark." Usage of Kerry: boys 36%, girls 64%. See also Kara.
Keri, Kerri, Kerrie, Kera, Keriann, Kerianne, Keriana, Kerianna, Kerilyn, Kerrianne, Kerra

KETIFA: *(ke-tee-fah)* (Arabic) "Flowering."

KETURAH: *(ke-TOO-rah)* (Hebrew) "Sacrifice." Biblical; the second wife of Abraham.

KEVINA: *(KEV-i-nah)* (Contemporary) "Handsome child." Feminine form of Kevin.
Kevia, Keva

KEZIAH: *(ke-ZYE-ah)* (Hebrew) "Cassia; sweet-scented spice." Biblical; one of the three fair daughters of Job.
Kezia, Kesiah

KHADIJAH: *(kah-DEE-jah)* Muhammad's first wife, named in the Koran as one of the four perfect women. (The others were Fatima, Mary, and Aisha.)
Kadija, Kaja

KHRISTINA: Variant form of Christin and Christina. See also Kristina, Krista and Krystal.
Khristyna, Khrystina, Khrystine, Khristine, Khrystyne, Khristeen, Khrystyn, Khristin, Khristen, Khristyana, Khristie, Khristy, Khrysta, Khristal, Khrystal, Khris, Khrystalline

"KI-" names: (Contemporary) Blends of "Ki-" plus variant endings, with pronunciation emphasis on the second syllable. See also "Ka-" and "Ke-" names.
Kiana, Kianna, Kiani, Kianni, Kiauna, Kiahna, Kiandra, Kiandria, Keiana, Keianna, Keanna, Kiauna, Kijana, Kiona, Kionah, Kionna, Kioni

KIARA (253): *(kee-AR-ah)* (Contemporary) Rhyming variant of Ciara and Tiara. Kiera *(KEER-ah)* is a feminine form of Kieran, (Irish/Gaelic) "dusky; dark-haired." See also Kira and Kyra.
Kiera, Kierra, Keira, Kiarra

KIKI: *(kee-kee)* (Spanish) Pet form of Enriqueta, from Henrietta.
Kiko

KILEY: (Irish/Gaelic) "Good-looking." See also Kylie
Kilee

KIM : (English) Short form of names beginning with

"Kim-." Usage: boys 18%, girls 82%. Also a Vietnamese name, "precious metal; gold," used for both boys and girls.

KIMBERLY (28): (English) "King's wood." Place name and surname.

Kimberley, Kimberlee, Kimberli, Kimberlyn, Kimberleigh, Kymberly, Kymberlee, Kymberlie, Kymberli, Kym

KIMI: *(kee-mee)* (Japanese) "Happiness"; "upright; righteous."

Kima

KIMIKO: *(KEE-mee-koh)* (Japanese) "Righteous child"; "heavenly child."

KINA: *(KEE-nah)* (Hawaiian) "China." Also the Hawaiian equivalent of Tina.

KIOKO: *(kee-OH-koh)* (Japanese) "Child born with happiness."

KIRA (481): (Russian) "Lady." See also Kiara and Kyra.

Kiri, Kirra, Kiran, Kiriana

KIRBY: (English) "Church farm." Place name and surname; boys 32%, girls 68%.

KIRSTEN (180): (Scandinavian/Scottish) Variant form of Christine.

Kirstin, Kiersten, Kerstin, Kirstyn, Kyrstin, Kierstin, Kirstine; Kirstie, Kirsty, Kirsti, Kirstee (Scottish)

KISHI: *(kee-shee)* (Japanese) "Happiness to the earth." Surname.

KITRA: (Hebrew) "Crowned one."

KITTY: Pet name for Katherine.

Kitlyn

KLARISSA: (German) "Bright, shining and gentle." Variant form of Klara. See also Claire.

Klara, Klaire

KODI: "Helpful." See also Codi.

Kodie, Kodee

KOEMI: *(koh-AY-mee)* (Japanese) "A little smile."

KOLBY: "Dark; dark-haired." See also Colby.

Kolbie

KOLINA: *(ko-LEEN-ah)* (Swedish) Variant form of Katharine.

KORA: (Greek) "Maiden." See also Cora.
Korena, Koren, Koreen, Koral, Koralise, Korissa, Koressa

KORI: See also Cory.
Korie, Kory, Korey, Korri, Korrie, Koree, Korry

KORIN: "Maiden." See also Corinne.
Korrin, Korinne, Koryn, Korynn, Korynne, Korine, Korina, Korinna, Korrine, Koreena, Korrina

KOURTNEY: Variant form of Courtney.
Kortney

KRISANDRA: Variant form of Chrisann and Chrysandra.
Krisanne, Krishana

KRISTA (144): (Czech) Variant form of Christine; also a variant spelling of Christa. See also Christa and Christy.
KRISTY (294), KRISTI (311), Kristie, Krysta (Polish), Krysti, Krystie, Krissa, Kryssa, Krissa, Krissi

KRISTEN (56): Variant form of Christian. See also Christen, Khristina and Kirsten.
KRISTIN (72); Kristyn, Krysten, Krystin, Kristan, Krystyn, Krystynn, Kristeena

KRISTINA (70): (Scandinavian) Variant form of Christina. See also Khristina.
Krystina (Czech); Krystyna (Polish); Krysteena, Kristena, Kristyna, Kristeena, KRISTINE (207), Krystine, Kristeen, Kristyne, Kristian (Danish); Kristiana, Kristianna, Kristiane, Kristianne, Krystiana, Krystianna

KRIZIA: *(KREE-zha)* (Polish) Short form of Krystyna. See also Krista.
Krysia

KRYSANTHE: (Greek) "Golden flower." See also Chrisann.

KRYSTAL (94): Variant form of Crystal. The "K" reflects the Greek spelling, *krystallos*. See also Crystal.
KRYSTLE (392), Kristal, Kristel, Kristell, Krystel,

Krystelle, Kristella, Krystalyn, Krystalynn, Kristalyn, Kristalena, Krystabelle, Kristabelle

KUMIKO: *(KOO-mee-koh)* (Japanese) "Companion child; drawing together."

KYLIE (135): "Chief." A feminine form of Kyle. See also Kaila and Kiley.

KYLA (419), Kylah, Kylee, Kyley, Kyli, Kyleigh, Kylea, Kylene, Kyleen, Kylianne, Kylin

KYOKO: *(kee-OH-koh)* (Japanese) "Mirror."

KYRA: *(KEER-rah* or *KYE-rah)* "Enthroned." Variant form of Cyra, feminine form of Cyrus. See also Kiara, Kira and Cyrah.

Kyrie (Greek) "lady," Kyria, Kyrene

L

"LA-"names: (Contemporary) Blends of "La-" plus various endings, with pronunciation emphasis on the second syllable, which may or may not begin with a capital. Lakeisha, Latasha, Latisha and LaToya are listed separately. Lacacia, Lachelle, Lacinda, Lacretia, Lacoya, Laday, Ladonya, LaDonna, LaGina, Lajuana, LaJoyce, Lakendra, Lakia, Lalani, Lalita, Lanae, Lanai, Lanelle, Lanesha, Lanessa, Laniece, Lanetta, Lanette, Lanika, Lanisha, Lanita, Lanora, Laporsha, Laquana, Laquanda, Laquesha, Laquita, Larae, LaRay, LaRee, LaRhonda, Laronda, Larisha, Lasandra, LaShae, Lashanda, LaShawn, Lashawnda, LaTanya, Latavia, Latina, Latonia, Latonya, Latoria, Latrice, Latreece, LaTricia, Latrisha, Lavette, Lavonda, Lavonna, Lavonne, LaWanda

LACEY (145): French nobleman's surname carried to England and Ireland after the Norman Conquest.

Lacy, Lacie, Lacee, Laci, Laycie, Lace, Lacene, Lacina, Lacyann, Laciann

LAEL: *(LAY-el)* (Hebrew) "Belonging to God." A biblical male name rarely used for girls.

LAILA: *(LAY-lah)* (Persian/Arabic) "Dark; born at night." Variant form of Leila. See also Leila.
Layla (Swahili), Laylah

LAINA: (English) "Path, roadway." Feminine variant form of Lane.
Layna, Layne, Laine, Laney, Lanie, Lainie, Lania

LAKEISHA: *(lah-KEE-shah)* (Contemporary) Lakeisha and its variant forms are rhyming variants of Leticia. See Leticia, Latisha and Keisha.
Lakesha, Lakisha, Lakeshia, Lakiesha, Laquisha

LALIA: *(LAH-lee-ah)* (Spanish) Short form of Eulalie. Lala is the Hawaiian equivalent of Lara.
Lali, Lala, Lalla (Arabic) "lady"

LANA: *(LAN-ah* or *LAHN-ah)* "Fair, good-looking." Short form of Alana. Also (Hawaiian paraphrase) "afloat; calm as still waters."
Lanna, Lanice, Lanni

LANDRA: *(LAHN-drah)* (Spanish) Short form of Landrada, a saint's name meaning "counselor."

LANI: *(LAH-nee)* (Hawaiian) "The sky; heavenly; royal."

LARA: *(LAR-ah)* (Latin) "Protection." From *lares*, referring to the individual gods of Roman households, the protectors of home and fields. Lara is popular in Russia as a girl's name, and is also a Spanish surname and place name.
Laralaine, Laramae, Larinda, Larina, Larita, Lari

LARAINE: Variant form of Lorraine.
LaRayne, Larraine, Lareina (Spanish) "the queen," Larena

LARISSA (414): Variant form of Lara.
Larisa (Russian), Laryssa, Laressa

LATASHA (444): *(la-TAH-sha)* A "La-" name based on Natasha, "birthday." See also Natasha and Tasha.
Latashia, Latoshia

LATISHA: *(la-TEE-sha)* A "La-" name developed from a variant form of the medieval name Letitia. See also Lakeisha, Leticia and Tisha.

Laticia, Latesha, Lateisha, Letitia

LATOYA (475): (Spanish) "Victorious one." Derived from a short form of Victoria, LaToya has been made familiar today by singer LaToya Jackson. See also Toya.

LAURA (25): (Latin/English) "The laurel tree." In use for at least eight centuries, Laura has many variant forms. See also Lora and Laurel.

Laurie, Laureen, Laurene, Laurena, Lauraine, Lauralee, Lauralyn; Lauretta (Italian); Laurita (Spanish); Laurinda, Laurana

LAUREL (405): Literally, the laurel tree, also called the sweet bay tree; symbolic of honor and victory. See also Laura.

Laurelle, Laural, Lauriel

LAUREN (12): (Latin/English) "From Laurentium, the place of the laurel trees." Feminine form of Lawrence. The earliest feminine form of the name was Laurentia, dating from the time of the early Romans; Lauren has come into use only in this century.

Lauryn, Laurenne

LAVERNE: *(la-VERN)* (French) "Woodland."

Lavern

LAVINA: *(la-VEEN-ah)* (Spanish) From Lavinia (Latin), a Roman given name of uncertain meaning.

Lavinia, Levina, Luvina, Luvenia

LEA: *(LAY-ah)* (Hawaiian) The goddess of canoe makers. Also a Spanish form of Leah.

LEAH (102): (Hebrew) Biblical; Leah was Jacob's first wife, mother of Dinah and six of his twelve sons. See also Lee.

Lia (Italian/Spanish), Leatrice

LEALA: *(lee-AL-ah)* (French) "Loyal, faithful."

Leola

LEANDRA: *(lee-AN-dra)* (Greek) "Lioness." Feminine form of Leander.

LEANNA (399): (Gaelic) "Loving." See also Liana

LEANNE (499), Leann, Leeann, Leana, Leeanne, Leianna

LECIA: *(LEE-sha)* Short form of names like Alicia or Felecia, used as an independent name.
Lisha

LEDA: *(LEE-da)* (Greek) Mythology; queen of Sparta, mother of Helen of Troy.
Leyda, Leida, Lyda, Leta

LEE: (English) "Meadow." Surname. Usage: boys 87%, girls 13%. Lee is often chosen as a middle name.
Leigh

LEILA: *(LEE-la, LAY-la or LYE-la)* (Persian/Arabic) "Dark." Lela is a French soundalike name referring to loyalty. See also Laila and Lyla.
Leilah; Lelia (Latin); Leela, Lela, Leyla

LEILANI: *(lay-LAH-nee)* (Hawaiian) "Child of heaven; heavenly flowers."
Lei "wreath of flowers," Leia

LENA: Name ending used as an independent name. See also Lina.
Leena

LEONIE: *(LAY-o-nee or lay-OH-nee)* (French) "Lion, lioness. Feminine form of Leon.
Leona, Leonela, Leondra, Leondrea, Leonda

LEONORA: (Italian) "Shining light." Variant form of Eleanor.
Leonor, Leonore (French) Lenore (German), Lenora (Russian), Leora

LEONTYNE: *(LEE-an-teen or LAY-an-teen)* Feminine variant of Leon made familiar by operatic singing star Leontyne Price.
Leontina

LEORAH: *(lee-OR-ah)* (Israeli) "Light to me."
Leora

LESLIE (99): *(LESS-lee or LEZ-lee)* (Scottish) A name of royalty. Once considered a male name, Leslie now is used almost entirely for girls (96%). The Lezlie spelling preserves the original Scottish pronunciation.
Lesley, Leslee, Lezlie

LETICIA (204): *(le-TEE-sha)* (Latin) "Great joy." From the medieval name Letitia. See also Keisha, Lakeisha and Latisha.
Letitia, Letisha, Letty, Laetitia

LEVANA: *(le-VAHN-ah)* (Latin) "Raise up." Roman mythology; Levana was goddess/protectress of the newborn.
Livana

LEXANDRA: *(lex-ANN-dra)* (Contemporary) Variant form of Alexandra.
Lexann, Lexi, Lexie, Lexine; Lexa (Czech)

LIANA: *(lee-AHN-ah)* Short form of names like Jillian and Juliana. See also Leanna.
Lia, Lianna, Lianne, Liane, Liann, Lian, Li (Chinese)

LIBBY: Diminutive of Elizabeth.

LIBERTY: (English) Literally, freedom.
Librada (Spanish)

LICIA: *(LEE-sha)* Short form of Alicia.

LIDA: *(LEE-dah or LYE-dah)* (Russian) Diminutive name ending used as a given name; also a variant of Lydia.

LIESL: *(LEES-ul or LEE-zul)* (German) Short form of Elizabeth.
Liezel, Liezl

LILIANA (223): (Latin) Variant form of Lillian, from Lily, the flower name.
LILLIAN (398), Lilian, Lilliana, Lilianna, Lillianna; Liliane (French); Lilianne, Lilliann, Lilliane

LILIBETH: Blend of Lily and Elizabeth.
Lilibet, Lilybeth, Lilybell

LILY (438): A flower name; the lily is a symbol of innocence and purity as well as beauty.
Lilia (Latin); Lilly, Lillie; Lilli (German); Lili (French)

LIN: (Chinese) Family name. Also an English short form for names beginning with "Lin-," in rare use for boys and girls.

LINA: An ending of names like Carolina, used as an independent name. See also Lena.
Lyna

LINDA (122): (German/English) "Lime tree; linden tree." Originally derived from linde, a Germanic name element referring to the lime tree, today Linda is associated by most parents with the Spanish word *linda*, meaning "beautiful." See also Lynda.
Lindy, Lindee, Lindi, Lindalee

LINDEN: The linden tree.

LINDSEY (51): (Scottish/English) Meaning uncertain; may refer to a lake or to a place of linden trees. Lindsay is a surname of some of the major Scottish and English noble families. See also Lyndsey.
LINDSAY (71), Linsey

LINNEA: *(le-NAY-a)* (Scandinavian) A name from nature; in Sweden, a small blue flower.
Linnae, Lenae, Lynae, Lynnae, Linna

LINNETTE: (French/English) "Songbird." See also Lynette.
Linnet

LIORA: *(lee-OR-a)* Variant form of Laura and Lora.

LISA (53): *(LEE-sa)* "My God is bountiful." Short form of Elisabeth. See also Liza.
Lise (French)

LISANDRA: *(le-SAN-dra)* (Greek) "Liberator." Feminine form of Lysander. Lissandra is an Italian short form of Alexandra; Lizandra is a contemporary blend of Liz and Alexandra; Lizann, a blend of Liz and Ann.
Lissandra *(li-SAHN-dra)*, Lizandra, Lizann, Lizanne, Lysandra

LISSA: Short form of names like Melissa, Lissandra and Alyssa.
Lyssa

LITA: *(LEE-tah)* Diminutive ending now used as an independent name.
Leta

LIV: (Latin) Short form of Olivia. Liv is also a Scandinavian given name made familiar by actress Liv Ullman.

Livia is an ancient Roman name as well as being a short form of Olivia.

Livia, Lyvia

LIZA: *(LYE-za* or *LEE-za)* Short form of Elizabeth and Eliza. See also Lisa.

Liz, Leeza, Lyza, Lizzie

LIZETTE (283): (Contemporary) Variant form of Elizabeth.

Lissette, Lisette (French), Lysette, Lyzette, LIZBETH (448), LIZETH (498), Lizbet, Lisbet, Lisabet, Lyzbeth, Lizabeth, Lisbeth, Lisabeth

LLESENIA: (Latin) "Of the Essenes." Variant form of Esenia. See also Jessenia and Yesenia.

LOIDA: *(LOY-dah)* Variant form of Leda.

Loyda

LOIS: (Greek) "Pleasing." Biblical; a first-century Christian, the grandmother of Timothy.

LOLA: (Spanish) Short form of Dolores.

Lolita

LONDON: (English) Place name and surname.

LONI: *(LAH-nee)* Variant form of Alona. Usage of Lonnie: boys 78%, girls 22%.

Lona *(LOH-na)*, Lonnie, Lonni, Lonna

LORA: Variant form of Laura. See also Lori and Loretta.

Lorah, Lorinda, Lorita, Loree, Loranna, Loreana

LORELEI: *(LOR-a-lye* or *LOR-a-lay)* (German) A rocky cliff on the Rhine River, dangerous to boat passage, has been poetically personified as the Lorelei, whose singing lures men to destruction.

Loralei

LOREN: Variant form of Lawrence, from the Latin Laurentius, meaning "from Laurentium." Usage of Loren: boys 53%, girls 47%. See also Lauren.

Lorin (French); Loryn, Lorren, Lorrin, Lorryn

LORENA (238): *(lo-REEN-ah* or *lo-RAY-nah)* Variant form of Laura or Lora. See also Lorraine.

Lorene, Lorenia, Loreen, Loreene, Lorenna, Lorrina

LORENZA: *(lo-REN-zah)* Feminine form of Lorenzo, from Lawrence.

LORETTA: Diminutive form of Laura or Lora. Loreta is a saint's name.
Lorette, Loreta

LORI (345): Variant of Lora.
Lorianne, Loriann, Lorian, Loria, Loriana, Loriel, Lorilee, Lorilynn, Lorinda, Loris

LORNA: (Scottish) Feminine form of Lorne, from Loren, made familiar by the heroine of Blackmoore's novel *Lorna Doone.*

LORRAINE: Name of the province in France, and a family name of French royalty. See also Laraine and Lorena.
Lorraina, Loraine, Loraina, Lorayne

LOTUS: A flower sacred to the Hindus and Chinese; Buddha is always depicted as sitting on a lotus.

LOUISE: (French) Feminine form of Louis, ''renowned fighter.''
Louisa, Louiza, Louella

LOURDES: (Basque) Miracles of healing are attributed to the site in France where the Virgin Mary reportedly appeared to a young girl. See also Bernadette.

LUANA: *(loo-AHN-ah)* (Hawaiian) ''Content, happy.'' Also contemporary blends based on Lou and Ann, Anna.
Luann, Luanna, Luanne, Luanda, Louann

LUCIA (414): *(loo-CEE-ah)* (Latin) ''Light, illumination.'' Feminine form of Lucius.
LUCY (419) (English), Lucie, Luciana, Lucianna (Italian), Lucienne, Lucette (French); Luci; Lucita (Spanish)

LUCILLE: *(loo-CEEL)* (French) Diminutive form of Lucia.
Lucila (Spanish); Lucilla (Italian); Luciela, Lucilia; Lucienne, Lucile (French)

LUCINE: *(loo-CEEN)* (Latin) ''Illumination.'' Mythology; name of the Roman goddess of childbirth, giver of first light to the newborn. Also a reference to Mary as the Lady of the Light; see Luz.
Lucina, Lucena (Spanish), Lucinda, Lucinna

LUCRECIA: *(loo-KREE-shah)* The name of a Roman matron who committed suicide in public protest against dishonor. See also Crecia.
Lucretia, Lucrece (French)

LUISA: *(loo-EE-sah)* (Spanish) ''Renowned fighter.'' Feminine form of Louis.
Luiza, Luisana, Luzelena, Luella (Spanish)

LULU: (Swahili) ''Precious''; (Tanzanian) ''pearl''; (Hawaiian) ''calm, peaceful; protected.'' Also a pet form of names like Louise and Louella.

LUMINA: *(loo-MEEN-ah)* (Latin) ''Brilliant, illuminated.''

LUNA: *(LOO-na)* (Latin) ''The moon.''

LUPITA: *(loo-PEE-tah)* Short form of Guadalupe.
Lupe

LUZ (471): *(looz)* ''Almond tree.'' Biblical; an early name of the town of Bethel. Also a reference to Mary as ''Our Lady of Light''; see Lucine.
Luziana, Luzelena, Luzette

LYDIA (291): (Greek) ''From Lydia.'' Biblical; a Christian woman called ''a seller of purple.''
Lidia

LYLA: See also Leila.
Lila, Lilah

LYNDA: See also Linda.
Lyndi, Lyndee, Lyndall

LYNDSEY (479): See also Lindsey.
Lyndsay, Lyndsie, Lynsey, Lynzee, Lynzie, Lynsie

LYNETTE: (English/French) Variant form of Linnette, or a diminutive of Lynn. In the Arthurian tales, Lynette accompanied Sir Gareth on a knightly quest. See also Lynn and Linnette.
Lynnette, Lynnet, Lynelle, Lynessa

LYNN: (Gaelic) ''Lake, pool.'' Used as a short form, an independent name (especially middle name) and as a feminine ending in many name blends, like Kaylyn. See also Lynette.

Lynne, Lyn, Lynna, Lynlee, Lynley.

LYRIC: (Latin/French) "Of the lyre." Literally, the words of a song.

Lyrica, Lyra

M

MABEL: (English) "Lovable." Short form of Amabel.

Mable, Maybell, Mabelle (French)

MACHIKO: *(MAH-chee-koh)* (Japanese) "Child who learns truth; beautiful child." Machiko is the name of the current empress of Japan.

MACKENZIE (291): (Gaelic/Scottish) "Son of Kenzie; fair, favored one." Usage: boys 27%, girls 73%. See also McKenzie, "Mc-" names and Kenzie.

MACY: (English/French) From a medieval male name, possibly a form of Matthew or a reference to the mace, a medieval weapon.

Maci, Macey, Macie, Macee

MADELINE (206): *(MAD-a-linn)* (French) "Woman from Magdala"; (English) Variant form of Madeleine. See also Magdalena.

Madeleine *(mad-LAYNE)*, Madelaine, Madelon (French); Madalyn, Madalynn, Madelyn, Madelynn, Madilyn; Madalena (Spanish); Madelena, Madelina, Madelene, Madalene, Maddie, Maddy; Madia, Madina, Madena (Spanish); Malena (Scandinavian)

MADISON (192): (English) Surname derived from Matthew, "gift of Jah," or Matilda, "strong fighter." The mermaid heroine Madison in the hit film *Splash* probably influenced the adoption of the surname as a girl's name. Usage: boys 6%, girls 94%.

MADONNA: (Italian) "My lady." A form of respectful address, like the French *madame*. Also used to signify the Virgin Mary, or a work of art depicting her as a mother. See also Donna and Mona.

MAEKO: *(mye-EE-koh)* (Japanese) "Truth child."

MAEMI: *(mah-AY-mee)* (Japanese) "Smile of truth"; "true smile."

MAEVE: *(ma-EEVE)* (Irish) Maeve, the legendary warrior queen of ancient Connacht, is described in the *Tain*, the Celtic equivalent of the *Iliad*, as "tall, fair . . . carrying an iron sword."

MAGDA: (German) Short form of Madeline.

MAGDALENA: (Spanish/Czech) "Woman from Magdala." Variant form of Madeline. Biblical; Mary Magdalene came from the Magdala area near the Sea of Galilee.
Magdalen, Magdalene

MAGGIE (370): Short form of Margaret; usage as an independent name has increased due to a revival of interest in "old-fashioned" names.
Maggy, Maggi

MAGNOLIA: A name from nature; the magnolia flower.

MAHALA: *(mah-HAH-la)* (American Indian) "Woman."
Mahalia

MAHINA: *(mah-HEE-nah)* (Hawaiian) "Moon, moonlight." The Hawaiian equivalent of Diana, goddess of the moon.

MAI (471): (French) "May." Roman mythology; Maia (source of the name May for the calendar month) was the goddess of spring growth. Maiya *(MY-ah)* is a Japanese surname meaning "rice valley." See also May and Maya.
Maia, Maiya, Mae, Maelee, Maelynn

MAIDA: (English) "Maiden, Virgin." Maita *(mah-EE-tah)* (Spanish)

MAIRA (387): See Mayra.

MAISIE: Nickname for Margaret or Marjorie.

MAJESTA: *(MAJ-ess-ta* or *ma-JESS-ta)* (Latin) "Royal bearing, dignity."
Majesty, Maja

MALANA: *(ma-LAH-nah)* (Hawaiian) "Buoyant, light."
Malina "calming, soothing"

MALIA: *(ma-LEE-ah)* (Hawaiian) Variant form of Mary. Also a Spanish variant form of Maria.

Malea, Maleah, Maleia

🖉 MALLORY (163): (English/French) English surname that came into great favor as a girl's name during the eighties and completely eclipsed its former quiet use as a boy's name. The role of the daughter named Mallory on the TV series "Family Ties" was no doubt the major influence in bringing the name into popularity.
Malorie, Mallorie, Malori, Mallori

MAMIE: Short form of Mary and Miriam. See also Mimi.
Mayme

MANDISA: *(man-DEE-sah)* (African) "Sweetness."

MANDY (463): Short form of Amanda.
Mandi, Mandie, Manda, Mandalyn

MANON: *(man-AWN)* (French) Diminutive form of Marie.

MANUELA: *(mahn-WAY-lah)* (Spanish) "With us is God." Feminine form of Manuel.

MARA: *(MAHR-ah)* (Russian/Czech) Variant form of Mary or Mark. See also Maureen.
Maralinda, Maraquina

MARCELLA: (Latin) "Of Mars." Feminine form of Marcellus. Mythology; Mars, the Roman god of fertility, for whom the spring calendar month March was named, came to be identified with the Greek god Ares, god of war. See also Marcia and Maricela.
Marcelle, Marchelle (French), Marcelina, Marceline, Marcelyn, Marcelline, Marcellina, Marcelinda

MARCIA: *(MAR-sha)* (Latin) "Of Mars." Feminine form of Marcus. See also Marsha and Marcella.
Marcy, Marci, Marcie, Marcena, Marciana, Marcianne, Marcila, Marcine

MARGARET (138): (Greek) "Pearl." A saint's name. Historical; the name of nine queens of England, Scotland, France and Austria. See also Marjorie.
MARGARITA (329) (Spanish), Marguerite (French); Margret, Margrete (Scandinavian); Margareta, Margarete, Margarette; Margita (Czech/Polish); Madge, Margie, Margeen, Margette, Meg, Meggie

MARGO: (Hungarian) Variant form of Margaret.

Margot, Margaux, Margeaux (French)

MARI: Variant form of Mary; also a favored prefix for blending with other names. See also Maribel and Maria.

MARISOL (220) (Latin) "Mary *soledad*; Mary alone," Maricruz (Latin) "Mary of the Cross," Marycruz, Marilu, Marilou, Marilena, Marilene, Marilee, Maribeth, Marilisa, Maridel, Marita

MARIA (35): (Latin) Variant form of Mary, popular with both Spanish and non-Spanish cultures. Marie, the French variant, was the preferred form of Mary in England until about the time of the Reformation. Mariah *(ma-RYE-ah)* is quietly but steadily used today. Maria and Marie are very often blended with other names and suffixes. See also Mary and Mari.

MARIE (257), Maree (French); Marya (Slavic); Mariah, Marielena, Marialena, Marialinda, Marialisa, Marieanne, Mariko; Marika (Czech)

MARIANA (384): (Latin) Variant form of Mary. Shakespeare gave the name Mariana to a woman noted for her loyalty in *Measure for Measure*. See also Mary and Miriam.

Marianne, Marian, Marianna, Mariann; Mariane (French); Maryan, Maryon (English surname forms); Marien (Dutch); Mariam; Maryam (Greek); Marianda

MARIBEL (221): "Beautiful Marie." Blend of Mari and Belle. See also Mary.

Maribell, Maribelle, Maribella

MARICELA (360): (Spanish) Variant form of Marcella.

MARISELA (365), Maricella, Maricelia, Maricel

MARIELA: (Spanish/French) Diminutive form of Marie.

Mariel, Mariella, Marielle, Mariele, Marietta, Mariette

MARIGOLD: (English) "Mary's gold," a reference to the flower and to the mother of Jesus.

MARIKO: *(mah-REE-koh)* (Japanese) "Ball, circle."

MARILLA: "Shining sea." Variant form of Muriel.

Marilis, Marella

MARILYN (378): (English) Blend of Marie or Mary and Lyn.

Marilynn, Marylynn, Marylin, Marylyn, Maralyn, Marlyn

MARINA (248): *(mah-REE-nah)* (Latin) "Of the sea."

Marin, Maryn, Marena, Mareen, Mareena, Marinna, Marinella, Marinelle, Marinda

MARISE: *(mah-ree-say)* (Japanese) "Infinite, endless; torrent." Surname.

MARISSA (73): "Of the sea." Variant form of Marie or Maris.

MARISA (244) (Spanish/Swiss); Mareesa, Marysa; MARITZA (316) (German); Mariza; Marisha (Russian); Maryssa, Maressa; Maryse (Dutch); Maris, Marisabel, Maricia, Merissa, Meris

MARJAN: (Polish) Variant form of Mary.

Marjanne, Marjon

MARJORIE: (English) Variant form of the French Margerie, from Margaret.

Marji, Marja, Marjo, Margerie, Margery (English)

"MARK-" names: (Contemporary) Feminine names that probably are based on Mark, though Marketa is a Czech form of Margaret. See also Marquise.

Markie, Markee, Markia, Marketa, Markita, Markeda, Markeeta, Markeia, Markeisha, Markesha, Markisha, Markiesha, Marqui, Marquee, Marquel

MARLA: Variant form of Marlene or Marlo. Also used as a prefix to form other variants. See also Marlee.

Marlo, Marlette, Marlisa, Marlise, Marliss, Marlissa, Marlyssa, Marlyse, Marlys

MARLEE: (English) "Marshy meadow." May also be used as a variant form of Marlene. See also Marla.

Marley, Marlie, Marleigh

MARLEN: Feminine form of Marlon or variant of Marlene. Marlin is sometimes used for boys also.

Marlyn, Marlin, Marlynn, Marlenne

MARLENE (231): *(mar-LEEN* or *mar-LAYNE)* Variant form

of Madeline. Some contemporary names are spelled
phonetically to ensure the desired pronunciation.

Marlena, Marleen, Marleene, Marleena, Marlina, Mar-
line, Marleina, Marlaina, Marlayna, Marlayne, Mar-
linda, Marlana

MARNI: (Israeli) "Rejoicing." Marnie is a variant form of
Marina.

Marnie, Marnee, Marnell, Marnisha

MARQUISE: *(mar-KEES)* The feminine equivalent of the
French title Marquis fits the favored "Mark-" name pattern. Variants are contemporary. See also "Mark-"
names.

Marquisha, Marquisa; Marquesa *(mar-KAY-sah)* (Italian); Marquita (Spanish); Marquette, Marquetta, Mar-
queta

MARSHA: Variant form of Marcia.

MARTHA (165): (Aramaic) "Lady." Biblical; the sister of
Mary and Lazarus.

Marta (Spanish)

MARTINA: (Latin/English) "Warrior of Mars"; (Spanish)
Feminine form of Martin. Martinique (French) is a West
Indies island.

Marteena; Martine (French); Martinique *(mar-ten-NEEK)*

MARVELL: (Latin) "Wonderful, extraordinary."

Marvella, Marvela, Marvelyn, Marvadene, Marva

MARVINA: *(mar-VEEN-ah)* "Renowned friend." Feminine form of Marvin.

MARY (44): (Hebrew) "Bitter," "rebellious"; (English)
Variant form of Miriam. Biblical; the virgin mother of
Christ. Mary became the object of great veneration in the
Catholic Church. Through the centuries, names like Do-
lores and Mercedes have been created to express aspects
of Mary's life and worship. Mary is also frequently used
in blends and compounded names. See also Maria, Mari,
Maribel and Mariana.

Maryann, Maryanne, Maryanna, Marybel, Marybell,
Marybeth, Maryjo, Marylou, Marylu, Marylee

MATILDA: (German) "Strength for battle."
  Matilde (French/Spanish), Mattie
MATSUKO: *(MAHT-soo-koh)* (Japanese) "Pine tree child."
MAUDE: (French) Variant form of Matilda.
  Maudie
MAUREEN: (Irish) Variant form of Moira and Mary. Maurissa and Maurisa may also be feminine forms of Maurice. See also Mara and Morisa.
  Maura, Maurianne, Maurissa, Maurisa
MAVIS: *(MAY-viss)* (English/French) "Song-thrush."
MAXINE: (English) "The greatest." Feminine form of Max.
  Maxi, Maxie, Maximina
MAY: (Latin) "Maia, the month of May." Also used as a short form of Mary. See also Mai.
  Mayleen, Maylene
MAYA: *(MYE-ya)* (Spanish) Short form of Amalia; also a variant form of Maia. See also Mai.
MAYDA: (English) "Maiden." See also Maida.
MAYRA (95): (Irish) Variant form of Mary. See also Moira and Myra.
  MAIRA (387), Mairi, Maire
"Mc-" names: (Scottish/Irish) Surnames occasionally used as given names for girls, especially names that sound like Michaela. See also Mackenzie, McKenzie and Michaela.
  McCall, McKayla, McKay, McKell, McKella, McKenna
MCKENZIE: (Scottish/Gaelic) "The fair one." See also Mackenzie, "Mc-" names and Kenzie.
  McKensie
MEDINA: "City of the Prophet." The city where Muhammad began his campaign to establish Islam.
MEDORA: A literary creation; Medora is a romantic heroine in Lord Byron's narrative poem *The Corsair*.
MEERA: (Israeli) "Light." See also Mira.
  Meira
MEGAN (10): *(MEG-an, MEE-gan* or *MAY-gan)* (Welsh)

Variant form of Margaret, based on the short form Meg.
Phonetic spellings of Megan are used to ensure one of
the three pronunciations.

MEGHAN (130), MEAGAN (177), Meaghan, Maygan,
Maegan, Meeghan, Meegan (Gaelic) "soft, gentle,"
Meggan

MEIKO: *(may-EE-koh)* (Japanese) "A bud."
Mieko *(mee-EH-koh)* "already prosperous"

MELANIE (89): *(MEL-a-nee)* (Greek/French) "Dark."
Melanee, Melaina, Melaine, Melana, Melania (Latin)

MELIA: *(me-LEE-ah)* (Hawaiian) "Plumeria."

MELINDA (195): (Greek/Latin) "Honey-sweet."
Melina, Malinda, Melynda

MELISANDE: *(mel-a-SAHND)* (German/French) "Strength,
determination." Variant form of Millicent.
Melisandra *(mell-a-SAHN-dra)*

MELISSA (13): (Greek) "Bee." Mythology; the name of
a nymph.
Melisa *(ma-LEE-sah)*, Meliza *(ma-LYE-zah)*, Melise *(ma-
LEESE)*, Melisse, Melisha, Missy

MELITA: *(mah-LEE-tah)* (Spanish) Short form of Carmelita. Malita is a variant form of Maria.
Malita

MELODY (311): (Greek) "Music, song."
Melodie, Melodi, Melodee

MELORA: *(ma-LOR-ah)* (Latin) "Make better."

MELVA: "Friend of Michael." Feminine form of Melvin.
Melvina

MERALDA: *(mer-AHL-dah)* (Latin) "Emerald." Short
form of Esmeralda.

MERCEDES (213): *(mer-SAY-dees)* (Latin) "Mercies."
Used in reference to Mary as "Our Lady of Mercies."
See also Mercy.
Mercedez

MERCER: (English/French) "Merchant." Surname in rare
use as a given name for boys and girls.

MERCY: (French/Latin) "Compassion, forbearance." A virtue name. See also Mercedes.

Mercie, Mercia, Mercina, Mercilla

MEREDITH (270): (Welsh) "Great lady." Formerly considered a boy's name, in America Meredith now is used almost entirely as a girl's name.

MERLE: See Meryl

MERRY: (English) "Mirthful, joyous." The Finnish name Meri means "sea."

Merrie, Merri, Merrilee, Meridel, Meri

MERYL: (French) "Blackbird." Variant form of Merle. Female usage favors Meryl and Merla; Merle is in rare use for boys and girls.

Merla, Merryl, Maryl, Merle, Mirla, Myrla, Merlyn

MIA (388): (MEE-ah) (Israeli) Feminine short form of Michal. Mia is also used as a short form of English and Latin names containing "mia." See also Miya.

MICAH: (MYE-cah) (Hebrew) "Who is like Jah?" Biblical; a prophet and writer of the Book of Micah. Usage: boys 86%, girls 14%.

Micaiah (mee-KYE-ah)

MICHAELA (257): (mih-KAY-lah) Feminine form of Michael. Michaela is one of the most frequently misspelled names; phonetic spellings are effective, but care needs to be taken to avoid unnecessary awkwardness or spelling difficulties. See also "Mc-" names.

Micaela, Mikaela, Mikayla, Mychaela, Mikella, Mikelle

MICHAL: (MYE-kal) (Hebrew) "Who is like God?" Biblical; Feminine form of Michael. Michal was King Saul's daughter, the first wife of David.

Mychal, Mical, Michaelyn, Michaeline, Micole

MICHELLE (16): (mi-SHELL) French feminine form of Michael.

MICHELE (315), Mychelle, Mychele, Michela, Michella

MICHIE: (mee-chee-AY) (Japanese) "Gateway; gracefully drooping flower."

MICHIKO: *(MEE-chee-koh)* (Japanese) "Child of beauty"; "wisdom."

MIDORI: *(mee-DOR-ee)* (Japanese) "Green."

MIKI: *(MEE-kee)* (Japanese) "Three trees together." Miki (Hawaiian) "Quick, nimble." Mikki is sometimes used as a short form of names like Michaela.
Mika (Japanese) "new moon," Mikko, Mikki

MILDRED: (English) "Gentle strength."

MILIANI: *(mee-lee-AH-nee)* (Hawaiian) "Gentle caress." Miliana and Milana are Latin feminine forms of Emeliano.
Miliana, Milana

MILLICENT: (German/French) "Strength, determination." See also Melisande.
Millie

MIMI: *(mee-mee)* (French) Pet name for Miriam or Marie. Also used as a Spanish pet name for names like Mira, Maria and Noemi. See also Mamie.

MINA: *(MEE-nah)* (German) "Love." Name endings (mina and mena) and diminutives used as independent names.
Minna, Minnie, Minette, Minnette, Mena, Meena

MINDY (352): Short form of Melinda, frequently used as an independent name.
Mindi, Mindie, Mindee, Minda (Hindi)

MINERVA: *(mi-NER-va)* (Latin) Mythology; name of the Roman goddess of wisdom.

MIRA: Variant form of Myra and Miranda. See also Meera.
Miri, Miriana

MIRANDA (140): (Latin) "Worthy of admiration." In Shakespeare's *The Tempest*, Miranda is an innocent girl raised and educated on an isolated island by her magician father.

MIRELLA: (Latin) Feminine form of Mireya, from Amariah. (Hebrew) "Jehovah has said."
Mireille, Mirelle, Myrelle, Mireya

MIRIAM (358): Hebrew form of Mary. See also Mariana.

Myriam

MISCHA: *(MEE-sha)* (Russian/Slavic) Nickname for Michael, rare use for girls as well as boys.
Miesha, Misha

MISTY (223): The English word used as a contemporary given name for girls. See also Mystique.
Misti, Mistie, Mystee, Mysti

MITZI: *(MIT-see)* (German) Pet name for Mary and Marie. Mitsu is a Japanese surname meaning "shine, reflect."
Mitzy, Mitsu

MIYA: *(MEE-yah)* (Japanese) "Three arrows"; "temple." See also Mia.

MODESTY: (Latin) "Without conceit; modest." A virtue name.
Modesta, Modestine

MOHALA: *(mo-HAH-lah)* (Hawaiian) "Petals unfolding; shining forth."

MOIRA: (Scottish) Variant form of the Irish Maire, from Mary. Phonetic spelling is Moyra. See also Mayra and Myra.
Moyra

MOLLY (104): Variant form of Mary. In use since the late Middle Ages, recently revived in popularity, probably in part due to actress Molly Ringwald. See also Polly.
Mollie, Mollee, Molli, Molley

MONA: *(MOHN-nah)* (Gaelic/Irish) "Noble." Mona is also an Italian short form of Madonna. Most famous name bearer: the Mona Lisa, a portrait painted by Leonardo da Vinci, which has itself inspired name blends. See Madonna.
Monisha, Monalisa, Monalissa

MONICA (60): (Latin) Variant form of Mona.

MONIQUE (98) *(moh-NEEK)* (French); Monika (German)

MONSERRAT: *(mohn-sir-AHT)* (Latin) "Jagged mountain." The name of a mountain in Spain, a monastery and a celebrated image of the Virgin Mary.

Montserrat

MONTANA: *(mon-TAN-nah)* (Latin/Spanish) "Mountain." The name of the western state used as a given name. Usage for boys and girls is about equal.

MONTEENE: (Latin/French) "Mountain." Variant form of Montaigne.

Montina

MORENA: *(moh-RAY-nah)* (Spanish) "Brown, brownhaired."

Moreen, Morella

MORGAN (78): (Welsh) "Bright sea." Usage for girls increased sharply during the eighties, to about 76% (24% for boys) probably due in part to actress Morgan Fairchild. Morgaine and Morgayne are medieval Irish forms.

Morganne, Morgann, Morgana, Morgaine, Morgayne

MORIAH: *(moh-RYE-ah)* (Hebrew) Biblical; the name of the mount of the Temple of Solomon in Jerusalem.

MORISA: (Spanish) Feminine form of Maurice. See also Maureen.

Morissa

MORWENNA: (Welsh) "Ocean waves."

MURIEL: (Celtic/Irish) "Shining sea."

MYISHA: *(mye-EE-shah)* (Arabic) "Woman, life." Variant form of Aisha.

Myesha, Myeisha, Myeshia, Myiesha

MYLA: (Contemporary) "Merciful." Feminine form of Myles.

Mylene, Myleen, Milena

MYRA: (English) Poetic invention, possibly a variant of Mayra. See also Moira.

Myrah, Myriah

MYRNA: (Aramaic/Arabic) "Myrrh; sweet oil." Also a Gaelic name meaning "beloved."

Morna (Irish), Mirna

MYRTA: *(MIR-ta)* Variant form of Myrtle, a nature name based on the evergreen shrub that was sacred to Venus as a symbol of love. Myrtle is very rarely used today.

Myrtle

MYSTIQUE: *(miss-TEEK)* (French) "Air of mystery." The use of Mystique as a contemporary name for girls is probably an outgrowth of the popularity of the name Misty.
Mystica, Mistique

N

"NA-"names: (Contemporary) Blends of "Na-" plus various endings, with pronunciation emphasis on the second syllable.
Nakisha, Nakeisha, Nakia, Nakita, Nalani, Naquita, Nareesha, Natahnee, Natavia, Natisha, Notosha, Natoya

NADIA (365): *(NAH-d'yah)* (Russian/Slavic) "Hope." Also (Arabic) "dew-drenched."
Nadhia, Nadya, Nadja

NADINE: *(NAY-deen)* (French) Variant form of Nadia.
Nadeen *(nah-DEEN)*

NANA: *(NAH-nah)* (Hawaiian) Month of spring and the Hawaiian name of a star. The Spanish Nana is a pet form of Ana.
Nani "beauty, splendor."

NANCY (68): *(NAN-cee)* (French/English) Variant form of Anne.
Nanci, Nancey, Nancie

NANETTE: (French) "Favor, grace." Variant form of Ann.
Nannette, Nan, Nann, Nanine

NAOMI (285): *(nay-OH-mee)* (Hebrew) "Pleasantness." Biblical; an ancestress of Jesus and mother-in-law to Ruth.
NOEMI (363) *(no-AY-mee)* (Spanish), Neomi, Noemy, Neoma

NARA: (Celtic) "Contented."
Nareen, Nareena, Nareene

NARIKO: *(nah-REE-koh)* (Japanese) "Child who is humble"; "gentle, soft; child who climbs high."

NATALIE (39): *(NAT-a-lee)* (Latin/French) "Birthday," especially referring to the birthday of Christ. The "h" is silent in the French form Nathalie; some American variants (like Nathalee) are phonetically spelled to retain the "h" sound.

NATALIA, Natalya, Natalee, Nathalie, Nathaly, Nathalee, Nathalia

NATASHA (90): (Russian) Variant form of Natalie. See also Latasha.

Natashia, Natasia, Natascha

NATHANIA: *(na-THAN-ya)* "God has given." Feminine form of Nathan and Nathaniel.

NAZNEEN: *(nahz-NEEN)* (Persian) "Exquisitely beautiful; charming." The name is meant to convey the superlative sense of the charm of a beloved woman or child.

NEDDA: Feminine form of Ned, the equivalent of Edda.

Nedra

NEEMA: (Swahili) "Born in prosperity."

NEILA: *(NEE-lah)* (Gaelic) "Champion." Feminine form of Neil.

Neelie, Neely

NEIVA: *(NEE-vah)* (Spanish) "Snow." Feminine form of the Spanish word *nieve*. Neva is the name of a river in Russia, and Neff is a related German surname in rare use as a girl's name.

Neyva, Neva, Neff

NELLY: Short form of Eleanor and Helen.

Nellie, Nell, Nella, Nelida (Spanish)

NEREIDA: *(ne-RAY-dah)* (Greek) "Sea nymph; daughter of Nereus." Greek mythology; the Nereids were deities of the seas, mermaids.

Nereyda, Nerida, Nerissa, Narissa

NETTIE: Short form of names ending in "-nette."

Netty, Netta

NIA: *(NEE-ah)* Short form of names with the "-nia" ending, used as an independent name after the fashion of Mia.

NICHELLE: *(nee-SHEL)* (Contemporary) "Victorious maiden." Blend of Nichole and Michelle.

Nichele

NICOLE (11): *(ni-KOHL)* (French) Feminine form of Nicholas. (See historical note in boys' index.) During the Middle Ages names that seem feminine today, like Nicolet and Nicol, were actually male names. See also Nikki.
NICHOLE (139), Nicholle, Nichol, Niccole; Nicola (Italian); Nicolette (French); Nicoletta (Italian); Nickole, Nikole, Nikkole, Nycole

NIDIA: (Latin) "Nest."
Nydia

NIKKI (326): Short form of Nicole. "Nic-" and "Nik-" variants are used in many cultures. Greek mythology; Nike *(NYE-kee)* was the name of the goddess of victory. Nikki *(NEE-kee)* is also a Japanese surname with the potential meaning "two trees."
Nikita (Russian); Nikia, Niki (Greek); Nikkie, Nike, Nicki, Nickie; Nicci (Italian)

NINA (264): *(NEE-nah* or *NINE-ah)* Diminutive name ending based on Anne, used as an independent name, especially in Russia.
Nena, Neena

NINON: *(nan-AWN)* (French) Variant form of Anne. Ninon de Lenclos was a seventeenth-century aristocrat famous for her wit and beauty.
Ninette, Nynette

NISHA: *(NEE-sha)* Popular contemporary name ending, also used as an independent name.
Niesha, Neesha, Nyssa *(NISS-ah)*

NITA: *(NEE-tah)* (Spanish) Diminutive ending used as an independent name. Nita *(nee-tah)* is also a Japanese surname meaning "full of compassion."

NOELANI: *(no-ah-LAH-nee)* (Hawaiian) "Mist of heaven."
Noe *(noh-AY)* "mist; misty rain"

NOELLE: *(no-ELL)* (French) "Birthday." Feminine form of Noel. Commonly used in reference to Christ's birth and the Christmas festival. Usage of Noel: boys 80%, girls 20%.

Noel, Noell, Noella, Noele

NOLA: Feminine form of Nolan.

Nolene, Nolana

NONA: (Latin) "Nine."

NORA: Short form of names like Eleanora. In Ireland, the diminutive "-een" was added to form Noreen.

Noreen, Norene, Norah, Noreena, Norine, Norabel, Norissa

NORELL: (no-RELL) (Scandinavian) "From the north." Occasional use of this surname as a given name may be due to the perfume. Narelle is a variant currently popular in Australia.

Narelle

NORIKO: (noh-REE-koh) (Japanese) "Child of cere-mony"; "law, order."

NORMA (306): Feminine form of Norman.

NOVA: (NOH-vah) (Latin) "New." Astronomy; a nova is a star that suddenly releases a tremendous burst of energy, increasing its brightness many thousandfold.

NURI: (Arabic) "Light."

NYLA: "Champion." Feminine form of Nyles, from Neil.

Nila

O

OCEANA: (oh-SHAH-nah or oh-see-AHN-ah) (Greek) "Ocean." Feminine form of Oceanus. Greek mythology; Oceanus was a Titan, the father of rivers and water nymphs.

OCTAVIA: (ock-TAHV-yah) (Latin) "Eighth." Feminine form of Octavius. A clan name of Roman emperors. See also Tavia.

Octaviana

ODELIA: (oh-DEEL-ya) (French) "Wealthy."

Odile (oh-dyle), Odilia, Odila, Odella, Odette

ODESSA: *(oh-DESS-ah)* (Greek) "Wandering, quest"; (Latin) Variant form of Odysseus.

OHARA: *(oh-hah-rah)* (Japanese) "Small field." Surname.

OLA: (Hawaiian) "Life; well-being." Also (Nigerian) "precious."

OLETHA: *(oh-LEE-tha)* (English/Scandinavian) "Light, nimble."

OLEXA: *(oh-LEKS-ah)* (Czech) Feminine form of Alexander.

OLGA: (Scandinavian/Russian) "Holy, devout."

OLIDA: *(oh-LEE-dah)* (Latin) Variant form of Olivia.
Oleta

OLINA: *(oh-LEE-nah)* (Hawaiian) "Joyous."
Oleen, Oline

OLINDA: (Latin) A poetic name created in the sixteenth century.
Olynda

OLIVIA (134): *(oh-LIV-ee-ah)* (Latin) "The olive tree." Feminine form of Oliver. Biblical; the olive tree is a symbol of fruitfulness, beauty and dignity. Today "extending an olive branch" traditionally signifies an offer of peace.

OLYMPIA: *(oh-LIM-pee-ah)* (Greek) "From Olympus." One of the many saints' names with origins in mythology. Mount Olympus was the home of the ancient Greek gods.
Olimpia.

OMEGA: *(oh-MAY-gah)* (Greek) "Large." The last letter in the Greek alphabet.

ONDREA: (Czech) "Womanly, brave." Variant form of Andrea.
Ondra

OONAGH: (Irish) Variant form of the English Una.
Oona

OPAL: (Sanskrit) "Gemstone, jewel." A gemstone possessing a unique iridescence of colors.

OPHELIA: *(oh-FEEL-yah)* (Greek) "Help." Name of the

unfortunate maiden who loved Hamlet in Shakespeare's
play *Hamlet*.

Ofelia (Spanish)

OPHRAH: *(OHF-ra)* (Hebrew) "Young deer" or "place of
dust." A biblical place name. Oprah Winfrey, actress and
TV talk show hostess, has made this very rare name familiar to the present generation.

Ophra, Oprah

ORAH: (Israeli) "Light."

Oria

ORALIA: *(oh-RAYL-yah)* (Latin) "Golden." Variant form
of Aurelia.

Orelia

ORIANA: *(or-ee-AHN-ah)* (Latin) "Dawning."

Orianna, Oriane *(or-ee-AHN)* (French), Oreana

ORINDA: (Latin) A seventeenth-century poetic name.

OSANNA: Short form of the Latin *hosannah*, a chanted
prayer meaning "save, we pray."

P

PAGAN: *(PAY-gan)* (English/Latin) "Country dweller."
Once a common medieval given name, Pagan fell out of
favor as a given name when it became a term used for an
irreligious person or someone who believed in more than
one god.

PAIGE (133): (English/French) "Young attendant." A page
in medieval households was usually a young boy whose
service was the first step in his training as a knight.

Page, Pagett

PAISLEY: *(PAYS-lee)* The name of a patterned fabric that
was at one time the principle product manufactured in
Paisley, Scotland.

PALMIRA: *(pal-MEE-rah)* (Greek/Latin) "Palm; land of
palm trees." Feminine form of Palmer; also the name of
an ancient oasis-city in the Arabian desert. See historical
note under Zenobia.

PALOMA: *(pa-LOH-mah)* (Latin) "Dove."

PAMELA (252): (Greek) "Honey; all sweetness." A poetic invention from the sixteenth century.
Pam, Pamella

PANDORA: (Greek) "All-gifted." Greek mythology; Pandora was gifted with powers and desirable attributes from all the gods, then given charge of a mysterious box she was forbidden to open. When she opened the box, every kind of mankind's ills flew out.

PARIS: The name of the French capital used as a given name for both girls and boys. Usage of Paris: boys 34%, girls 66%.
Parisa, Parris, Parrish

PARTHENA: *(par-THEEN-ah)* (Greek) "Virgin." A name that refers to the Parthenon, Athene's temple in Athens.

PATIENCE: (Latin) "Enduring, forbearing." One of the virtue names, rarely used today.

PATRICIA (74): (Latin) "Noble; a patrician." The Romans once were divided socially and politically into two major classes, the plebeians and the patricians. To be patrician meant one was highly ranked, an aristocrat.
Patrice (French), Patrisha, Patrina, Patrisse, Patrizia, Patryce, Patty, Patsy, Patti, Patria

PAULA (339): (Latin) "Little." Feminine form of Paul.
PAULINA (419), Pauline, Paulene, Paulette, Pauletta, PAOLA (463) (Spanish/Italian), Paolina, Paulita, Pavla (Czech), Pauli (German)

• PAYTON: (English) Surname in rare use as a given name. Usage for boys and girls is about equal.
Peyton

PAZ: *(pahz)* (Spanish) "Peace," from the Latin word *pax.* In Catholic use, a reference to "Our Lady of Peace."

PEARL: A jewel name. See also Perla.
Pearla, Pearlie, Pearlinda, Pearline, Perle

PEGGY: Rhyming pet name from medieval times, based on Margaret (Meggy). Today, Peggy is almost always treated as an independent name.

PENNY: (Greek) "Weaver's tool." Short form of Penelope. Greek mythology; Penelope, wife of Ulysses, fended off suitors by weaving during the day and unraveling at night a tapestry she said had to be completed before she would wed another husband. The name has come to signify a loyal, capable and clever woman.
Penelope *(pen-NELL-a-pee)*, Pennie

PEONY: *(PAY-uh-nee* or *PEE-uh-nee)* (Greek) "Praise-giving." A flower name. As a Chinese name motif, the peony signifies riches and honor.

PERDITA: *(per-DEE-tah)* (Latin) "Lost." Shakespeare created this name for a young heroine in *The Winter's Tale*.

PERI: (Greek) In Greek mythology, an *oread*, nymph of mountains and caves. In Persian fable, a fallen angel. Pera and Perita are Spanish short forms of Esperanza.
Pera, Perita, Perah (Israeli) "flower"

PERLA (450): (Spanish) Variant form of Pearl.
Perlita

PERRI: Feminine variant form of Peter. See also Petra.
Perris, Perrianne, Periannus, Perrine, Perrin

PERSIS: *(PER-sees* or *PER-siss)* (Greek) "Woman of Persia." Biblical; a first-century Christian woman commended by Paul.

PETRA: Feminine variant form of Peter. See also Perri.
Petrina, Peta, Pier, Pierette, Petronella

PHAEDRA: *(FAY-dra)* (Greek) "Shining." Phaedra is derived from Phoebus, "the sun," another name for Apollo.
Phedre, Phadra, Fedra

PHILIPPA: (English) "Fond of horses." Feminine form of Philip.
Philana, Philina, Pippa

PHOEBE: *(FEE-bee)* (Greek) "Pure; bright, radiant." Biblical; a Christian woman who aided Paul and others. Greek mythology; a reference to Apollo, the god of light.
Phebe (Spanish)

PHYLICIA: (Contemporary) Blend of Felicia and Phyllis, made familiar today by actress Phylicia Rashaad.
Philicia

PHYLLIS: (Greek) "Green branch."
Phillida, Phyliss

PIA: *(PEE-ah)* (Latin) "Pious, reverent."

PILAR: *(pee-LAR)* (Latin) "Pillar." In Catholic tradition, a reference to a marble pillar connected with an appearance of the Virgin Mary.

PIPER: (English/French) "Plays the pipes; organ-player." Surname very rarely used today as a given name. Actress Piper Laurie has made the name somewhat familiar.

POLA: (Latin/Arabic) "Poppy." Short form of Amapola.

POLLY: One of the medieval rhyming nicknames, based on Mary (Molly). Moll and Poll, at one time widely used, are virtually never used today as given names. See also Molly.

PORTIA: *(POR-sha)* (Latin) Feminine form of a Roman clan name. Portia was used by Shakespeare as the name of a clever, determined young heroine in *The Merchant of Venice*. Today, the similar sounding name Porsche is used almost as often, though probably more in reference to the sports car than to Portia.
Porsha, Porsche, Porcha, Porscha, Porschia

PRECIOUS: (English/French) "Of great value; highly esteemed." A name of endearment. In Catholic tradition, also a reference to the "precious blood of Christ."
Precia, Preciosa

PRIMA: *(PREE-mah)* (Latin) "First." The Spanish word *primavera* signifies the "first green," springtime.
Primavera

PRINCESS: (English) Feminine form of Prince. A "title" name.
Princesa (French); Princessa (Italian)

PRISCILLA (124): *(pris-SILL-ah)* (Latin) "Of ancient times." Biblical; a first-century Christian missionary. Priscilla was a favored name with the Puritans of En-

gland; Longfellow gave the name to the heroine of his
poem *The Courtship of Miles Standish*.

PRISMA: (Greek) "Cut, sawed." Prisms are cut pieces of
glass that can be used to separate light into the rainbow
spectrum.
Prysma

PRUDENCE: (Latin) "The exercise of caution and wisdom." One of the virtue names.

Q

QUEENA: Variant of the English title used as a given name.
Queenie, Queen, Quenna

QUERIDA: *(kare-EE-dah)* (Spanish) "Beloved, darling."

QUINN: (Gaelic/Irish) "Counselor." Usage: boys 77%,
girls 23%. Quincy is very rarely used for girls.
Quincy

R

"RA-"names: (Contemporary) Blends of "Ra-" plus various endings, with pronunciation emphasis on the second
syllable.
Ranelle, Ranessa, Ranisha, Rashanda

RACHEL (19): *(RAY-chel)* (Hebrew) "Ewe." Biblical; Jacob's wife, described as being "beautiful in form and
countenance." Rachelle is a variant pronunciation. See
also Raquel, Rochelle and Richelle.
RACHAEL (126), Raechel, Raychel, Rachelann, Rach-
elanne, RACHELLE (243) *(ra-SHELL)*, Rachell; Rach-
ele (Italian); Rashelle

"RAE-": Short form of Rachel; also used as a prefix in
contemporary names, following the "Ra-" name pattern.
See also Ray.
Rae, Raeann, Raeanne, Raeanna, Raedell, Raedine, Rae-
lee, Raelena, Raelyn, Raelynn, Raelynne, Raelene, Rae-
leen, Raelina, Raelani

RAFAELA: (*rah-fah-AY-lah*) (Spanish) Feminine form of Raphael. (Hebrew) "God has healed".
Raphaella

RAINBOW: The English word used as a given name. See also Iris.

RAISA: (*rah-EE-sah*) (Russian) "Rose." See also Rosa.
Raiza, Raissa

RAMAH: (Israeli) "High."

RAMONA: (Spanish) "Guards wisely." Feminine form of Ramon, Raymond.
Ramie, Ramee

RANA: (*RAH-nah*) (Scandinavian) "Catcher." Scandinavian mythology; Rana was the goddess of the sea. Rani is a Hindu title meaning "royal, queen."
Rani, Ranae

RANDI (364): Feminine form of Randy, or short form of Miranda, used as a given name.
Randee, Randa

RAQUEL (173): (Spanish/Portuguese) Variant form of Rachel.
Raquelle, Raquela, Racquel, Racquell, Roquel

RASHEEDA: (Arabic/Swahili) "Righteous."
Rasheedah, Rashida

"RAY-"names: (Contemporary) Feminine variants using Ray as a prefix. See also "Rae-" and "Ra-" names.
Rayann, Rayanna, Rayana, Rayleen, Raylene, Raylynn, Raynisha, Raynesha, Raynell, Rayeann, Raye, Raycine

RAYA (Israeli) "Friend."

RAYNA: Short form of Lorraine and Reynalda.
Raina, Reyna, Rayne, Raine, Raynee, Rainey, Rainee, Rainie

REANNA: (*ree-ANN-ah*) (Contemporary) See Rhiannon.
Reanne, Reannon, Reannah, Reeanne

REBECCA (24): (Hebrew) "Tied, knotted"; (English) Variant form of Rebekah. Biblical; Rebekah, noted in the Genesis account as a maiden of beauty, modesty and kindness, became the wife of Abraham's son Isaac.

REBEKAH (173); Rebeca (Spanish); Reba

● REGAN: (*REE-gan* or *RAY-gan*) (Gaelic/Irish) "Reigning, kingly."
Reagan, Ragan

REGINA (303): (*re-JEEN-ah*) (Latin) "Queen."
Regine, Regeena, Regena

REIKO: (*RAY-koh*) (Japanese) "Pretty; lovely child."
Rei

RENA: (*REE-nah*) Name ending used as an independent name.
Reena, Reene, Rina

RENEE (185): (*ren-NAY*) (French) "Reborn." Phonetic spellings of Renee have resulted in a number of contemporary variants. "Ren-" is also used as a prefix with various endings to create new names.
Renae, Rene, Renaye, Renay, Renita; Renata (Spanish); Renisha, Reneisha, Renne, Rennie

REXANNE: (Contemporary) Blend of Rex and Anne. These names are also used as feminine forms of Rex.
Rexanna, Rexana, Rexine

REYNALDA: (Scandinavian) "Powerful force"; (Latin) Feminine form of Reynold. See also Rayna.

RHEA: (*REE-ah*) (Greek) "Flowing." Greek mythology; Rhea was the mother of Zeus, Poseidon, Hera and Demeter. Rhea is also a Welsh name referring to a river in Wales.
Rhia, Rhaya, Rhae, Reya

RHIANNON: (*ree-ANN-an*) (Gaelic/Welsh) "Maiden," with contemporary variants. Celtic mythology; name of the Welsh horse goddess described in legend as dressed in shining gold and riding a pale horse. See also Reanna.
Rhianna, Rheanna, Rheanne, Rhiann, Rhiannan, Rhianon, Rhiana, Rhyan, Riana, Rianna, Rianne, Riane, Riannon, Riona

RHODA: (*ROH-dah*) (Greek) "Rose." See also Rosa.

RHONDA: (*RON-dah*) (Welsh) "Fierce waters."
Ronda, Rhonette, Rhona

RIA: Short form of names beginning or ending with "-ria" or "-rie," in rare use as a given name.
Rie

RICHELLE: (*ri-SHELL*) (Contemporary) Feminine blend of Richard and Rachelle. Also related feminine short forms based on Ricky, Rickie or Frederica.
Rikki, Ricki, Riki, Rikkie, Ricci, Ricca

RILEY: (*RYE-lee*) (Irish) Surname of unknown origin. Usage: boys 83%, girls 17%. See also Rylee.

RIMA: (*REE-mah*) (Spanish) "Rhyme, poetry." Literary; in Hudson's *Green Mansions*, Rima was an elusive maiden of the South American rain forest who spoke the language of animals and birds.

RISA: (*REE-sah*) (Spanish) "Laugh, laughter."
Rise (*ri-ZAY*) (French); Reesa

RITA (444): (Spanish) Short form of names ending in "-rita," especially Margarita.

RIVA: (*REE-vah*) (French) "Riverside."
Reva

ROBERTA: (English/French/German) "Famed; bright, shining." Feminine form of Robert. Usage of Robbie: boys 77%, girls 23%. See also Robin and Bobbi.
Robertha, Robbie

ROBIN (188): (English) Variant form of Robert, in popular use as a boy's name since the medieval days of Robin Hood, now used for girls as well. Usage today: boys 25%, girls 75%. See also Roberta.
ROBYN (319), Robynn, Robynne, Robena, Robina

ROCHELLE (352): (*roh-SHELL*) (French) "Rock, stone." See also Rachel.
Rochele; Rochella (Italian); Roshelle

ROCIO (337): (*roh-SEE-oh*) (Latin) "Dew." Refers to Mary as "Our Lady of the Dew."

RODERICA: "Famous ruler; red." Feminine form of Roderic.

ROLANDA: "Renowned in the land." Feminine form of Roland.

Rolande (French)

ROMINA: (Latin) "Woman of Rome." Roma is the name of the capital of Italy used as a given name. Romi and Romy are similar sounding German pet names.

Roma, Romana, Romalda, Romelia, Romi, Romy

RONNIE: Short form of Veronica or feminine variant of Ron and Ronald. Roni (*ROH-nee*) is also an Israeli name meaning "song."

Ronni, Roni, Rona, Ronae, Ronay, Ronisha, Ronnette, Ronelle, Ronica, Ronika

ROSA (166): (Latin) "Rose." This is the most popular flower name for girls and has many variants and compounds. Rosa is the Latin form, Rose is English, and both are frequently used in English-speaking countries. See also Roza, Rhoda and Raisa.

Rosalie (French); Rosanna; Rosana (Spanish/Portuguese); Rosanne, Rosalee, Rosabelle, Rosalba; Rosalia, Rosella (Italian); Rosalyn, Rosaline, Rosalina; Rosaleen (Irish); Rosalin, ROSE (336), Roseann, Roseanne, Roseanna, Roselia, Rosey, Rosie, Rosetta, Rosette, Roselyn, Roslynn, Roslyn, Rosio, Rosita, Rosina, Rosine, Rosy, Rossana, Rossanna

ROSALIND: (Latin) "Beautiful rose." A sixteenth-century poetic creation by Spenser.

Rosalinda (Spanish); Rosalynd; Rosalinde (German)

ROSAMOND: (Latin/French) "Rose of the world; rose of purity."

Rosamund, Rozamond, Rozamund

ROSARIO: (*roe-ZAR-ee-oh*) (Spanish/Portuguese) "Rosary." The rosary refers to devotional prayers honoring Mary. Usage: boys 84%, girls 16%.

ROSEMARY (450): Blend of Rose and Mary; also refers to the fragrant herb, which in folklore is the emblem of remembrance.

Rosemarie

ROSHANA: (Contemporary) Blends with "Ro-" as a prefix plus various name endings.

Roshawn, Roshawna, Roshaunda

ROWAN: (*ROH-an*) (Gaelic/Scandinavian) "Red-berry tree." Rowena was the name of one of the heroines in Sir Walter Scott's *Ivanhoe*.

Rowena (*roh-EEN-ah*), Roanna, Roanne

ROXANNE (225): (Persian) "Dawn." Roxandra is a contemporary blend of Roxanne and Alexandra, appropriate since Roxanne was the Persian princess Alexander the Great married during his travels of conquest.

ROXANA (413) (Spanish), Roxanna; Roxane (French); Roxann, Roxandra, Roxie, Roxy, Roxi, Roxene

ROYA: Feminine name based on Roy and Royal.

Royalle, Royanna, Royleen, Roylene

ROZA: Variant form of Rosa and Rose. The "z" spelling reflects French, Slavic or Yiddish influence; in contemporary usage, it is also a phonetic means of ensuring the stronger consonant pronunciation of "z" over the softer "s." See also Rosa.

Rozalyn, Roz, Rozalee, Rozanna, Rozlyn, Rozana, Rozella, Rozelle, Rozetta

RUBY (253): (Latin) "Red." A jewel name; the value of a ruby sometimes exceeds that of a diamond.

Rubi, Rubie, Rubina, Rubena, Rubianne

RUDI: "Renowned wolf." Feminine form of Rudy, from Rudolf.

Rudie

RUE: (English) "Regret." The name of an herb used for cooking and in medicine. In Shakespeare's *Hamlet*, Ophelia called rue the "herb-grace o' Sundays." Actress Rue McClanahan has made this name familiar today.

RUI: (*ROO-ee*) (Japanese) "Troublesome, tears, affection."

RUSTI: "Red." Feminine form of the nickname Rusty.

RUTH (230): (Hebrew) "Companion." Biblical; Ruth was the young Moabite widow who said to her Hebrew mother-in-law Naomi, "Where you go, there shall I go also; your people will be my people, your God my God."

Ruthie, Ruthanne, Ruthann, Ruthellen

RYANN: "Kingly." Feminine form of Ryan.
Ryanne, Ryane, Ryana, Ryanna

RYLEE: See also Riley. Ryley is in rare use for boys and girls.
Ryley, Rylie, Rylina

S

SABINA: (*sah-BEE-nah*) (Latin) "Of the Sabines." A saint's name in use at least since the second century. See also Sabra.

SABLE: (*SAY-bel*) (Slavic) "Black." A highly prized fur, dark brown, almost black. Also used in French and English heraldry as a term for black.
Sabelle (*sa-BELL*)

SABRA: (*SAY-bra*) (Israeli/Arabic) "Thorny." A name signifying one who is native-born, especially in Israel. Also a variant form of Sabina.

SABRINA (105): (*sa-BREE-nah*) (Latin) The name of a Celtic nymph said to have inhabited the Severn River in England.
Sabreena, Sabrena, Sabryna, Sabrinna, Sabreen, Sabrene

SACHI: (*SAH-chee*) (Japanese) "Benediction, fortunate."
Sachiko (*SAH-chee-koh*) "Blessed child; fortunate child."

SADE: (shah-DAY or *shar-DAY*) Short form of Folasade (*fol-lah-shah-DAY*), a Yoruban/African name meaning "honor confers a crown." The West Indian singer Sade has greatly influenced popularity of the name and the *shar-DAY* pronunciation. Sadie is a short form of Sarah. Saida is a variant form of Zaida (Arabic) "huntress; fortunate." See also Sharde.
Sadie, Saida, Sada, Sayda, Sadee, Sadia, Sadina

SADIRA: (*sa-DEER-ah*) (Persian) "Lotus."

SAGE: (English/French) "Wise one." Usage for boys: 59%, girls 31%.
Saige

SAHARA: (*sah-HAH-rah*) Rare variant form of Sarah. Sahara is also an Arabic name meaning "wilderness." See also Zahara.

Saharah, Sahra (Arabic)

SALLY (429): (English) Variant form of Sarah. The variants of Salina are more derivative of Sally than of the similar sounding name Selene.

Sallie, Sallee, Salina, Salena, Saleena

SALOME: (*sa-LOH-may*) (Hebrew/Greek) "Peace." Feminine form of Solomon. Biblical; the name of one of Christ's disciples, probably his mother Mary's sister. Also, the name of a beautiful woman who danced before Herod and requested the head of John the Baptist on a platter.

SAMANTHA (8): (*sa-MAN-tha*) Blend of Sam plus Anthea, and a feminine variant of Samuel. Samantha became very popular in the sixties due to the TV show "Bewitched" and has kept a high ranking among name choices ever since.

SAMI: (Arabic) "Exalted." Also a feminine form of Samuel.

Sammie, Sammi-jo, Sammi, Samma, Samia, Samina

SANDRA (91): (*SAN-dra* or *SAHN-dra*) "Helper of mankind." Short form of Alexandra. Sondra and Saundra are contemporary phonetic spellings.

SANDY (210), Sandi, Sandie, Sandee, Sanda, Sondra, Saundra

SANTANA: (*sahn-TAHN-ah*) (Latin) "St. Ann." The surname Santana is familiar today due to the Latin jazz-rock star of that name. Other "saint" related names: Santora, (Italian) "sainted;" Sante (French) "health;" Santina (Italian) "little saint."

Santora, Sante, Santina, Santanna, Santara

SAPPHIRE: (Arabic) "Beautiful." From the Sanskrit "beloved of Saturn." Sapphire is used as a jewel and color name. Sapphira is very rarely used, probably because the biblical Sapphira was a woman who was executed by God for lying. Safira (Spanish) is based on Ceferino, from Zephyr, the name of a third-century pope.

Sapphira, Safira

SARAH (5): (Hebrew) "Princess." Biblical; originally called Sarai, Sarah shared an adventurous nomadic life with her husband Abraham; she is described as being exceptionally beautiful even into her older years.

SARA (30), Sarabeth, Sarajane, Sarajean, Saralee, Saralyn, Saralynn, Sarahlee, Sarahlynn, Saramae, Sarai, Saray, Saraya, Sari, Sarrah, Sarra, Saira, Sairah, Sayra, Sarahi, Sariah; Sirke (Israeli/Finnish)

SARINA: Variant form of Sara. See also the soundalike name Serena.

Sarena, Sarita (Spanish/Portuguese), Sareen (Irish), Sarene, Sareena, Sarinna

SASA: (*sah-sah*) (Japanese) "help, aid."

SASHA (189): (*SAH-sha*) (Russian) Short form of Alexander, formerly used as a boy's name, now almost entirely used for girls.

Sascha, Sacha, Sasheen (Irish)

SATIN: (French/English) The name of the luxury fabric used as a given name.

Satina (*sa-TEE-nah*)

SAVANNAH (208): (Spanish) Literally, a grassland or treeless plain. Usage of Savannah as a given name for girls may be influenced by its sounding like Samantha, and by its use in a film called *Savannah Smiles*. See also the similar sounding name Sivanah.

Savanna, Savanah, Savana, Savonna

SCARLETT: (English/French) Surname referring to the bright red color, brought into use as a given name primarily by Margaret Mitchell's heroine in the novel *Gone with the Wind*.

Scarlet, Scarlette

SEANA: (*SHAWN-ah*) Feminine form of Sean. See also Shana, Siana and Shawna.

Seanna

SELENA: (Greek) "Goddess of the moon." Greek mythology; Selena was sister to Helios, the sun. For Salina and variants, see Sally. See also Celina.
Selina, Selene (Greek/French), Selenia, Selenne

SELMA: (English/German) "God's protection." Feminine short form of Anselmo.

SERAFINA: (*ser-ah-FEE-nah*) A Latin saint's name from the Hebrew word *seraphim*, "burning ones," referring to a class of angels.
Seraphina

SERENA (483): (Latin) "Serene, calm." When spelled Sirena, the name could be a reference to the Sirens, creatures of Greek mythology who by their irresistible singing lured seamen to their doom. See also Sarena.
Serina, Sereena, Serene, Syrena, Sirena, Sirenia

SERENITY: (English/French) One of the virtue names, referring to a calm and serene temperament.

"SHA-"names: (Contemporary) Blends of "Sha-" plus various endings, with pronunciation emphasis on the second syllable. Of all the contemporary "prefix" names, names beginning with "Sha-" are the most popular. Some may be duplicates of existing names from African, Arabic, Israeli, or other cultures. The Shavon variants listed here are also found under the Siobhan listing. See also "Cha-" names, Charlene, Shanice, "Shan-" and "She-" names.
Shadia, Shadira, Shadonna, Shakeena, Shakira, Shalaina, Shalaine, Shalana, Shalane, Shalaya, Shalee, Shaleena, Shalena, Shalene, Shalia, Shalina, Shalisa, Shalise, Shalita, Shaliza, Shalonda, Shalynn, Shamaine, Shamara, Shameka, Shamika, Shanel, Shanelle, Shanell, Shannell, Shania, Shanae, Shanay, Shanea, Shanedra, Shanee, Shanessa, Shanetta, Shanika, Shaniqua, Shanique, Shanita, Shannae, Shaquise, Shaquita, Sharae, Sharaia, Sharana, Sharay, Sharaya, Sharayah, Sharaye, Sharona, Sharonda, Sharonna, Shareen, Shareena, Sharell, Sharelle, Sharena, Sharene, Sharice, Sharika, Sharina, Sharisa, Sha-

rise, Sharissa, Sharita, Shavaugn, Shavon, Shavona, Shavonda, Shavonna, Shavonne

SHAINA (463): (*SHAY-nah*) (Israeli) "Beautiful." Shaina and its variants may also be contemporary feminine forms of Shane.

SHAYNA (455), Shayne, Shaena, Shainah

SHALIMAR: (Persian) The rare use of Shalimar as a given name for girls today is probably due to the perfume Shalimar. Chanel, Norell, Dior, Ciara and Aviance are other perfume names in use today as girls' names.

"SHAN-" names: (Contemporary) With pronunciation emphasis on the second syllable. See also Shantel, "Sha-" and "She-" names.

Shanda, Shandi, Shandra, Shandelle, Shandel, Shandell, Shandon, Shante, Shantee, Shantae, Shantai, Shantoya, Shantrice

SHANA (485): Feminine form of Shane. Shana has been made familiar today by journalist Shana Alexander. See also Seana and Shawna.

SHANNA (491), Shannah, Shani

SHANI: (*SHAH-nee*) (Swahili) "A marvel; wondrous."

SHANICE: (*sha-NEESE*) An especially favored "Sha-" name, rhyming with the variant forms of Janise.

Shaniece, Shaneice, Shanise, Shanese, Shannice

SHANNON (69): (Gaelic/Irish) "Wise." Today, usage of this surname as a given name is almost entirely for girls (95%).

Shannan

SHANTEL (461): "Singer." Contemporary variant form of Chantel, following the "Shan-" name pattern.

Shantell, Shantelle, Shantal

SHARDE: (*shar-DAY*) (Yoruban/African) "Honor confers a crown." Phonetic variant form of Sade, the short form of Folasade.

Shadae, Shardae, Sharday, Shardai

SHARI: Variant form of Sarah or phonetic form of Sherry.

Shara, Sharee

SHARIK: (*sha-REEK*) (African) "God's child; one on whom the sun shines."

SHARLENE: Variant form of Charlene and Charla.

Sharla, Sharlee, Sharly, Sharleen, Sharlyn, Sharlynne, Sharlina, Sharlana, Sharlaine, Sharlane, Sharlan, Sharlisa, Sharletta, Sharlamaine

SHARMAINE: See Charmaine.

SHARON (272): (Hebrew) "The plain of Sharon." Biblical place name; the Song of Solomon describes the beloved Shulamite woman as a flower of Sharon.

Sharron, Sharyn, Sherron

SHASTA: (American Indian) Tribal name, the name of a mountain in California, and the name of the Shasta daisy. Shasta may also be used as an alternative to Chasta or Chastity.

Shastina

SHAWNA (280): Feminine variant of the Irish names Shawn and Shaun, from John. See also Seana, Siana and Shana.

Shauna, Shawnna, Shawnice, Shawniece, Shawnda, Shawndelle, Shawnee, Shawni, Shawneen, Shawntae, Shawnte, Shawntay, Shaunna, Shaunte, Shauntay, Shaunice, Shaunda, Shaundee, Shaunelle

"SHE-"names: (Contemporary) Blends of the "She-" plus various endings, with pronunciation emphasis on the second syllable. See also Sherisa, "Sha-" and "Shan-" names.

Shelanna, Shelisa, Shelonda, Shenelle, Sherae, Sheraya, Shevonda

SHEA: (*shay*) (Irish) Surname. Usage: boys 57%, girls 43%. Shai is an Israeli name meaning "gift," and Shaya is an Israeli diminutive of Isaiah. Some of the contemporary variants also may be intended as variants of Sheila.

Shay, Shae, Shaye, Shaya, Shayla, Shaylah, Shaela, Shaila, Shaylene, Shayleen, Shaylynn, Shaylynne, Shaylyn, Shealynn, Shailyn, Shayda, Shayana, Shaelee

SHEBA: (*SHEE-bah*) The name of a kingdom in southern

Arabia, noted for its great wealth. Biblical; the queen of Sheba who journeyed to Jerusalem to see for herself if accounts about Solomon's great wisdom and wealth were true.

SHEENA (356): (Scottish) Variant form of Jane. Increased interest in this name today is probably due to singer Sheena Easton.
Sheenah

SHEILA (405): (Irish) Variant form of Celia.
Sheela, Sheilah

SHELBY (253): (English/Scandinavian) "Willow farm." English surname used as a given name for girls (84%) and boys (16%).
Shelbi, Shelbie

SHELLEY: (English) Surname used as a given name for girls and as a short form of names like Michelle, Rochelle and Shirley.
Shelly, Shelli, Shellee

SHERIDAN: (Gaelic/English) "Bright." English surname in rare use as a given name for boys (39%) or girls (61%).

SHERISA: (Contemporary) Variant based on Cherise, or Sherry. See also "She-" names.
Sherise, Sherissa, Sherita, Sherrina, Sherronda

SHERRY (496): Short form of Sharon and the many names beginning with "Sher-." Sherry also may be used in reference to the wine, after the fashion of Brandy. See also Cherie.
Sheri, Sherri, Sherree, Sherrie, Shereen

SHERYL: Variant form of Cheryl. The Sheryl spelling ensures the soft "sh" pronunciation. Sherilyn is a blend of Sheryl and Marilyn, and some of the names listed here also could be considered variant forms of Shirley. See also Cheryl.
Sherril, Sherrill, Sherill, Sharrell, Sherell, Sherelle, Sherrell, Sherrelle, Sherelene, Sherilyn, Sherylann, Sherylayne, Sherlynn, Sherlene

SHILOH: (SHY-loh) (Hebrew) "The one to whom it belongs." Rare usage is about equal for boys and girls. See historical note in boys' index.

Shyla, Shylah, Shilo, Shyloh

SHIRAE: (*shee-rah-EH*) (Japanese) "White bay"; "white creek."

SHIRLEY (500): (English) "Sunny meadow." See also Sheryl.

Shirleen, Shirlee, Shireen, Shirell, Shirelle (*she-RELL*)

SIANA: (*see-AHN-ah* or *SHAWN-ah*) Variant of Sian (*SHON*), a Welsh form of Jane. See also Seana, Shawna and Shana.

Sian, Sianna

SIBYL: (Greek) "Prophetess, oracle." See also Sybil and Cybil.

SIDNEY: See Sydney.

SIENNA: (*see-EN-ah*) (Latin) "From Siena." The city of Siena in Italy; also a brownish red color.

SIERRA (161): (*see-ERR-ah*) (Latin) "Mountains, mountainous." A name associated with environmental concerns due to the Sierra Club. Usage today may be influenced by its sounding like Ciara. Serra is a Latin surname, perhaps used in honor of Spanish missionary Junipero Serra.

Serra

SIGRID: (Scandinavian) Variant form of Siegfried.

SILVANA: (*sil-VAHN-ah*) (Latin) "Woodland; forest"; (Italian) Feminine form of Silvanus.

Silvanna (*sil-VAN-ah*)

SILVIA (370): (Latin) "Wood, forest." Silvia and Sylvia are about equally used today. Shakespeare used Silvia for a heroine's name in *Two Gentlemen of Verona*. See also Sylvia.

SIMONE (483): (*see-MOHN* or *see-MUN*) (French) Feminine form of Simon.

Simona, Symone, Simonne

SINEAD: (*sha-NADE*) (Gaelic/Irish) Variant form of Janet.

Sinead has been made familiar to Americans today by rock singer Sinead O'Connor.

SIOBHAN: (*sha-VAHN*) (Irish) Variant form of Joan. The unusual Irish spelling of Siobhan has not caught on with American parents nearly so well as has the sound pattern of the name, as shown by the "Sha-" names listed here. Shavaugn, Shavon, Shavonna, Shavonne, Shavona, Shavonda

SIRENA: See also Serena.
Siri (Scandinavian); Siriana

SIVANAH: (*see-VAH-nah* or *SEE-van-ah*) (Israeli) "Of the month of Sivan." See also Savannah.

SKYE: Skye and Sky are used as nicknames for Skyler and Skylar, as nature names, and possibly in reference to the Isle of Skye in Scotland. Usage: boys 15%, girls 85%. See also Schuyler in the boys' index.
Sky, Skyla, Skylar, Skyler

SKYLAR: Phonetic form of the Dutch surname Schuyler. Usage: boys 85%, girls 15%.
Skyler

SLOANE: (Gaelic/Scottish) "Fighter, warrior." Surname. Sloan is used for boys.

SOLANA: (*soh-LAH-nah*) (Latin) "Eastern wind." A saint's name.

SOLANGE: (*soh-LANZH*) (Latin/French) "Alone." Soledad and Sola are Spanish names with the same meaning.
Soledad, Sola

SONIA (197): (Russian) Variant form of Sophia. Sonya is a phonetic form.
SONYA (438); Sonja (Scandinavian); Sonni

SONNET: The word for the poetic form used as a given name for girls. Some of the world's most romantic poetry has been written in the form of sonnets.

SOPHIA (210): (*soh-FEE-ah*) (Greek) "Wisdom."
SOFIA (485) (Spanish), Sofiah, Sofie, Sophie, Sophy

SORRELL: (English/French) "Reddish brown."
Sorelle (French)

STACY (168): (English) Short form of the male name Eustace; (Latin) "productive; fruitful." Stacy and Stacey are surnames. Variants listed here for girls are most likely considered to be short forms of Anastacia rather than Eustace. Usage of Stacy and Stacey: girls 96%, boys 4%.
STACEY (159), Stacie, Staci, Stacee, Stacia, Stasia, Stasha

STARLA: Astronomical name based on "Star."
Starr, Star, Starlene, Starlena, Starlette, Starleena, Starlyn, Starlynn

STELLA: (Latin) "Star."

STEPHANIE (7): (Greek) "Crown, wreath"; Feminine form of Stephen. The name of the first Christian martyr was a favored name choice from the earliest centuries of the Christian era. Stephania, a Latin form of the name, was used for girls. The French form Stephanie became popular early in this century; it's been among the top ten names for the past fifteen years.
STEFANIE (348), STEPHANY (356), Stefani (Italian), Stephani, Stephania, Stefania, Stephaine (French), Stephine, Steffi, Stevana

STEVIE: Short form of Steven or Stephanie. Usage: boys 23%, girls 77%.

STORMY: Name from nature based on the English word and surname Storm.
Stormie, Stormi

SUMIKO: (*soo-MEE-koh*) (Japanese) "Child of goodness"; "beautiful child."

SUMMER (306): A nature name; the season used as a girl's name.

SUNNY: A nature name. Occasional usage is about equal for boys and girls.
Sunnie, Sunni, Sunita

SUSAN (169): (Hebrew) "Lily." Short form of Susannah. In the Apocryphal Book of Tobit, Susannah was a woman of courage who defended herself against wrongful accusation.

SUSANA (272): (Spanish) Suzana, Susanna, Susannah;
SUZANNE (355), Susanne, Susette, Suzette (French);
Suzanna, Suzannah, Susie, Susy, Suzan, Suzie, Suzy,
Suzi, Sue, Sueann, Sueanne, Sueanna, Suellen, Suelyn

SUZU: (*soo-zoo*) (Japanese) "Long-lived"; "round";
"crane."
Suzuko (*soo-ZOO-koh*) "spring, autumn child"; "peace
child."

SYBIL: (Greek) "Prophetess, oracle." See also Sibyl and
Cybil.
Sybille

SYDNEY (238): (English/French) "From St. Denis." In
current usage, Sidney is favored as a name for boys (56%
for boys, 44% for girls), and Sydney is favored for girls
(93% for girls, 7% for boys). See also Cydney.
Sidney, Sydnee

SYLVIA (268): See also Silvia.
Sylvie, Sylvina, Sylvana, Sylvonna

T

"TA-"names: (Contemporary) Blends of "Ta-" plus vari-
ous endings, with pronunciation emphasis on the second
syllable. See also "Te-" names.
Talani, Talanna, Talea, Taleah, Taleen, Talena, Talene,
Talona, Talyssa, Talicia, Talina, Talisa, Talisha, Tamika,
Tamica, Tameika, Tamisha, Tanaia, Taneece, Tanelle,
Tanika, Tanisha, Tanesha, Taniesha, Tanishia, Tarina,
Tashina, Tasheena, Tashana, Tashara, Tasharra, Tawana

TABITHA (191): (*TAB-i-tha*) (Aramaic) "Gazelle." Tabitha corresponds to the Greek name Dorcas; both names
are biblical, used to refer to the kindly woman, noted for
her good works, who was resurrected by Peter. The current popular revival of Tabitha as a name choice probably
was influenced by the child character Tabitha on the sixties' TV show "Bewitched." See also Dorcas.

TACY: (*TAY-cee*) (English/Latin) "Silence."

TAJA: (*TAH-zha* or *TAY-zha*) (Hindi) "Crown." Feminine form of Taj. Taji (*TAH-jee*) is a Japanese surname with the meaning "silver and yellow color."
Taisha, Taija, Tajia, Tajah, Taji, Tajiana

TALIA: (*TAL-ya*) (Hebrew) "Lamb, lambkin." From Taliah. Talia is also a short form of Natalia, or a variant form of Thalia (Greek).
Talya, Tahlia, Taliah

TALITHA: (*ta-LEE-thah* or *TAL-i-thah*) (Hebrew) "Child." Biblical; a reference to the resurrection of Jairus's daughter when Jesus said, "Child, arise."

TALLIS: (English/French) "Woodland." English surname in rare use as a girl's given name.

TAMA: (*tah-mah*) (Japanese) "Well-polished"; "globe, ball." Surname.
Tamae (*tah-mah-EH*) "ball, bell."

TAMARA (234): (*TAM-a-rah*) (Hebrew) "Palm tree"; (Russian) Variant form of Tamar. Biblical; one Tamar was the astute and persistent daughter-in-law of Jacob's son Judah, another was a daughter of King David noted for her great beauty.
Tamar (*TA-mar*), Tamra, Tamarah, Tamryn

TAMEKO: (*tah-MAY-koh*) (Japanese) "Child of good"; "advantage."

TAMI: (*TAH-mee*) (Japanese) "Let people see benefit."
Tamiko (*tah-MEE-koh*) "child born with green grass (born in spring)"

TAMMY (431): Short form of Thomasina and Tamara.
Tammi, Tammie, Tam, Tami, Tammie-jo, Tamlyn, Tamilyn

TANI: (*TAH-nee*) (Slavic/Spanish) Spanish short form of Estanislao, "make famous," from the name borne by several Slavic kings and three saints.
Tanis

TANYA (176): (Russian/Slavic) Short form of Tatiana or Titania. See also Tawny.
TANIA (382), **TONYA** (368), Tahnee, Tahni, Tahna,

Tahnia, Tana (African), Taina (Scandinavian), Tanee, Tanamarie

TARA (83): (*TAH-rah*) (Irish) "Hill." Ancient Tara was the site of the "stone of destiny" on which Irish kings were crowned. Today Tara is better known as the name of Scarlett O'Hara's plantation in Margaret Mitchell's *Gone with the Wind*. See also Terra.

Tarah, Tarrah, Tarra, Taralynn, Taralyn

TAREE: (*tah-ree-EH*) (Japanese) "Bending branch."

TARYN (339): (Contemporary) Blend of Tara and Erin.

Tarin, Tarryn, Tarynn

TASHA (260): Short form of Natasha, the Russian form of Natalie. See also Latasha.

Tashia, Tashi, Tassa, Tassie, Tasia, Tazia (Italian), Tosha, Toshiana

⊸TATE: (Scandinavian) "Cheerful." Surname in rare use as a given name for boys or girls.

Tatum

TATIANA (303): (*tah-sh'AHN-ah*) (Russian) Feminine form of Tatius, a Roman family clan name. A saint's name. See also Tiana and Tanya.

Tatianna

TAURA: (*TAW-rah*) An astrological name, the feminine form of Taurus. (See boys' index.) Taura (*tah-OO-rah*) is also a Japanese surname meaning "many lakes" or "many rivers."

Taurina

TAVIA: (*TAY-vee-ah*) Short form of Octavia.

TAWNY: Tawney is an English surname, but the many contemporary variants of this sound probably are based on Tanya or the literal meaning of tawny: the warm sandy color of a lion's skin.

Tawni, Tawnya, Tawnee, Tawney, Tawnie, Tawnia, Tawna

TAYA: (*tye-YAH*) (Japanese) "Valley field"; "house in the field." Surname.

TAYLOR (82): (English) "Tailor." Surname frequently

used as a given name for girls and boys. Current usage is about 57% for boys, 43% for girls.

"TE-" names: (Contemporary) Blends of "Te-" plus various endings, with pronunciation emphasis on the second syllable. See also "Ta-" names and Tiana.

Teanna, Teana, Telayna, Telisa, Telisha, Tenisha, Tenesha, Teona, Teonna, Tenaya

TEAGAN: (*TEE-gan*) (English/Irish) "Good-looking." Teagan is an Irish surname; contemporary usage as a girl's name probably is influenced by the rhyming similarity to Regan and Meagan.

Tegan, Teige (*teezh* or *tayzh*)

TEAL: A name from nature; the bird or the color, a deep greenish blue.

Teela

TEDDI: Feminine form of Teddy.

TEMPEST: (English) "Turbulent, stormy." Surname; may also be used as a nature name. Child actress Tempestt Bledsoe has brought attention to the name in recent years.

TEMPLE: (English/Latin) The surname Temple refers to the medieval priories and settlements of the Kinghts-Templar, a military religious order. In rare use for boys and girls.

TENEILLE: (*te-NEEL*) (English/French) Surname rarely used as a given name for girls, made familiar by the pop musical duo Captain and Teneille.

Tenille

TERA: (*teh-RAH*) (Japanese) "Calm (unwavering in flight) arrow." Surname. Terami (*ter-AH-mee*) is a Japanese surname meaning "viewing the temple." Tera is also a Spanish diminutive of Teresa.

Terami

TERESA (155): (*te-REE-sah* or *te-RAY-sah*) (Spanish/Italian) Variant form of Theresa. The popularity of two saints, Teresa of Avila and Therese of Lisieux, has resulted in the creation of many variants. See also Theresa, Terri and Tessa.

Teresita (Spanish); Tereza (Italian); Terese, Teressa, Terez, Tressa

TERRA: (*TARE-ah*) (Latin) "Land; the planet earth." Terra ensures the pronunciation "*TARE-ah*" rather than "*TAHR-ah*" of the similar name Tara. See also Tara.

Terrah, Teralyn

TERRI: Short form of Teresa. Variants are contemporary blends. Usage of Terry: boys 80%, girls 20%. See boys' index for historical note.

Teri, Terry, Terrie, Terika, Terilynn, Teriann, Teriana, Teryn, Terrin, Terryn

TESSA (370): Short form of Teresa.

Tess, Tessia, Tessie

THALIA: (*THAYL-yah*) (Greek) "Flowering." Mythology; Thalia was the Muse of comedy and one of the Three Graces, goddesses who were the embodiment of beauty and charm.

THEA: (Greek) "Goddess, godly." Thea is an independent name and a short form of names like Althea and Dorothea.

Tia, Tiah, Teah

THELMA: (Greek) "Will, wilful." A literary creation from the nineteenth century.

Telma (Spanish)

THEODORA: "God-given." Feminine form of Theodore.

Teodora (Spanish), Theadora

THERESA (227): (Greek) "From Theresia." See also Teresa.

Therese (French), Theressa

THOMASINA: "Twin." Feminine form of Thomas.

Tommie, Tommi, Tomasina, Tamsen, Tamsin

TIANA (455): (*tee-AHN-ah*) (Contemporary) Short form of Tatiana. See also Tatiana and "Te-" names.

Tianna, Tiani, Tiahna, Tiandra, Tiane, Tianne, Tiauna, Tiona, Tionna

TIARA (389): (*tee-ARH-ah*) (Latin) "Headdress." A tiara is a jeweled headpiece or demi-crown. Tierra is the Spanish word meaning "earth."

Tierra, Tiarra

TIFFANY (20): (Latin/French) English form of a French surname based on the Greek Theophania, a name referring to the Epiphany, the manifestation of divinity.

Tiffanie, Tiffani, Tiffney

TINA (204): (*TEE-nah*) A name ending used as an independent name and in combination with other names as in Tinamarie.

Teena, Tinamarie

TISHA: (*TEE-sha*) Independent name created from short forms of Leticia and Latisha.

Tiesha

TOMIKO: (*toh-MEE-koh*) (Japanese) "Happiness child"; "wealthy child."

Tomie (*toh-mee-EH*) "fruitful branch"; "wealthy."

TONI (306): Short form of Antonia and Antoinette, with contemporary variants based on Toni.

Tonette, Tonia, Tonell, Tonisha, Toniesha

TONYA (368): See Tanya.

TORI: (Scottish/English) Tori short forms and independent names are mostly derived from Victoria, but may also be the feminine use of surnames. (See Tory in boys' index.) In Japanese, Tori means "bird." Usage of Tory: boys 62%, girls 38%. The rarer use of Torey and Torrey is about equal for boys and girls.

Tory, Torrey, Torri, Torrie, Torey, Torry, Torree, Toriana

TOSHI: (*TOH-shee*) (Japanese) "Mirror reflection."

TOYA: (*TOY-ah*) (Spanish) Short form of Victoria, also a Japanese surname meaning "house door" or "door into the valley." See also LaToya.

Toyana

TRACY (184): (English/French) Surname dating from before the Norman Conquest. Usage: girls 85%, boys 15%.

TRACEY (471) (Irish), TRACI (476), Tracie, Tracee

TRINA: (*TREEN-nah*) Short form of names with the

"-trina" ending; Trena is a Latin term meaning "triple," and the names are sometimes used in reference to the Trinity.
Treena, Trena, Trinadette, Trini

TRISHA (279): Short form of Patricia, used as an independent name. See also Teresa for similar sounding variants.
Tricia, Trish, Trissa, Trisa, Trishana

TRISTA: (Latin/French) "Sadness." Feminine form of Tristan. The spelling of Trysta suggests the English word *tryst*, usually taken to mean a romantic appointment. Usage of Tristan: boys 84%, girls 16%.
Tristan, Tristen, Tristin, Tristina, Tristyn, Trysta

TRIXIE: "Brings joy." Short form of Beatrix.

TRUDY: (German) "Strength." An independent name formed from the suffix of names like Gertrude.

TWYLA: (English) The use of Twyla as a girl's given name today is probably due to dancer/choreographer Twyla Tharp and to a character in a novel by Zenna Henderson.
Twylla, Twila

TYRA: (*TEER-ah* or *TYE-rah*) (Scandinavian) "Of Tyr, god of battle."
Tyla, Tylena

U

ULA: (*OO-la*) Short form of Eulalie.

UNIQUE: (*you-NEEK*) (Latin) "Only one." Use of the English word as a given name may be influenced by its sounding like Monique.

URSULA: (*UR-soo-lah*) (Latin) "She-bear." A medieval saint's name.

V

VALENCIA: (*vah-LEN-cee-ah*) (Latin) "Strong." From Valentinus, a saint's name.

VALENTINA: (Latin) "Strong." Feminine form of Valentinus.

Valen, Valene, Valyn

VALERIE (109): (English/French) "Strong, valiant"; Feminine form of Valerius, a Roman family clan name.
Valeria (Italian/Spanish); Valarie, Valaree

VAN: (Dutch) "Of." The Dutch equivalent of "de" in French names. When some early immigrants to America dropped this prefix from their surnames, they converted it to a given name. Today Van is used for both boys (55%) and girls (45%).

VANESSA (23): An early eighteenth-century literary name created by Jonathan Swift. Vanessa sounds like Venetia, another name of the period. See also Venicia.
Vanesa (Spanish)

VANNA: Short form of Ivana, the Russian feminine form of John, or a variant form of Vanessa. Vanda is a Czech form of Wanda.
Vanda, Vanetta

VELMA: Variant form of Wilma or Wilhemina.
Valma (Finnish)

VELVET: (English/French) The name of the soft-napped fabric used as a given name.

VENECIA: (ve-NEE-sha) (Contemporary) Variant form of Venetia, the Latin form of Venice. See also Vanessa.
Venice, Venitia, Venicia, Venita

VENUS: (VEE-nus) (Latin) Roman mythology; Venus was the goddess of beauty and love, equivalent to the Greek Aphrodite.

VERA: (Latin) "Truth"; (Russian) "faith."
Verla, Verena

VERITY: (Latin) "Truthfulness." One of the virtue names.

VERNA: Short form of Laverne, or a feminine form of Vern or Vernon, with contemporary variants.
Vernisha, Vernita

VERONICA (63): (ver-RON-ni-kah) (Latin) "True image." Vernice and Verenice are Spanish variants of Bernice.

Veronika (Czech); Veronique (French); Vernice, Verenice, Verenise

VIANNA: (*vee-ANN-ah*) Short form of Viviana. Vianca is a Spanish variant of Bianca. See also Vivian.
Vianna; Viana (Portuguese); Vianca, Viona, Vina

VICTORIA (48): "Conqueror." Feminine form of Victor.
Viktoria (Czech); Vittoria (Italian); Vicky, Vicki, Vickie, Vikki, Viki

VIDA: (*VEE-dah* or *VYE-dah*) Short form of Davida. Vida is also the Spanish word for "life." Veda may be used in reference to the Hindu Veda (Sanskrit) "knowledge."
Veda

VIENNA: (*vee-EN-ah*) (Latin) The name of the Austrian city, used as a given name.

VIOLET: (English) One of the earliest flower names. Shakespeare used the Latin form Viola for the enterprising heroine in *Twelfth Night*.
Violeta (Spanish); Violetta (Italian); Violette (French); Viola

VIRGINIA (257): (Latin) "Chaste, virginal."
Virgina, Virgena, Virgene (*ver-JEEN*)

VIRIDIANA: (*ver-REE-dee-AHN-ah*) (Latin) "Green." An Italian saint's name.

VIVIAN (399): (Latin) An ancient personal name. Once considered to be a male name, today Vivian is almost entirely viewed as a feminine name. In Malory's *Morte d'Arthur*, Vivien was the Lady of the Lake, also the enchantress of Merlin. See also Vianna.
Viviana, Vivianna, Vivianne, Viviane (French), Vivien, Vivienne

VONDRA: (Czech) "Womanly, brave." Variant form of Andrea.

W

WANDA: (German) "Kindred; of the same stock."

WAVA: (*WAY-vah*) (English) Rare variant form of Ava or Evelyn that came into use at the turn of the century.

WENDY (131): A created name that first appeared in James Barrie's *Peter Pan*.
Wendi

WESLEE: (English) "West meadow." Feminine form of Wesley.
Weslia

WHITLEY: (English) "White meadow." English surname now coming into use as a given name for girls, probably influenced by its sounding like Whitney, and by the character on the TV show "A Different World."

WHITNEY (66): (English) "Fair island." Formerly in rare use as a boy's name, today the English surname Whitney is almost solely used as a girl's name.

WILLA: "Resolute protector." Feminine form of William.
Wilma, Wilhelmina (German/Dutch)

WILLOW: (English) Literally, the willow tree, noted for its slender, graceful branches and leaves.

WINIFRED: (Welsh) "Reconciled, blessed." Winifred, a martyred Welsh princess, traditionally is called the patron saint of virgins.
Winnie

X

XANDRA: (*ZAN-drah*) (Spanish) "Defender of mankind." Variant form of Alexandra. See also Zandra.

XANTHE: (*ZAN-thah*) (Greek) "Yellow, blond."

XAVIERA: (*ecks-say-vee-EHR-ah*) "Bright, splendid." Feminine form of Xavier.

XENIA: (*ZAYN-yah*) (Greek) "Welcoming." See also Zenia.
Xena (*ZAY-nah*), Xia

XIOMARA: (*zho-MAH-rah*) Feminine form of Xiomar. See also Geomar.

XUXA: (*SHOO-sha*) Nickname for Susana used by the hostess of a very popular children's TV show in Brazil.

Y

YASMIN: (Arabic) "Jasmine flower." See also Jasmine.
Yasmine, Yazmin, Yasmeen

YESENIA (113): (Latin) "Of the Essenes"; (Spanish) Meaning uncertain. See also Jessenia and Llessenia.
Yessenia, Yecenia

YNES: "Chaste." Variant form of Ines and Inez, from Agnes. See also Inez.
Ynez

YOLANDA (353): (Spanish) Variant form of Yolande, a French form of Violet.
Yolonda

YONINAH: (*yoh-NEE-nah*) (Israeli) "Little dove."

YSABEL: Variant form of Isabel.

YUMIKO: (*you-MEE-koh*) (Japanese) "Arrow child."

YURIKO: (*you-REE-koh*) (Japanese) "Lily child" or "village of birth."

YVETTE (195): (French) "Archer's bow." Feminine form of Yves.

YVONNE (274): (French) Feminine form of Yves.
Yvonna

Z

ZAHARA: (African) "Flowering." Also used as a variant form of Sarah. See also Zaira and Sahara.
Zahra, Zarah

ZAIDA: (Arabic) "Huntress" or "fortunate." See also Sade.
Zayda, Zada

ZAIRA: (Arabic) "Dawning;" (Italian) Variant form of

Zara. The Zara names are sometimes used as exotic phonetic forms of Sarah. See also Zahara.
Zara, Zayra, Zarina, Zareena

ZALIKA: (Swahili) "Well-born."
Zuleika (Arabic)

ZANDRA: (Spanish) Variant form of Alexandra. See also Xandra.

ZANETA: (*zah-NEE-tah*) A saint's name; variants also may be used as feminine forms of Zane.
Zanita, Zanetta

ZELDA: "Patience." Short form of Grizelda. The similar sounding Zelde is a Yiddish name meaning "happiness."
Zelma, Zelde

ZENIA: "Welcoming." Variant form of Xenia. The similar sounding name Zinnia is a flower name; Zena is a short form of Zenobia.
Zinnia, Zina

ZENOBIA: (*ze-NOH-bee-ah*) Queen Zenobia (third century B.C.) was ruler of the wealthy city of Palmyra in the Arabian Desert.
Zena

ZITA: (*ZEE-tah*) (Spanish) Short form of names like Rosita.

ZIVAH: (Israeli) "Radiant."

ZOE: (*ZOH-ee*) (Greek) "Life."
Zoey

ZOHRA: (Arabic) "Blossom." Biblical; Zorah was the name of a city in Judah where Samson was born.
Zora (Slavic) "dawn"

ZSA ZSA: (Hungarian) Pet name for Susan.

ZULEMA: (*zoo-LEE-mah* or *zoo-LAY-mah*) (Hebrew/Arabic) "Peace." Variant form of Salome and Solomon.
Zulima

SUGGESTIONS FOR FURTHER READING

Browder, Sue. *The New Age Baby Name Book*. Warner Books, 1974.

Dunkling, Leslie, and William Gosling. *The Facts on File Dictionary of First Names*. Facts on File, 1983.

Hanks, Patrick, and Flavia Hodges. *A Dictionary of Surnames*. Oxford University Press, 1988.

Lower, Mark Antony. *A Dictionary of Surnames*. Wordsworth Editions Ltd., 1988.

Root, Eileen M. *Hawaiian Names—English Names*. Press Pacifica, 1987.

Withycombe, E. G. *The Oxford Dictionary of English Christian Names*. Oxford University Press, 1977.

Woods, Richard D. *Hispanic First Names*. Greenwood Press, 1984.